THE

YOGA SŪTRAS OF PATAÑJALI

A Study Guide for Book II
Sādhana Pāda

Translation and Commentary
by Baba Hari Dass

Edited with an Introduction by Dayanand Diffenbaugh
Notes by Dharma Dass Budding

SRI RAMA PUBLISHING
Santa Cruz, California

Sri Rama Foundation is the non-profit parent organization of Sri Rama Publishing. It was created in 1974 to support needy children in India. All proceeds from the sale of this book support Shri Ram Ashram, an orphanage, school, and free medical clinic near Haridwar, India in the Himalayan foothills. Founded by Baba Hari Dass in 1984, the Ashram, shown above, is now home to nearly 65 children. The school, Shri Ram Vidya Mandir, educates over 500 children from pre-kindergarten through 12th grade. There is a separate facility for the free medical clinic. Please see www.sriramfoundation.org.

Additional Editing
Sarada Diffenbaugh
Veda Prakash Ahlen
Dharma Dass Budding

Design & Production
Veda Prakash Ahlen
Patricia Bacall
Anitā Bridgman

Photographs
Sadanand Ward Maillard
Dharma Dass Budding

Sri Rama Publishing
P.O. Box 2550
Santa Cruz, CA 95063
(408) 842-8117 phone
www.sriramfoundation.org

ISBN-10: 0-918100-23-2
ISBN-13: 978-0-918100-23-8
First Edition, 1st Printing

Regarding the First Edition
This study guide is intended for use as an aid to students. Please send any comments to veda.prakash@ashtangyoga.org or to the publisher via mail or fax.

© 2008 Sri Rama Publishing

Acknowledgements

There have been several excellent translations of both the *Yoga Sūtras* of Patañjali and their classical commentaries. The author and editors are especially grateful for the following works:

The translation of Vyāsa's commentary with the additional commentary of Swāmi Hariharānanda Āraṇya, published by SUNY Press in Albany, NY;

The translation of Vyāsa's commentary and the extensive survey of the classical commentaries on *Sādhana Pāda*, by Pandit Usharbudh Arya, published by Himalayan Publishers in Honesdale, PA;

The translation of Vyāsa's commentary with the gloss of Vāchaspati Miśhra by Rāma Prasāda, published by Munshiram Manoharlal Publishers in New Delhi, India; and

The Hindi translation and commentary of Dr. Vimalā Karṇātak. Her doctoral thesis was published in book form in 1974 by Kashi Hindu Vishvavidyalaya.

Bābā Hari Dāss

A Note on the Text

The format of this book follows a traditional presentation of the *Yoga Sūtras*. Each *sūtra* starts with the original Sanskrit. Below it is the identical text transliterated into roman letters with diacritical marks. This allows people unfamiliar with the Devanāgari script (the Sanskrit alphabet) to pronounce the Sanskrit words. Next, Bābā Hari Dāss's translation of the Sanskrit into English is in bold type. This is followed with a word by word breakdown of the *sūtra*. Below that is the extended commentary.

The study of the *Yoga Sūtras* cannot be separated from its technical language. For this reason, we have retained the use of Sanskrit terminology in the commentary. Whenever possible, we have included a translation along with the Sanskrit terms, which are in italics every time they appear. In the appendix, there is a glossary of the terms used in the text.

The *sūtras* are terse and condensed phrases. The Sanskrit terms are richer and more evocative than their English counterparts. There are multiple possible interpretations for many of the concepts and terms used. For this reason, there cannot be a complete translation of each term in just a few words. Sometimes the same word will have different meanings in different contexts.

Diacritical marks are used throughout the text. These are the marks that distinguish various letters in the Devanāgari script (the Sanskrit alphabet), which has nearly twice as many letters as the Roman alphabet. The diacritical marks will be of service to those interested in the study of Sanskrit, and can be ignored by others.

In finalizing the text, every effort has been made to use gender neutral language. Unfortunately, the English language is flawed; it does not easily permit gender neutral references. Sanskrit, on the other hand, assigns a grammatical gender to every noun, even if the object itself has no masculine or feminine qualities. It would be incorrect to assign these qualities to the object when the gender refers only to the word.

A difficult example of this is the word, *drashṭri* (seer). The seer is beyond all qualities, including all masculine and feminine qualities, yet the word itself is a masculine word, and it requires the use of the pronoun *his* in Sanskrit.

The truths addressed in the *Yoga Sūtras* transcend all duality, including all differences in race, culture, or gender. In spite of the limitations of language, neither the author nor the editors intend any bias in these areas.

Transliteration Schematic

अ	a	a	ख	kha	kha	द	da	da
आ	ā	ā	ग	ga	ga	ध	dha	dha
इ	i	i	घ	gha	gha	न	na	na
ई	ī	ī	ङ	ṅa	ṅa	प	pa	pa
उ	u	u	च	cha	ca	फ	pha	pha
ऊ	ū	ū	छ	chha	cha	ब	ba	ba
ऋ	ṛi	ṛ	ज	ja	ja	भ	bha	bha
ॠ	ṝi	ṝ	झ	jha	jha	म	ma	ma
ऌ	ḷ	ḷ	ञ	ña	ña	य	ya	ya
ए	e	e	ट	ṭa	ṭa	र	ra	ra
ऐ	ai	ai	ठ	ṭha	ṭha	ल	la	la
ओ	o	o	ड	ḍa	ḍa	व	va	va
औ	au	au	ढ	ḍha	ḍha	श	śha	śa
अं	aṁ	aṁ	ण	ṇa	ṇa	ष	ṣha	ṣa
अः	aḥ	aḥ	त	ta	ta	स	sa	sa
क	ka	ka	थ	tha	tha	ह	ha	ha

The method used for transliterating Saṅskṛit is a slight variation on the international norm. The traditional method requires greater study for correct understanding. Instead, most readers will find this anglicized method easier to follow. The left column is the Devanāgari letter followed by the transliteration as used in this Study Guide. The separate right column is the international norm, which is different in just a few letters, such as *śha*, *ṣha*, *cha*, and *ṛi* (or *śa*, *ṣa*, *ca*, and *ṛ*).

Finally, hyphens have been inserted in the transliteration of the Devanāgari *sūtra* as an aid to reading. In Saṅskṛit, single words are combined using *sandhi* (rules of combination). This can make for very long strings of letters without any spaces. As this is unfamiliar to most Western readers, hyphens have been added at the conjuncts of two words. They are grammatically insignificant, but should facilitate the reading and recognition of the Saṅskṛit terms.

Invocation

ॐ नमो अविद्याविहीनाय ह्यस्मितारहिताय च।

रागद्वेषप्रहीणाय निर्भयाय नमो नमः ॥१॥

समाहिताय शान्ताय निःसङ्गाय निराशिषे।

आत्मानं जानते सम्यक् स्वस्थाय च नमो नमः ॥२॥

संस्थितस्त्वयि वाह्यात्मा त्वमन्तरात्मनि स्थितः।

वितर्कविहीने हार्दे आकाशे मे महीयताम् ॥३॥

त्वयि मे सर्वम् ॐॐॐ आत्मनि मे त्वम् ॐॐॐ।

स्मारय स्मारय ॐॐॐ चित्तं शामय शामय ॐ ॥४॥

स्मराणि सोऽहम् ॐॐॐ शान्तं चिन्मयमों माम् ॐ।

त्वत्स्थं केवलम् ॐॐॐ स्मराणि शुद्धमों माम् ॐ ॥५॥

Om namo avidyā vihīnāya hyasmitā rahitāya cha
Rāga-dvesha-prahīṇāya nirbhayāya namo namaḥ

Samāhitāya śhāntāya niḥsaṅgāya nirāśhiṣhe
Ātmānaṁ jānate samyak svasthāya cha namo namaḥ

Saṁsthitastvayi vāhyātmā tvamantarātmani sthitaḥ
Vitarka-vihīne hārdde ākāśhe me mahīyatām

Tvayi me sarvam om om om ātmani me tvam om om om
Smāraya smāraya om om om chittaṁ śhāmaya śhāmaya om

Smaraṇi so'ham om om om śhāntaṁ chinmayamoṁ mām om
Tvat sthaṁ kevalam om om om smarāṇi śhuddhamoṁ mām
om

Translation

My homage to that Being who is devoid of all misapprehension, free from the feeling of "me" and "mine," above desire and hate, and bereft of all fear.

My homage to that Being who is in perfect quiescence and peace, calm, beyond all attachments, above all cravings, who has got perfect knowledge of the transcendent Self and is self-contained.

My outer self (the body) is in Thee; You are present in my inner self, O Lord, You manifest yourself in my inner heart free from all perturbations and worries.

Om Om Om - My all is in You, and You are present in my inner Self; please direct me to be mindful of Thee. May I be led by my spirit; may I get peace of mind.

May I have constant remembrance of Thee and of my purified Self dwelling only in Thee. Om Om Om.

Contents

तपःस्वाध्यायेश्वरप्रणिधानानि क्रियायोगः ॥ १ ॥

tapaḥ-svādhyāy-eśhvara-praṇidhānāni kriyā-yogaḥ

Austerity, Self-study, and surrender to God constitute Kriyā Yoga (Practical Yoga).

समाधिभावनार्थः क्लेशतनूकरणार्थश्च ॥२॥

samādhi-bhāvanārthaḥ kleśha-tanū-karaṇārthaśh-cha

[Kriyā Yoga is practiced] for attaining samādhi and reducing the afflictions.

अविद्याऽस्मितारागद्वेषाभिनिवेशाः पञ्च क्लेशाः ॥३॥

avidyā-'smitā-rāga-dveṣhābhiniveśhāḥ pañcha kleśhāḥ

The five afflictions are ignorance, egoism, attraction, repulsion, and fear of death.

अविद्याक्षेत्रमुत्तरेषां प्रसुप्ततनुविच्छिन्नोदाराणाम् ॥४॥

avidyā-kṣhetram-uttareṣhāṁ prasupta-tanu-vichchhinnodārāṇām

Ignorance is the field for the other [kleśhas], which can appear as dormant, weak, interrupted, or operative.

अनित्याशुचिदुःखानात्मसु नित्यशुचिसुखात्मख्यातिरविद्या ॥५॥

anity-āśhuchi-duḥkh-ānātmasu nitya-śhuchi-sukh-ātma-khyātir- avidyā

Ignorance consists of seeing permanence in the impermanent, purity in the impure, pleasure in pain, and the Self in the non-Self.

यमनियमासनप्राणायामप्रत्याहारधारणाध्यानसमाधयोऽष्टावङ्गानि ॥२९॥

yama–niyamāsana–prāṇāyāma–pratyāhāra–dhāraṇā–dhyāna–
samādhayo–'shṭāvaṅgāni

Restraints, observances, posture, regulation of breath, withdrawal, concentration, meditation, and absorption are the eight limbs of yoga.

अहिंसासत्यास्तेयब्रह्मचर्यापरिग्रहा यमाः ॥ ३० ॥

ahimsā–satyāsteya–brahmacharyāparigrahā yamāh

The restraints are non-violence, truthfulness, non-stealing, continence, and non-possessiveness.

जातिदेशकालसमयानवच्छिन्नाः सार्वभौमा महाव्रतम् ॥ ३१ ॥

jāti–desha–kāla–samayānavachchhinnāh sārvabhaumā mahāvratam

They (the five restraints) become a great vow [when they are practiced] universally, not limited by space, time, life state, and circumstances.

शौचसन्तोषतपःस्वाध्यायेश्वरप्रणिधानानि नियमाः ॥ ३२ ॥

shaucha–santosha–tapah–svādhyāyeshvara–praṇidhānani niyamāh

The observances are purity, contentment, austerity, self-study, and surrender to God.

वितर्कबाधने प्रतिपक्षभावनम् ॥ ३३ ॥

vitarka–bādhane pratipakṣha–bhāvanam

When the mind is disturbed by negative thoughts, one should dwell on their opposites.

वितर्का हिंसादयः कृतकारितानुमोदिता लोभ क्रोध मोह पूर्वका मृदुमध्याधिमात्रा
दुःखाज्ञानानन्तफला इति प्रतिपक्षभावनम् ॥३४॥

vitarkā himsādayah krita–kāritānumoditā lobha krodha moha pūrvakā
mridu–madhyādhimātrā duhkhājñānānanta–phalā iti pratipakṣha–
bhāvanam

Negative thoughts cause violent or harmful actions. They are either performed directly, initiated through others, or tacitly approved. They may be caused by greed, anger, or delusion, and are in mild, medium, or intense degrees. Knowing that their result is endless pain and ignorance is dwelling on the opposite.

Introduction

Prologue

It is with much love and gratitude that we are publishing Bābā Hari Dāss's commentary on Book II of Patanjali's *Yoga Sūtras* as a study guide for all serious students of this timeless classical Yoga.

As with Babaji's previous commentary on Book I, the main points of the traditional commentaries of Śhri Vyāsa, Vāchaspati Miśhra, and Bhoja Rāj are included. We would also like to acknowledge the work of Vimalā Karnatika in compiling the traditional commentaries in a combined Hindi commentary. In addition to presenting the profound insights of these commentaries in modern language, Bābā Hari Dāss has added his own knowledge as expressed in thirty years of teaching students in America, based on an ancient lineage and timeless knowledge realized in the practice and in the person of a master *yogi*.

SĀDHANA PĀDA INTRODUCTION

What relevance does the wisdom of the ancient and timeless practice and philosophy of *yoga* have for us today? Has the world qualitatively changed such that the principles of life and the dynamics of consciousness as observed by the seers and teachers of ancient times are no longer relevant? Is modern culture's aim of freedom to pursue desires and experience the world through the senses a sufficient explanation and justification of life? In *Sādhana Pāda* the ageless methods for achieving freedom from desires are presented. These life-changing principles and practices are offered here so that they can be tested and experienced in the setting of modern life; the experience of peace that they bring can then be measured against the experience of a life spent fulfilling desires.

We can see that there has been a progression of the collective knowledge of humanity through the development of various technologies, which has allowed us to modify and control our environment. In all aspects of life, from cooking to computers, we use the knowledge and tools passed along to us by our families and cultures, and this knowledge is both sequential and cumulative. Language and culture itself are the symbols and understandings passed on through the generations by which we form our collective agreements.

"Progress" is the term given to the evolution of this knowledge and these technologies. We can also see that there are recurrent patterns within human behavior, appearing in all cultures, which have not significantly changed over the entire span of human existence. Violence, politics, community, family, and religion are but some examples of human behavior that has ongoing expression throughout human history.

It is in addressing the basic human condition, that of consciousness in a mind-body complex and the resulting behaviors, that we find the relevance of the ancient wisdom traditions such as the *Yoga Sūtras*. These traditions offer guidance and methods to restrain the "lower" impulses of humanity such as violence, greed, lust, and hate, and to cultivate the "higher" nature of the human spirit such as love, tolerance, charity, and forgiveness. There is an implication here that humanity has the potential to evolve in a qualitatively positive way and that the effort involved in this transformation is the challenge of human existence.

Within the spectrum of the spiritual traditions, the *Yoga Sūtras* of Patañjali blends philosophy with a variety of practical methods. Rarely do we find such a tradition that embraces experimentation and calls for experiential verification of the Truth expressed in its philosophy. The basic idea is that real change starts from within. If we cannot deal with our own egotism, anger, and attachment to desires, how can we expect the world to change?

In the process of the practice of *yoga* it becomes apparent how much the world we experience is colored by our projections. As soon as this coloring is removed, the perception of the world changes, becoming more truth bearing. If our attitude becomes more positive and less fearful, then our actions become more harmonious and the effect of our presence will bring peace to those around us.

In *Samādhi Pāda*, Book I of the *Yoga Sūtras*, Patañjali outlines the vast realm of consciousness within the human psyche that can be unlocked through *nirodha* (control of thought waves, restraint of mental modifications). The methods of achieving *nirodha*, mainly *abhyāsa* (practice) and *vairāgya* (dispassion), are also described. But for most of us, who at the beginning of *yoga* practice find it difficult to sit with a calm mind, *nirodha* seems unachievable and *samādhi* (super consciousness) seems like a distant state rather than an imminent and potential reality.

Fortunately Patañjali did not stop the exposition with an outline of philosophical principles and advanced methods of practice. In *Sādhana Pāda*, Book II of the *Yoga Sūtras*, Patañjali continues with a discussion of preliminary methods that can help an aspirant build a firm foundation for spiritual life and a more detailed exposition of the philosophy of *yoga* to facilitate the inquiry of the beginning aspirant.

COMPARISON OF *SAMĀDHI PĀDA* AND *SĀDHANA PĀDA*

In both *Samādhi Pāda* and *Sādhana Pāda*, Patañjali begins with a quintessential statement of the essence of philosophy and practice, and then in subsequent *sutras* breaks it down into components of refined explanation and methodology. In this sense, the two books are parallel in construction. Both begin with a definition of *yoga* and its method in generic form.

In *Samādhi Pāda* the core definition of *yoga* is given in Sūtra 2, "*Yogaśh-chitta-vritti-nirodhaḥ,*" or "*yoga* is control of thought waves in the mind." In *Sādhana Pāda*, Kriyā Yoga (the practical *yoga* of purification), is defined as *tapas* (austerity), *svādhyāya* (self-study), and *Īśhvara Praṇidhāna* (surrender to God). In both cases, *yoga* as a process is defined as purifying the mind, by which *yoga* the goal—peace, union, and self-realization—is achieved.

Furthermore, in both Book I and Book II, the underlying principle behind the methods given for achieving *yoga* is the removal of obstacles blocking the realization of the essential reality (the Self, the all pervading conscious principle, *puruṣha*). In *Samādhi Pāda*, the obstacles to be removed are presented as the thought waves or mental modifications. In *Sādhana Pāda* the obstacles are presented as the five *kleśhas*, or the afflictions of ignorance, egoism, attraction, repulsion, and fear of death. Sutra II:2 states that Kriyā Yoga is the weakening of the *kleśhas* and the establishing of *samādhi* or higher consciousness. Here again it is taught that removing the veils of ignorance reveals the natural state of yogic consciousness.

Sādhana Pāda is a prescription of purification practices for this category of *yogi* who is suffering from the afflictions. These methods of purification are Kriyā Yoga and Aṣhṭāṅga Yoga. These step-by-step methods prepare the aspirant for understanding the subtle principles of *yoga* and ultimately develop the capacity to intuit and stabilize higher consciousness (*samādhi*). The direct perception of the gross, subtle, and cosmic reality leads to discrimination and dispassion, which precede true *yoga* or union and the end of suffering.

SCOPE OF *SĀDHANA PĀDA*

Sādhana Pāda begins with the definition and explanation of Kriyā Yoga and proceeds with an exposition on the *kleśhas*, or afflictions (ignorance, egoism, attraction, repulsion, and fear of death). In the central part of *Sādhana Pāda*, Patañjali presents an explanation of the mechanics of creation based on the Sāmkhya philosophy of Kapila. This explanation covers both the individual or microcosmic creation, the cycle of rebirth (*samsāra*) created by actions (*karma*) and the latent potentiality of action (*samskāras*); as well as the universal creation, the interface of consciousness and matter activating the three *guṇas* (purity, activity, and stability), which are the qualities by which the creation is known. Furthermore, the purpose of creation, *bhoga* (experience) and *apavarga*

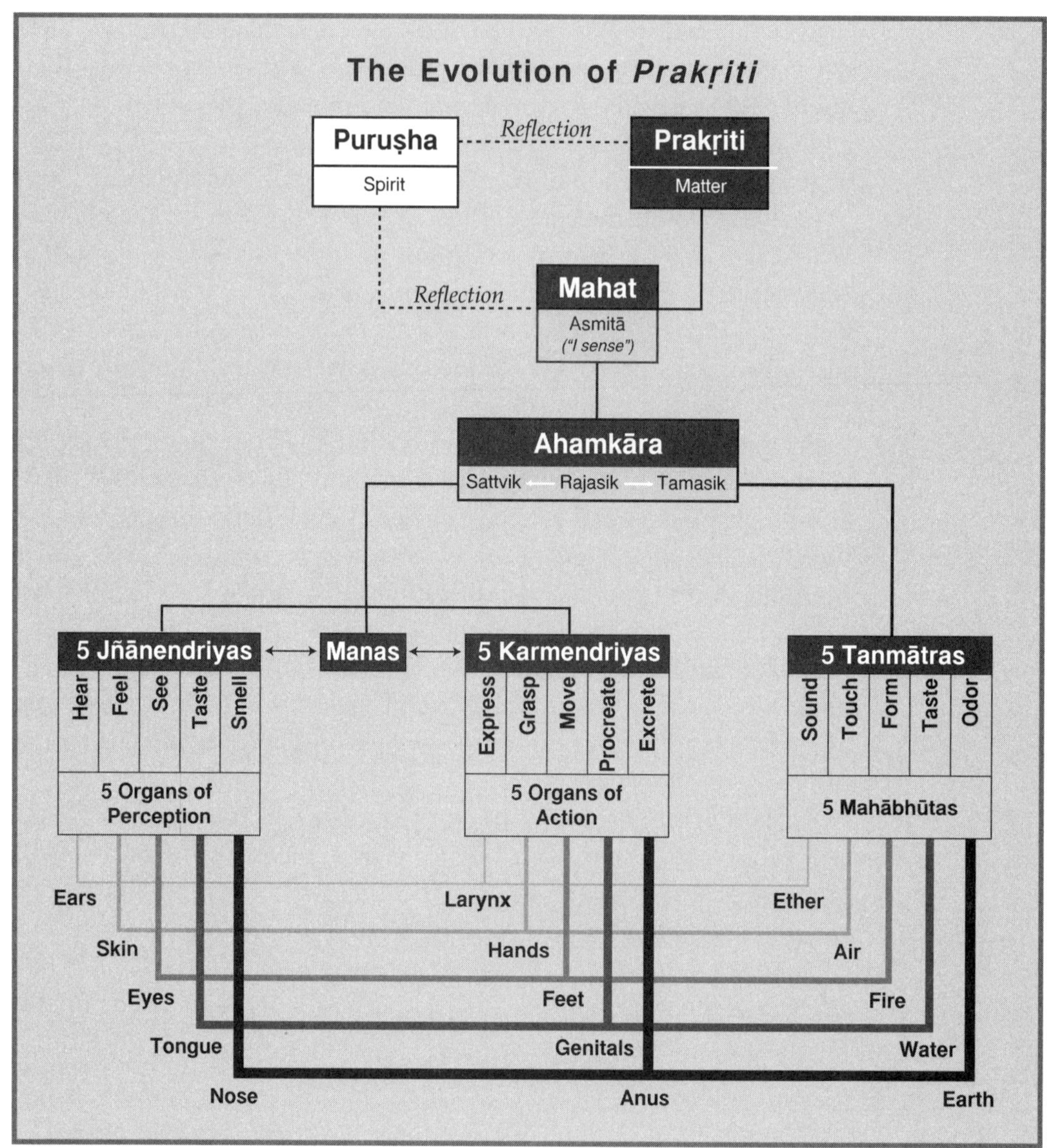

(liberation), is given. Finally the book culminates with the definition and explanation of Aṣṭāṅga Yoga.

Though Patañjali uses terminology from Sāṁkhya philosophy like *puruṣa* (consciousness), *prakṛti* (matter), *guṇas* (qualities - *sattva, rajas, tamas*), *indriyas* (sense organs), *tanmātras* (energetic essence of the five elements), and the *mahābhūtas* (five elements - earth, water, fire, air, space), there is a clear distinction between Sāṁkhya philosophy and practice and Yoga philosophy and practice. The Sāṁkhya philosophy of Kapila is essentially an atheistic philosophy that posits two eternal principles, consciousness (*puruṣa*) and matter (*prakṛiti*). The union of these two is the cause of the creation, bringing the experiential modality; the disunion of these two is the cause of liberation. The practice of Sāmkhya is based on the discrimination of the principles of creation leading to discriminative wisdom, which is the means to liberation and the end of suffering. It is a *jñāni* approach, beginning with an intellectual dialectic and progressing through deep reflection on the principles beyond words, and culminating in a direct experience of their essential reality. This type of analysis is included in *Sādhana Pāda* Sūtras 17-26; it is presented within the scope of a comprehensive practice. Classical Sāmkhya is a form of Jñāna Yoga, the *yoga* of knowledge, in which the mind and intellect are the main instruments used to achieve liberation. Kriyā Yoga, on the other hand, is the *yoga* practice in which the physical body is used in actions towards the spiritual goal. It is a practical approach and sometimes Kriyā Yoga is translated as practical *yoga*, as *Sādhana Pāda* is the book on practice.

Yoga philosophy differs from Sāmkhya in that Patañjali brings in the idea of *Īśhvara* or God the creator, preserver (savior) and destroyer of the whole creation. In *Samādhi Pāda*, Patañjali presents *Īśhvara* as being before the creation, outside the laws of creation, yet immanent within the creation. In Sūtra I: 28 the method of devotional surrender to God (*Īśhvara Praṇidhāna*) was given and equated with the most intense methods (*upāya*) of *sādhana* (spiritual practice). Here in *Sādhana Pāda*, surrender to God is again presented as part of a combined approach to spiritual practice that also includes intellectual reflection and inquiry as well as physical, mental, and moral disciplines.

The methods of *yoga* presented in *Sādhana Pāda* are presented in two broad categories: Kriyā Yoga (Sūtra II:2), the *yoga* of purificatory action, and Aṣhṭāṅga Yoga (Sūtras II:29), eight limbed *yoga*. Kriyā Yoga is defined in three broad generic categories of practice: austerity, self-study, and surrender to God. Kriyā is presented first as a more advanced method and the limbs of Aṣhṭāṅga Yoga are presented at the end of the book.

The eight limbs of Aṣhṭāṅga Yoga can be fit into the context of the three aspects of Kriyā Yoga, thus making Aṣhṭāṅga Yoga a more complete and expanded explanation of Kriyā Yoga. In this scenario, the moral precepts of *yama* and *niyama*, and the physical disciplines of *āsana* (postures) and *prāṇāyāma* (breath control) come within *tapas* (austerity). *Pratyāhāra* (withdrawing the mind from the sense objects) is the bridge between the external and internal limbs. It comes within self-study or *svādhyāya*, the deep reflection on the true nature of experience that accompanies the internalization of consciousness.

Nowhere in the *Yoga Sūtras* are moral precepts implied in yogic life more clearly and explicitly than in the presentation of Aṣhṭāṅga Yoga in the final sūtras of *Sādhana Pāda* (Sūtras II:28-52). The five restraints (*yama*) of non-violence, truthfulness, non-stealing, sexual continence, and non-possessiveness provide the guiding principles for virtuous action in the world. Then taken as "great vows" (Sūtra II:31), any one of these principles can be taken as a *sādhana* in itself. Mahatma Gandhi is an example of a reformer saint who practiced non-violence (*ahiṁsā*) and truthfulness (*satya*) without reservation concerning class, country, time, or situation.

The fixed observances (*niyama*) of purity, contentment, austerity, self-study, and surrender to God are the main precepts of yogic life. It is interesting to note that the observances include the three elements of Kriyā Yoga. In defining Kriyā Yoga, Patañjali removed *śhaucha* (cleanliness) and *santoṣha* (contentment) and included *tapaḥ* (austerity), *svādhyāya* (self study) and *Īśhvara Praṇidhāna* (surrender to God). These are identified in Kriyā Yoga as the three main methods to attain the spiritual goal. The complete discussion of *yama* and *niyama* as well as the limbs of *āsana* and *prāṇāyāma*, comprise the balance of the second book of Patañjali *Yoga Sūtras*.

The internal limbs of Aṣhṭāṅga Yoga (*dhāraṇā, dhyāna, and samādhi*) ultimately fall within *Īśhvara Praṇidhāna*, or surrender to God, because in these processes the ego of individuality along with its attachments and desires is transcended. While all three of these limbs may be practiced within the focus of *tapas* (austerity) and *svādhyāya* (reflection), in the Kriyā Yoga and Aṣhṭāṅga Yoga systems the complete surrender of the ego of individuality is called *Īśhvara Praṇidhāna*.

In the following outline of *Sādhana Pāda*, Kriyā Yoga, the *kleśhas*, as well as several philosophical topics are discussed. They include: ignorance (*avidyā*), which is the field of afflictions (*kleśhas*); the dynamic of consciousness (*puruṣha*) and matter (*prakṛiti*) and how these two eternal principles produce the 24 principles (*tattvas*); the cycle of action (*karma*), impression of action (*saṁskāra*), and desire (*vāsanā*) that sustains and conditions the cycle of rebirth (*saṁsāra*); the purpose of the creation being experience (*bhoga*) and liberation (*apavarga*); and reflections on pleasure, pain, and freedom, from the perspective of *yoga*.

KRIYĀ YOGA OVERVIEW

Kriyā Yoga, the first description of the preliminary practices of *yoga* offered by Patañjali in *Sādhana Pāda*, can be translated as "*yoga* of purificatory actions." It is also known as practical *yoga*. These actions of purification fit into three categories that work together to prepare the aspirant for one-pointed meditation and *samādhi* (*chitta vṛitti-nirodhaḥ*).

Tapaḥ

Austerity, the first category of discipline, is based on the idea of limiting desires. Placing or imposing limitation creates tension, friction, or heat within the mind of the aspirant. This heat in itself is purifying, and it gives first hand knowledge of "where we are at," for when we put limits on our behavior, the ego reacts and resists, and this gives visibility to our attachments. The discipline, if performed correctly, also gives energy and fortifying strength of will that can be applied towards the goal. Severe austerities performed beyond one's capacity are not recommended, as they can create depression, self-torture, and morbidity. Watching one's thoughts is a form of austerity. Breath control (*prāṇayāma*) is also an effective austerity as it puts one directly in touch with fear of death.

Svādhyāya

Self-study is the second category of purificatory action included in the prescription of Kriyā Yoga. Self-study includes scriptural study when the knowledge gained is applied in one's life. The application of reflection within self-study has different degrees. For example, the scriptures tell us that everything in life is transitory. One may pass a burning *ghāṭ* (cremation grounds) or a graveyard and for a moment have a thought of one's own mortality. This "graveyard dispassion" may last only for a moment, as the next thought may be of some opportunity for pleasure or ownership. The grief experienced at the death of a family member brings a much deeper experiential awareness of mortality, but all intellectual and inferential acknowledgment of one's own mortality evaporates in the face of the life-and-death struggle at the end of one's life. Patañjali says in Sūtra II:9 that fear of death dominates even the wise.

With this in mind, *svādhyāya*, or self-study, becomes a deeply personal and experiential inquiry into one's life and sense of being. An example of this type of inquiry is watching one's own self-interest in every thought, word, and action. This can be as painful as it is revealing, for virtually every action is rooted in self-protection, selfishness, comparison, and self-justification.

One of the ultimate spiritually directed forms of self-study is *Ātmā vichāra*, or inquiry into the nature of the Self: "Who am I?" Since we refer to "my body," "my senses," and "my intellect," the owner of the body, senses, and mind must be an entity different from the one asking the question. Inquiry into the nature of the Self is a path of self-realization. Ramana Mahāriṣhi is a well-known saint who developed and taught this method of self-awareness.

Īśhvara Praṇidhāna

Īśhvara Praṇidhāna, surrender to God, is the third prescription given in Kriyā Yoga. *Īśhvara Praṇidhāna* was already introduced in Sūtra 23 of *Samādhi Pāda* as a means of attaining *asamprajñāta samādhi* when practiced as an intense method by an intense *yogi* with intense urge. We see an example of this type of self-surrender to God when we read about Sri Rāmakriṣhṇa Paramahaṅsa reaching for Kālī Mā's sword to kill himself if he cannot see her living form. At that moment the sky opened up and he was merged in cosmic vision and bliss of self-realization.

For the *yogi* of less intense nature and urge, a method of self-surrender is given as part of Kriyā Yoga. This practice is keeping the presence of God in the

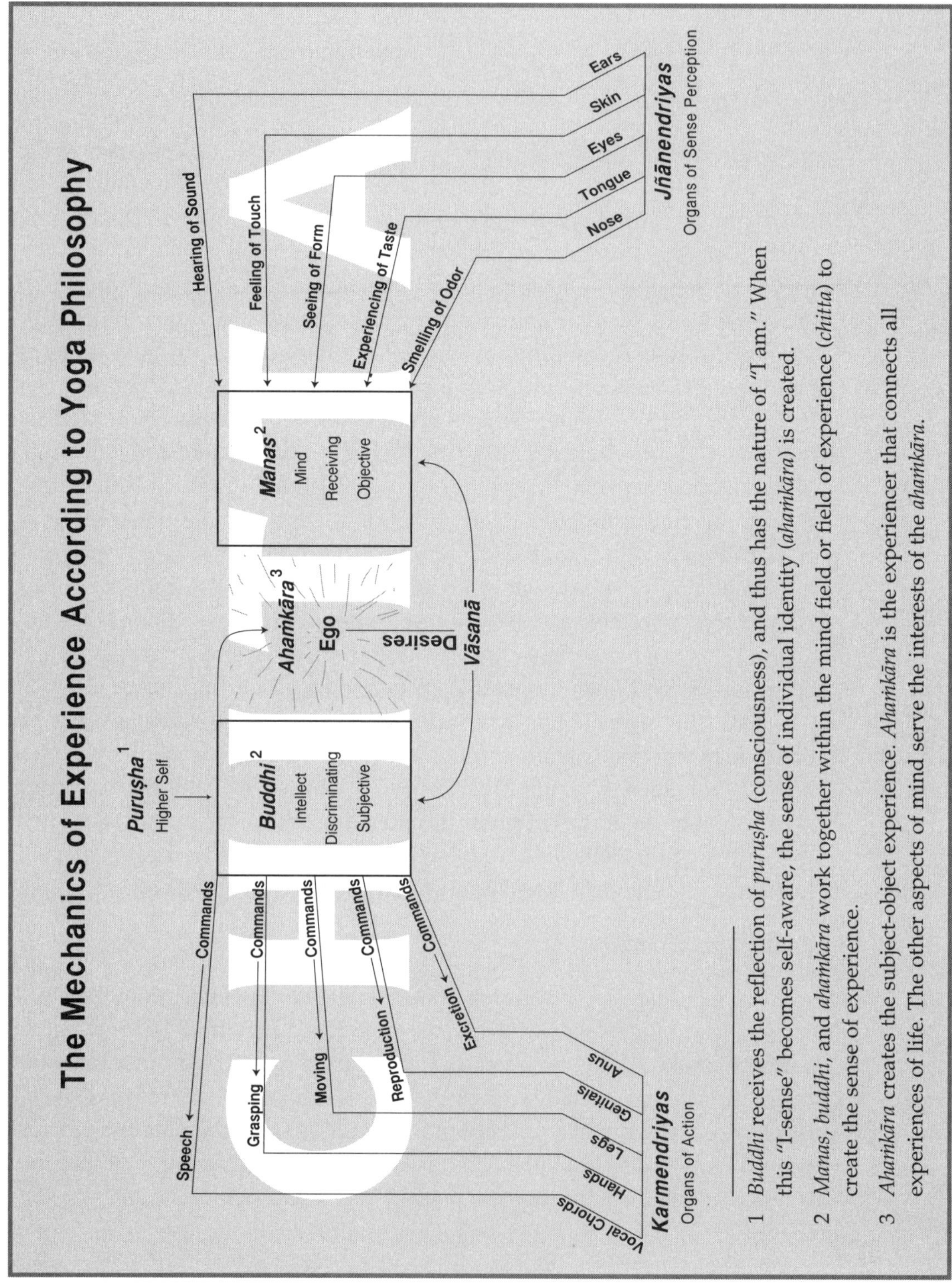

1 *Buddhi* receives the reflection of *puruṣa* (consciousness), and thus has the nature of "I am." When this "I-sense" becomes self-aware, the sense of individual identity (*ahaṁkāra*) is created.

2 *Manas, buddhi,* and *ahaṁkāra* work together within the mind field or field of experience (*chitta*) to create the sense of experience.

3 *Ahaṁkāra* creates the subject-object experience. *Ahaṁkāra* is the experiencer that connects all experiences of life. The other aspects of mind serve the interests of the *ahaṁkāra.*

heart at all times, seeing God in everyone and everything. Patañjali mentions *Īshvara Praṇidhāna* for a third time in Sūtra 45 of *Sādhana Pāda*, indicating ritualistic activities of surrender to God that may be integrated into one's daily life and practice such as *pūja* (prayer), or *yajña* (sacrifice).

KLEŚHAS

Sūtra II:24 can be stated, "Ignorance (*avidyā*) is the field of the afflictions (*kleśhas*)."

Implied in the concept of purification is the existence of impurity. In the first section of *Sādhana Pāda*, Patañjali introduces the *kleśhas* or afflictions (ignorance, egoism, attraction, repulsion, and fear of death), which are the generic forms of impurity. Actually, all five afflictions are forms of ignorance (*avidyā*). Ignorance is primordial, existing from the beginning of creation. It is in the seed of creation. In fact, all five afflictions are necessary for the creation to manifest. They are woven into the fabric of creation itself.

All spiritual traditions posit some sort of flaw—sin, evil, suffering, darkness, ignorance—the correction of which marks the achievement of the goal of perfection, transcendence, release, salvation, satori, which is the experience of merging with, or knowledge of, the Absolute (God, Self, Nirvāṇa, Tao, Peace, Reality). The goal is beyond the pairs of opposites, transcendent and imminent, yet it is achieved due to the condition of purity of mind developed by the practice of virtue.

Within the philosophy behind the *yoga* system there is no question of the existence of ignorance, though ignorance is a form of wrong cognition or mistaken identity (*viparyaya*). Without ignorance (*avidyā*) and its forms of egoism (*asmitā*), attraction (*rāga*), repulsion (*dveṣha*), and fear of death or clinging to life (*abhiniveśha*), the creation simply would not and could not exist. Nor would the stated purpose of creation, experience and liberation (Sūtra II: 18), be possible. Ignorance is the means by which the one becomes many and is the principle behind the evolution of the diversity of life forms (*eko ham, bahu shyam*, "I am one in many"). Furthermore, the piercing of the veil of ignorance by discriminative wisdom (*viveka khyāti*) brings the dissolution of the creation with its multiplicity of appearances and union with the One, non-dual reality that is the goal of *yoga*.

EXPERIENCE AND LIBERATION

What does the philosophical dialectic of the eternal principles of consciousness and matter and the 24 *tattvas* of creation mean for the aspirant who feels stuck in restlessness, distraction, and depression? First we have to look at the cause of our own "stuckness" and then we can see how our individual reality is actually a microcosm of the cosmic reality, which is explained in universal terms in the Sūtras. Actually, if we can accept on faith that there is a "spiritual reality," that consciousness is indeed separate from nature, this in itself creates freedom to move out of old patterns.

In *Sādhana Pāda*, Patañjali presents the overall purpose of the creation as experience and liberation of the Self, the embodied consciousness. The concepts of experience and liberation have direct relevance in every day life. The first consideration in applying these principles is to examine the nature of experience. According to the law of cause and effect, every thought, word, and action (*karma*) produces an effect. In yogic terminology, the effect of any action is a latent impression or *saṁskāra* that is stored in the mind (*chitta*). These impressions carry the latencies and predispositions that have the potentiality to create actions and color perceptions. In Sūtra II:12, Patañjali states that there is a reservoir of latent tendencies called *karmāśhaya* that are rooted in afflictions and will be experienced in present and future births. A person's personality is thus the cumulative expression of habits, predispositions, and desires coming from the experiences of this life and, by inference, past lives. It is clear that the mind is conditioned and experiences the objects of perception according to its likes and dislikes. In this way, the ego of individuality expresses its self-interest and is in turn bound by the limitations of its own predispositions. Thus people become trapped in habitual behavior even after the behavior is identified as hurtful.

As long as the mind is rooted in the *kleśhas* and perceiving the world in terms of its own self-interest, likes, dislikes, and fears, the cycle of action, impression, and desire continues. This is experienced on the microcosmic or individual level and it produces pleasurable and painful experiences. Sūtra II: 14 states that actions of virtue and vice result in pleasure and pain in one's birth, span of life, and experience. This is one of the purposes (*prayojana*) of creation; to give all kinds of experience (*bhoga*) through all the manifest forms of creation, to all sentient beings from the gods (*devas*) to single celled organisms.

The companion purpose of creation is liberation (*apavarga*). For the *yogi* with discrimination, all experiences are seen as painful because they do not lead to the goal of liberation (Sūtra II:15). Certainly all experiences have their place and the process of liberation comes in degrees as discrimination and dispassion develop. The beginning stages of this process start with examining one's own life and habitual thought process, which is discussed as part of *svādhyāya* or self-study. The liberating aspect of this is the development of the witnessing awareness that gives a more objective or dispassionate view of one's involvements in the world. This development starts with a desire to know the truth and progresses by honest introspection. To see ourselves this way is often humbling, but with this more objective view the opportunity for change is created. For example, if we catch ourselves before we react with judgment or anger, we create the opportunities for other responses to the situation, and we create a space for others to see and react to us differently. This is liberating from the deep entrenchment in habitual egoistic behavior.

A more profound level of the process of liberation happens in meditation. By focusing the mind on subtle principles such as inner light or sound, the inclination of the mind to go out to worldly objects, memories, and desires is confronted and gradually reduced. The mind is trained by regular *sādhana* practice and becomes habituated to the withdrawal from worldly preoccupation. The mind proficient in one-pointed concentration on subtle spiritual principles becomes absorbed in the reality of all-pervasive being and experiences a peace and freedom not found in the choices of worldly life. The discrimination, dispassion, and will to live a virtuous life are thus reinforced by the regular practice of meditation.

CONSCIOUSNESS AND MATTER

To explain more fully the origin and nature of the creation (*saṁsāra*), Patañjali brings the principles of Sāṁkhya to bear in the central philosophical section of *Sādhana Pāda*. Two eternal principles, consciousness (*puruṣha*) and matter (*prakṛiti*), constitute the absolute aspects of the ever-changing phenomenon of creation. In order to remove bondage and effect liberation, we have to remove the cause of bondage. Ignorance is the cause, and ignorance is uniting *puruṣha* and *prakṛiti* as if they were one entity; in ignorance the two are identified as one. This identity or "I-sense," known as *asmitā*, is the sense of being within each manifest entity.

Each entity in creation carries within its essential being the two eternal realities. Due to ignorance the conscious principle and the matter principle are not identified as distinct realities. The identification is with the "I-sense," the separate identity that expresses itself according to the nature of the entity. Whether it is a star, a planet, a plant, a rock, or a human being, every created thing or being in the creation is expressing its existence and has life force within it.

In reality, consciousness (*puruṣha*) is eternal, unchanging and all pervasive, while matter (*prakṛiti*) is eternal, mutable, but unconscious. Consciousness pervades matter like the sunlight illuminates everywhere. When the sunlight is blocked there is darkness; likewise when the interface of consciousness and matter is broken or blocked, there is *prālāyā* or suspension of the creation. This can either be a partial suspension (*kānda prālāyā*) or a complete suspension (*mahā prālāyā*) as in the end of the universal cycle. During the period of dormancy, between creations, *prakṛiti* holds the seed (*saṁskāra*) of creation. Thus matter (*prakṛiti*) exists in unmanifest or potential form as well as in manifest or active form (the creation).

Prakṛiti is characterized by three qualities: *sattva*—purity, essence, sentience; *rajas*—activity, life force, will; *tamas*—inertia, stability, perceptibility. These three qualities or *guṇas* are seen in every aspect of creation, in everything as well as every subjective awareness, perception, and action. The *guṇas* are in opposition to each other by nature of their characteristics and yet supportive of one another when there is predominance of any particular quality over the others. In creation the three *guṇas* are constantly unbalanced yet moving towards balance. This is the essence of the evolutionary process that moves from chaos to order and back to chaos with continual innovation and adoption to ever changing conditions.

As *prakṛiti* (matter) has an unmanifest state (*pradhāna*) as well as a manifest state (*saṁsāra*), the *guṇas* are either dormant or active. In the unmanifest state of matter the *guṇas* exist as the potential for manifestation. The qualities exist within the *guṇas* in seed form, but they do not mix or act together to produce anything.

The unmanifest is the cause of the manifest and also exists concurrently with the manifest as creative potentiality. The eternal existence of the unmanifest aspect of *prakṛiti* also allows for the possibility of liberation (*mokṣha*), which is the state of *kaivalya* or the isolation of consciousness (*puruṣha*) from matter (*prakṛiti*).

The static equilibrium of the unmanifest state of *prakṛiti* is disturbed due to the pervasive influence of *puruṣha* (consciousness), as a seed germinates due to the influence of the sun. In *mahat*, the first evolute of the interface of consciousness and matter, the *guṇas* exist in their cosmic form. *Mahat* is the first manifestation of evolution and the last knowledge of the involution before liberation.

THE 24 PRINCIPLES OF CREATION FROM THE PERSPECTIVE OF EVOLUTION AND INVOLUTION

From the association or union of consciousness and matter, all the evolutes of creation (*tattvas* or principles) come into manifest forms—from *mahat* to the elements (five *bhūtas*). Ignorance is the cause of this union, and experience and liberation are its purpose (Sūtras II:18 and 24). Thus the universal and individual reality is defined in terms of the evolution and involution of consciousness and matter. The flow and ebb, manifestation and dissolution of creation is a self-defining eternal process. Evolution produces experience (*bhoga*) of diversity, and involution gives rise to the knowledge leading to the establishment of non-dual reality (*kaivalya*), which is liberation (*apavarga*).

In the process of evolution, the principles (*tattvas*) appear in more diversified, denser, and tangible forms, as manifestation progresses. The process of involution, experienced in deep meditation through the states of *samādhi*, is exactly the reverse of the cause and effect sequence of evolution or creation.

In evolution, the first manifestation of the interface of consciousness and matter, *mahat*, has the nature of "I-sense" (*asmitā*). *Mahat* is the subtlest level of duality as it is the unqualified essence of being. When this universal "I sense" is identified in ignorance as an independent entity, the unqualified sense of being crystallizes into the ego of individuality, which is called *ahaṁkāra*, or ego sense. *Ahaṁkāra* identifies everything as "mine" or "not for me" and the grosser level of duality of self and other is born. The *ahaṁkāra* expresses itself in the form of subjective and objective realities. From *sattvik ahaṁkāra* comes the *manas* (recording mind) and sense capabilities (five *jñānendriyas*—organs of perception, and five *karmendriyas*—organs of action. From *tamasik ahaṁkāra* issues their objects, the five *tanmātras* (subtle elements or energies of hearing, feeling, seeing, tasting, and smelling). *Buddhi*, the discriminating faculty of mind is actually the aspect of *mahat* that serves the *ahaṁkāra*. The three aspects of mind, *manas*, *buddhi*, and *ahaṁkāra* along with the ten senses and subtle elements are collectively called the *antaḥkaraṇa* and constitute the subtle body. The gross body and gross objects are created by the five elements (*pañcha mahābhūtas*—space, air, fire, water, and earth). This is the most dense and final manifestation of the interface of consciousness and matter, which, of course, is constantly evolving. The *rajasik* form of *ahaṁkāra* is contact of subject and object, which is characterized by attraction, creating attachment and repulsion, which ultimately creates hatred.

In deep meditation, the mind traces back this lineage from effect to cause as each level of manifestation is pierced. The states of the *guṇas* (qualities of *prakṛiti*) that are discriminated by the concentrated mind are given in Sūtra II: 19 as particular, universal, indicator only, and that which is without indication. The particular (*viśheṣha*) refers to the gross or elemental reality that is perceived by the senses. The universal (*aviśheṣha*) is the subtle, energetic level of reality created by the *tanmātras*, which is the cause or essence of the gross physical reality. Indicator only (*liṅga mātra*) is *mahat* (*sattva buddhi*), which is the cause and essence of the subtle reality. That indicator is "I-sense" or sense of pure unqualified being, the substratum of all life and indeed all animate and inanimate existence. That which is without indication is the unmanifest state of the *guṇas* (*mūla prakṛiti*), which is the causeless cause (*pradhāna*).

The conscious principle (*puruṣha*) is the all-pervading awareness that is the motivating factor in both evolution and involution. Therefore, it is said in Sūtra II:21 that nature (*prakṛiti*) exists for the purpose of the Self (*Ātmā*), which is embodied consciousness (*puruṣha*). This is the concept of *puruṣhārtha* (the purpose of *puruṣha*), which is experience and liberation. In experience, consciousness is identified with matter or nature. Ignorance is the cause of this identification (Sūtra II:24). In liberation matter and consciousness are known to be separate by means of *viveka khyāti* (discriminative wisdom). It is nature or *prakṛiti* that goes through transformation. *Puruṣha* or consciousness is always separate, independent, and immutable. If this were not true, liberation would be impossible.

CONCLUSION

By repetition and elaboration, Patañjali develops the practice and philosophy of *yoga* to include all levels and natures of aspirants. In *yoga*, practice includes an array of different approaches including devotion (*bhakti*), selfless service (Karma Yoga), self-inquiry (*Ātmā vichāra*) and spiritual exercises such as Rāja Yoga. The basis of all these practices are presented in generic form in *Sādhana Pāda*, without references to specific deities, creeds, or lineages. For this reason, it is said that the principles of *yoga* are in all religions.

Reading a book cannot bring liberation from suffering, and understanding philosophical concepts does not bring higher consciousness. This testimonial knowledge can, however, provide a map of a path to liberation and a context for practice. Faith in the truth of the scriptures and association with truth-seekers (*satsang*) does not establish the reality of that truth, though these intentions and associations are necessary aspects of a genuine spiritual life. Even association with an enlightened master does not necessarily bring enlightenment, though without such guidance, inspiration, and example the attainment of spiritual awareness leading to liberation is very difficult.

Knowledge remains inferential until established by one's own practice and the Truth is directly perceived. If testimonial or inferential knowledge alone were sufficient means to attain liberation, then *Sādhana Pāda*, Book II of Patañjali's *Yoga Sūtras* would not be necessary.

Those spiritual aspirants who are inspired by the great philosophies and exemplary lives of saints and sages, and want to experience the truth for themselves, know that practice is where "the rubber meets the road" in spiritual life. Practice may be dynamic and ecstatic, but more often it may seem repetitive and uneventful. Whereas spiritual awakening may be a joyous or wondrous experience, it is often followed by another kind of pain, the pain of separation from the Divine Reality, the loss of transcendence. At some point an aspirant realizes how thick the layers of delusion are and how we are trapped in habitual patterns of hurtful behaviors. As depressing as this realization may be, the sincere aspirant must push on and continue their practice.

Those of us who have had the privilege of studying with Babaji have heard him give the answer "regular *sādhana*" to any number of questions about problems in spiritual life. He has likened a daily *sādhana* practice to "rowing your boat in the middle of the ocean." We may not see any progress because neither shore is visible, nevertheless there is still movement. Over time, *sādhana* practiced regularly and with consistent effort, is transformative. In the end, the truth realized through practice is not a speculative belief, but it is rather an experienced truth, which is irrefutable to the one who has become established in its awareness through his or her own efforts.

As we embark on the study of *Sādhana Pāda*, whether it is for the first time or the hundredth time, let us commit ourselves again to practice, discipline, and virtuous action. In preparation for contemplation of the timeless knowledge of Yoga, let us consider two ancient Vedic prayers to sanctify the aims of liberation from the afflictions or ignorance, freedom to know the Truth, and finding Peace in the infinite unbounded Self.

Om saha nā va vatu/Saha nau bhunaktu
Saha viryaṁ karavā-vahai
Tejasvinā-vadhitam-astu mā vidviṣhā-vahai
Om śhāntiḥ, śhāntiḥ, śhāntiḥ

Om. May God protect us both, teacher and the disciple.
May we be nourished and work together with great energy.
May our study be vigorous and fruitful.
May love and harmony dwell amongst us.
Om, Peace, Peace, Peace

Om asato mā sad gamaya
Tamaso mā jyotir-gamaya
Mṛityor-mā-amritaṁ gamaya
Sarveṣhām svasti-bhavatu
Sarveṣhām śhānti-bhavatu
Sarveṣhām pūrṇaṁ-bhavatu
Sarveṣhām maṅgalaṁ-bhavatu
Lokā samastāḥ sukhino bhavantu
Om Śhāntiḥ śhāntiḥ śhāntiḥ

From untruth lead us to truth
From darkness lead us to light
From death lead us to immortality
May all beings dwell in happiness
May all beings dwell in peace
May all beings attain oneness
May all beings attain auspiciousness
May happiness be unto the whole world
Om Peace Peace Peace

Dayanand Diffenbaugh
Mount Madonna 2008

Book II

Sādhana Pāda

On Yoga Practice

Hairakhan Bābā site, Śheetlākhet, Kumaon

Sūtra 1   तपःस्वाध्यायेश्वरप्रणिधानानि क्रियायोगः ॥ १ ॥

tapaḥ-svādhyāy-eśhvara-praṇidhānāni kriyā-yogaḥ

Austerity, Self-study, and surrender to God constitute Kriyā Yoga (Practical Yoga).

तपः	*tapaḥ*	austerity, purificatory action
स्वाध्याय	*svādhyāya*	Self-study
ईश्वर-प्रणिधान	*Īśhvara-praṇidhāna*	surrender to God, worship of God
क्रिया	*kriyā*	action, practical
योगः	*yogaḥ*	yoga

In the first book, *Samādhi Pāda*, Patañjali gave an elaborate explanation of the theories of *yoga*, its divisions, and its fruits (*samprajñāta* and *asamprajñāta samādhi*). He also gave the primary means (*upāya*) of *yoga* and explains the efficacy of practice (*abhyāsa*) and dispassion (*vairāgya*). For those *yogis* who have already attained stable-mindedness (*samāhita chitta*), which is the highest category of *yogi*, the instructions of *Samādhi Pāda* are sufficient to achieve perfection in *yoga*.

Now, in *Sādhana Pāda*, Patañjali gives practical methods for those *yogis* who have a distracted mental state (*vikṣhipta*), which is the average category of *yogis*. These practical methods (Kriyā Yoga) make the mind fit for one-pointed concentration (*ekāgra-dhyāna*) and help the aspirant achieve the steady mental state (*samāhita chitta*).

In the course of these first two books, Patañjali gives three types of *yoga* methods suitable for the three types of *yogis*:

1. *Abhyāsa-vairāgyābhyāṁ-tannirodhaḥ* (Sūtra I:12) "Mental modifications are controlled by persistent practice and dispassion." The practice of one-pointed concentration, with all distracting thoughts (*vrittis*) restrained by dispassion, creates rapid progress in *sādhana*. This method is sufficient for *yogis* of the highest category who already have stable minds (*samāhita chitta*).

2. *Tapaḥ-svādhyāy-eśhvara-praṇidhānāni kriyā-yogaḥ* (Sūtra II:1) "Austerity, Self-study, and surrender to God constitute Kriyā Yoga (Practical Yoga)." For those *yogis* of moderate disposition who have distracted minds (*vikṣhipta*), and who are not capable of one-pointed concentration (*ekāgratā*) and dispassion (*vairāgya*), the methods of Kriyā Yoga are prescribed. By austerity, the aspirant gains control over the body and life force (*prāṇa*). By self-study, the aspirant gains control over the mind. Surrender to God brings *samādhi* (higher consciousness leading to liberation).

3. *Yama-niyamāsana-prāṇāyāma-pratyāhāra-dhāraṇādhyāna-samādhayo-'ṣhṭāvaṅgāni* (Sūtra II:29) "Restraints, observances, posture, regulation of breath, withdrawal, concentration, meditation, and absorption are the eight limbs of *yoga*." For worldly-minded people who have confused minds, Aṣhṭāṅga Yoga is the best method to practice for spiritual development. Starting with the

rules and regulations of conduct, a foundation for spiritual life is made. Step by step, practices are introduced that lead the aspirant to greater control of the mind-body complex until one is fit for the internal limbs of concentration, meditation, and *samādhi*.

The impure mind cannot develop perfection in *yoga*. The impurities of the mind, which are caused by desires (*vāsanā*), can be removed by self-discipline. Kriyā Yoga is self-discipline, so it purifies the mind. The methods are three: austerities, Self-study, and surrender to God.

1. **Austerity** (*tapaḥ*). The word *tapaḥ* literally means "to heat up" or "to burn." In the processing of impure gold, the gold is heated by fire. This purifies the molten gold by removing the dross. In the practice of austerities, a limit is put on desires. This limit causes a purifying heat in the mind, and gradually all desires are removed.

   Austerity is discipline. Just as an expert horse trainer tames a wild horse by disciplining it, an aspirant gets control over the body, life force (*prāṇa*), senses, and mind by practicing austerities. The result of having the mind, body, senses, and life force under control is that the *yogi* is not disturbed by the pairs of opposites like heat and cold, pleasure and pain, and fame and ignominy. The *yogi* can then meditate without any physical, psychological, or emotional disturbances.

   Actions, afflictions, and desires are caused by *rajas* and *tamas guṇas*. Without practicing austerities, the effects of *rajas* and *tamas guṇas* cannot be removed. A yogi should observe those austerities that bring peace of mind (*chitta-prasādana*) and that do not harm the physical body and sense organs. Austerities that are performed out of self-interest should be avoided.[1]

2. **Self-study** (*svādhyāya*). By Self-study, the flow of the mind is diverted away from worldly attachment and desires and toward the spiritual goal of finding truth, reality, or God. Self-study is practiced in two ways:

   a. Studying scriptures and/or the repeated utterance of sacred *mantras*, such as *japa* of Om.[2]

   b. Self-inquiry (*ātma-vichāra*) is a method of reflecting on the ego center to understand how it colors our perceptions and veils our understanding of the real Self.

3. **Surrender to God** (*Īshvara-praṇidhāna*). In this verse, the practice of surrender to God is an intermediate practice, performed by worshipping God with complete devotion, by offering the fruits of all actions performed to God, or by

---

1 Sūtra II:32 gives a thorough explanation of the three kinds of austerity—physical, vocal, and mental—as well as the differences between *yogic* (*sāttvika*) austerity, worldly (*rājasika*) austerity, and harmful (*tāmasika*) austerity.

2 Sūtra I:28 explains the practice as *taj-japas-tad-artha-bhāvanam* (Constant repetition of Om while meditating on its meaning), which is given as a method of achieving *asamprajñāta samādhi*.

removing the ego of being a performer. Surrender to God purifies the mind by developing non-attachment to objects and actions performed.

The practice of *Īshvara-praṇidhāna* is listed three times in the first two books of the *Yoga Sūtras*. Surrender to God, as it was mentioned in Sūtra I:23 (*Īshvara-praṇidhānādvā*, "Or, by devotional surrender to God"), is an advanced practice for those aspirants with intense devotion and supreme dispassion. They can attain *asamprajñāta samādhi* by *Īshvara-praṇidhāna* alone, which in this case means keeping divine presence in the heart at all times. It is a way of feeling the omnipresence of God.

In this *sūtra*, *Īshvara-praṇidhāna* relates to the practical actions of worshipping God and service to God. In this practical method of surrender to God, the mind is purified and prepared for *samādhi* (super-consciousness).

In Sūtra II:32, surrender to God is mentioned again as one of the observances of *yoga* (*niyama*). There, it refers to practices such as *puja* (devotional offerings) and the mental assertion, "Not my will, but Thy will be done." It is a purification practice that can be done by any aspirant at any stage.

These three practices of Kriyā Yoga incorporate all the practices of *yoga*. However, in this *sūtra*, Patañjali is referring to the intermediate level of practice. *Tapaḥ*, for example, has many levels. It is included as one of the *niyamas* (observances) listed in Sūtra II:32, and yet all the practices of *yama*, *niyama*, *āsana*, *prāṇāyāma*, and *pratyāhāra* can be included in *tapaḥ*.

Even the specific practices are in varying degrees. The beginning practice of silence, for example, is simply not using the vocal chords as a means of expression. An intermediate level practice of silence, which would be included in this *sūtra*, is using the absence of speech as a means to restrain the thoughts in the mind. The beginning level is an austerity for worldly-minded practitioners because it reveals how many desires there are in the mind. The intermediate level, which is part of Kriyā Yoga, actually reduces the *kleśhas* (afflictions) and prepares the mind for *samādhi*.

Yogis who practice Kriyā Yoga are of the intermediate level. Even though their minds are distracted (*vikṣhipta*), they have fixed their aim in spiritual practice and can concentrate with moderate success. In order to purify their minds of restlessness and worldly desires and to attain *samādhi*, they can practice austerity, Self-study, and surrender to God.

Note
Patañjali begins the discourse on spiritual practice by describing Kriyā Yoga, or the methods of austerity, Self-study, and surrender to God. Austerity means to willingly accept the discomforts of limiting the ego. Self-study means to investigate the nature of the Self through inquiry or *japa* (repetition of a *mantra*). Surrender to God means to replace self-interest with devotion, or replacing the pursuit of pleasure and pain with worship or service to God. All three are

considered intermediate practices because they are for *yogis* who have clarified their aim with strong determination, but who are not yet capable of perfect concentration.

In order to understand how Kriyā Yoga works and why it is effective, we have to understand what the goal of *yoga* is and what the obstacles are. The goal of *yoga* is perfect inner peace. The primary obstacle to inner peace is mental agitation. The mind is agitated by desires and attachments, which are expressions of the individual ego. All experiences of life are motivated by ego, attachment, and desire, which are all strengthened by our experiences of life. It is a self-perpetuating cycle that stops only by some opposing force (*yoga*).

Each of the three practices of Kriyā Yoga weakens the cycle by breaking the ego's reign. The ego's primary activity is to pursue pleasure and avoid pain. It acts for its own benefit, in as direct a manner as possible. It is, however, willing to use all forms of indirect methods when direct means are proven unfavorable. This means that the ego is very tricky and very difficult to subdue.

The practice of austerity simply means to act with a non-selfish motive. Any time we will ourselves to act for some greater purpose than our own gratification, we are weakening the reign of the ego. In the beginning, there will always be some selfishness, but the practices themselves remove it gradually.

For example, the ego likes comfort. A *yogi* may choose an austerity of meditating for one hour every morning at 5 AM. Initially, this practice may be quite easy because the ego likes the idea of being a "meditator." But sooner or later, the *yogi* will find a strong desire to keep sleeping. Or, they may have a busy day and want to shorten the meditation. Or, their knees are tight and they want to stand up early. All of these are natural urges that arise out of the ego's desire for comfort. The practice of austerity means to meditate for an hour at 5 AM no matter what contrary desires may arise.

The reason austerities are so effective is because the mind is habitual. Whatever we do creates a pattern in the mind. The more we do it, the more firmly established the pattern becomes. Anyone who has broken a bad habit knows this. In the beginning, not performing the bad habit is extremely difficult and takes tremendous will power. But if there is no indulging in the habit, it goes away over time because the pattern in the mind is weakened and eventually removed altogether. This is true for both good and bad actions.

The *yogic* practice of austerity must have the intention of bringing peace to the mind. In verses XVII:14–19 of the *Bhagavad Gītā*, austerities are divided into categories: the three forms of body, speech, and mind, and the three qualities of pure (*sāttvika*), passionate (*rājasika*), and dull (*tāmasika*). Pure austerities are performed only for the sake of bringing peace to the mind. Passionate austerities are performed for some selfish gain, such as power and/or recognition, or for making the body more attractive. Dull austerities are misguided, harming the body and mind.

The practices of Self-study and surrender to God also weaken the ego and bring peace to the mind, but for very different reasons. All the power of the ego comes from misunderstanding. Technically, the ego is simply the notion, "I am this mind-body complex." All selfish actions stem from this notion and are meant to benefit the mind-body complex that is "me." But what *yoga* tells us is that this notion is not the whole truth. It is *a* truth; it gives the world its reality. Nevertheless, it requires an identification, a union, of two separate principles. The "I" and the body are ultimately separate. The ego unites them, which is required for all experiences of the world, but outside the ego, the union doesn't exist.

The ego rules the mind because it links the "I" with the mind and body. If the "I," which is another name for the self, were not identified with the mind and body, the ego would have no power. Self-study, therefore, is the set of practices that investigates the nature of the self to discover its origin. When the origin is found to be separate from the body, the ego loses the battle and peace is attained.

There are two main categories of Self-study. The first is inquiry. This is an intellectual process in which the mind studies itself. At first, the nature of experience is discovered to be a mental process. Then, the various aspects of the mind are identified separately until it seeks the source of consciousness. When the intellect finally discovers that the Self, which is the source of consciousness, is separate from all aspects of the mind (*viveka khyāti*), all false notions of the ego are destroyed and the mind remains at peace.

The second category is study of the scriptures and/or repetition of a *mantra*. These methods bring the mind into contemplation of the nature of the Self. The scriptures use words to describe the Self, and the mind uses them directly. In the repetition of the *mantra*, the sounds direct the mind away from its normal worldly concerns and toward the silence of the Self.

Finally, in surrender to God, the "I" is consciously replaced as the motivation for action. Instead of acting for "my own" benefit, the *yogi* decides to act out of devotion to God or as an agent of God. At first, there may be some confusion about what God's will is, but the intention itself is what matters. Again, like a habit, when self-interest is consciously abandoned in order to perform actions for God or for others as a service to God, the ego is weakened. When this surrender becomes complete, the ego is dissolved and the mind rests in peace.

These three methods of Kriyā Yoga are also listed in other places in the *Yoga Sūtras*. The differences are simply of degree and proficiency. Here, they are performed specifically for reducing the afflictions (*kleśhas*) and attaining *samādhi*, which is further described in the next *sūtra*.

Temple and terraced hillside, Kakari Ghāṭ, Kośhi River, Kumaon.

Sūtra 2   समाधिभावनार्थः क्लेशतनूकरणार्थश्च ॥२॥

samādhi-bhāvanārthaḥ kleśa-tanū-karaṇārthaśh-cha

[Kriyā Yoga is practiced] for attaining *samādhi* and reducing the afflictions.

समाधि	*samādhi*	trance, super-consciousness
भावनार्थ	*bhāvanārtha*	for developing the state of
क्लेश	*kleśha*	afflictions
तनू	*tanū*	reduce, attenuate
करणार्थ	*karaṇārtha*	for the purpose of
च	*cha*	and

In this *sūtra*, the purpose of Kriyā Yoga is established. Kriyā Yoga is for those aspirants with a distracted mind who cannot attain one-pointed concentration. The distractions in the mind are the afflictions (*kleśhas*), and until the mind is purified of the afflictions, it cannot achieve *samādhi* (super-conscious absorption). Therefore, the purpose of Kriyā Yoga is to purify the mind—by reducing the afflictions—so that it may attain *samādhi*.

The *saṁskāras* of affliction (*kleśhas*) exist eternally in the mind field (*chitta*) as seeds or potential. The *kleśhas*, which are described in the next *sūtra* as *avidyā* (ignorance), *asmitā* ("I-amness"), *rāga* (attraction), *dveṣha* (repulsion), and *abhiniveśha* (fear of death), are life in the world. Without them, individuality (*ahaṁkāra*) and experience (*bhoga*) are impossible. But for the *yogi*, they are obstacles to *samādhi*.

When the mind is involved in worldly life (*saṁsāra*), the afflictions are in their active state (*udāra*). Through the practice of austerities (*tapaḥ*), the body, life force (*prāṇa*), and mind are purified and the *kleśhas* are reduced (*tanū*). Through the practice of Self-study (*svādhyāya*), the mind and intellect are purified and one develops the inclination to achieve Self-realization. Through the practice of surrender to God (*Īshvara-praṇidhāna*) one acquires steadiness of mind (*samāhita chitta*) and achieves *samādhi*.

Kriyā Yoga removes the impurities of the mind that give rise to worldly qualities such as passion, attachment, restlessness, and dullness. Without removing these qualities it is not possible to achieve *samādhi*. The impure mind is based on the afflictions. Therefore, when the mind is purified by the practices of Kriyā Yoga, the hold of the afflictions is first weakened and then attenuated, and the mind dwells in the *sāttvika* (pure) state. The inclination of the *sāttvika* mind is toward *samādhi*.

In Sūtra I:12, Patañjali stated *abhyāsa-vairāgyabhyām-tannirodhaḥ* (the modifications are controlled by persistent practice and dispassion). The practices of Kriyā Yoga weaken the hold of the afflictions and prepare the aspirant for *abhyāsa* (the regular practice of one-pointed meditation) and *vairāgya* (dispassion for the finite world). The result of *abhyāsa* and *vairāgya* is *samādhi*. The fruit of *samādhi* is discriminative wisdom (*viveka khyāti* or *prasaṁkhyāna*), which is the realization of the Self (*puruṣa*) as separate from the intellect (*buddhi tattva*). This knowledge removes the primary affliction of ignorance (*avidyā*), from which the other afflictions evolve. The removal of ignorance is therefore the removal of all five afflictions.

In the state of ignorance (*avidyā*), there exists an erroneous belief, "I am this mind-body complex." The Self, which is pure consciousness alone, is not known to be greater than its limited role as individualized consciousness within the mind-body complex. This erroneous belief linking the Self to the mind and body is known as *avidyā saṁskāra* (the impression of ignorance). It exists in all human beings in seed form and provides the basis for all types of individual experience.

When *sāsmitā samādhi* (super-consciousness with "I-sense" alone) is achieved, the pure "I-sense" is identified as existing independently from the mind. By discriminative wisdom (*viveka khyāti*), the seed of *avidyā saṁskāra* (the notion, "I am this mind-body complex") gets roasted, which means that it cannot germinate again. Once stability in discriminative wisdom is achieved, no actions experienced through that mind-body complex have the ability to create new *saṁskāras* (impressions based on the *kleśhas*). The purpose of experience (*bhoga*) is thus finished in that *yogi's* mind.

When the purpose of experience (*bhoga adhikāra*) is finished and the seeds of affliction are roasted in the fire of wisdom (*prasaṅkhyāna*), supreme dispassion (*paravairāgya*) develops. The *saṁskāras* of *paravairāgya* are the *saṁskāras* of restraint in *dharma megha* (cloud-pouring virtue) *samādhi*, and gradually they replace all worldly *saṁskāras* (see Sūtras I:50 and IV:29).

The discriminative awareness (*viveka khyāti*) of the difference between pure consciousness (*puruṣa*) and the mind itself is the highest knowledge possible in creation. *Viveka khyāti*, however, is still a *vritti* (thought wave in the mind). For the mind that has developed supreme dispassion, even that highest knowledge appears to the *yogi* as inferior to perfect control (*nirodha*) in which the mind is absolutely still. The *yogi* thus becomes unattached even to that knowledge.

In Sūtra I:50, Patañjali states, *taj-jaḥ saṁskāro-'nya-saṁskāra-prati-bandhī* (The latent impression produced from that [*samādhi*, wisdom] is opposed to the formation of other latent impressions). The more the afflictions attenuate, the subtler and more profound the *samādhi* becomes. This process of replacing the *saṁskāras* of affliction with the *saṁskāras* of restraint goes on until the afflictions are totally removed and *asamprajñāta samādhi* (*samādhi* beyond all knowledge) is achieved. When *asamprajñāta samādhi* is perfected, final liberation (*kaivalya*) results.

By themselves, the *kleśhas* are never extinguished or even weakened, so without the practice of Kriyā Yoga, the *kleśhas* perpetuate themselves indefinitely. In contrast, Kriyā Yoga and *samādhi* work together. The first attenuates the afflictions so that *samādhi* can be attained. Then the knowledge attained in the highest *samādhis* roasts the afflictions so that they can never become active again.

Note

In this *sūtra*, the goal of Kriyā Yoga is explained as reducing the afflictions and attaining *samādhi*, which places it as an intermediate level practice. These practices are not necessary for advanced *yogis* because they have already reduced the afflictions and can attain *samādhi* at will. They are also not appropriate for beginners whose aim is still not fixed and whose minds are incapable of concentrating. Instead, the practices of Kriyā Yoga are for *yogis* whose aim and commitment to *sādhana* are well established, and who can concentrate well at some times but not others.

The first book of the *Yoga Sūtras* provided the advanced practices designed to perfect *samādhi*. *Samādhi* is a categorically different type of concentration from normal meditation. In normal meditation, the mind retains multi-tiered thinking in the form of "I (the mind-body complex) am concentrating on an object (that is separate from me)." The feeling of separateness from the object is never abandoned.

In *samādhi*, the mind's identification with the mind-body complex as a separate entity is disrupted temporarily. The mind becomes so completely absorbed in the object of concentration that the separating activity of the mind is suspended. The object itself fills the mind completely.

Many levels of *samādhi* were described in detail in *Samādhi Pāda*. As the mind becomes proficient in each level, it develops the ability to go even deeper into the nature or cause of the object. The culmination of *samādhi* is discriminative wisdom (*viveka khyāti*) in which the Self is identified as separate from the mind. When *viveka khyāti* is perfected, the Self becomes identified only with itself (Sūtra I:3) and liberation is attained.

The purpose of Kriyā Yoga is to prepare the mind for *samādhi* by reducing the afflictions. The afflictions, which are described in detail in the next *sūtra*, are the five energies that keep the mind revolving in its separate identity and preclude *samādhi*. Once *samādhi* is attained, it generates momentum that roasts the very potential of the afflictions to sprout.

This, however, doesn't happen all at once. Everything about the mind cycles, so the practices of Kriyā Yoga continue to be necessary even after the first levels of *samādhi* are attained. It is only when the *yogi* can become established in *samādhi* at will that they can be fully replaced by the advanced practices of *Samādhi Pāda*.

The beginning practices of *yoga* are described primarily in Sūtras II:29 – 48. In the next *sūtra*, the five afflictions are introduced.

Frontispiece of Śhiva Temple, Jageshwar, Kumaon.

Sūtra 3 अविद्याऽस्मितारागद्वेषाभिनिवेशाः पञ्च क्लेशाः ॥३॥

avidyā-'smitā–rāga–dveṣhābhiniveśhāḥ pañcha kleśhāḥ

The five afflictions are ignorance, egoism, attraction, repulsion, and fear of death.

अविद्या	*avidyā*	ignorance, nescience
अस्मिता	*asmitā*	egoism, "I amness"
राग	*rāga*	attachment, attraction
द्वेष	*dveṣha*	repulsion, aversion
अभिनिवेशः	*abhiniveśhaḥ*	fear of death, clinging to life
पञ्च	*pañcha*	five
क्लेशाः	*kleśhāḥ*	afflictions

That which causes suffering and obstructs self-development is called an affliction (*kleśha*). There are five core afflictions upon which all painful experiences are based: ignorance (*avidyā*), egoism (*asmitā*), attraction (*rāga*), repulsion (*dveṣha*), and fear of death (*abhiniveśha*).

These five energies are the root cause of all suffering. They appear in the mind (*chitta*) in the form of thoughts (*vritti*). All thought waves that are based on the afflictions and that strengthen the afflictions fall within the category of painful thoughts (*kliṣhṭa vrittis*) as defined in Sūtra I:5.[1] Non-painful thoughts (*akliṣhṭa vrittis*), on the other hand, are those that weaken the hold of the *kleśhas*.

Painful *vrittis* are based on the *kleśhas* and are regarded as *viparyaya* (wrong cognition), which is the false conception of an object in which the real form of the object does not correspond to the image in the mind (Sūtra I:8). All *vrittis* require the root cognition, "I am an individual." This very idea that there is an individual experiencer of creation is itself a wrong cognition, a combination of ignorance (*avidyā*) and egoism (*asmitā*), and is the root of the other *kleśhas*.

The function of the *kleśhas* is to create ignorance, attachment, and aversion in the mind. Collectively, these promote the functioning of creation, or the wheel of birth and rebirth (*saṁsāra*). Actually, the evolution of creation cannot be separated from the activity of the *kleśhas* because all motivation for expanding the experience of the world comes from these five. The specific condition of the afflictions within living beings is the cause of their rebirth in a particular class or species (*jāti*). It also determines their length of life (*āyu*) and the nature of their experiences (*bhoga*), as described in Sūtra II:13.

When *puruṣha* (pure conscious principle) is reflected in *prakṛiti* (pure matter principle), *rajas guṇa* (quality of activity) becomes unbalanced and disturbs the equilibrium of the unmanifest *prakṛiti* (*avyakta*). The three *guṇas* start interacting and give rise to the cosmic intellect (*mahat*). *Puruṣha* is reflected in *mahat*, creat-

---

1 The *vrittis* are further classified into five categories in Sūtra I:6: valid proof (*pramāṇa*), wrong cognition (*viparyaya*), imagination (*vikalpa*), sleep (*nidrā*), and memory (*smṛiti*).

ing the nature of "I-sense" (*asmitā*). This causes *mahat* to appear as if it were conscious, whereas in reality it is a mixture of consciousness and matter. This incorrect appearance is the first affliction known as ignorance (*avidyā*).

Immediately, the "I-sense" becomes identified as a separate entity, which is known as the ego of individual existence (*ahaṁkāra*). This notion of a separate existence is based on ignorance, and it is the second affliction called egoism (*asmitā kleśha*). All the subtle and gross senses, objects, and experiences are manifested from these principles. Objects are experienced either as attractive (*rāga*), which creates attachment, or repulsive (*dveṣha*), which creates aversion or negative attachment. The end effect of objective experience is the fear of death or clinging to life (*abhiniveśha*).

The purpose of manifest creation is the experience and liberation of the *puruṣha* (individualized consciousness). Since all experiences are ultimately based on the primary affliction of ignorance (*avidyā*), the manifestation of each individual's world (*saṁsāra*) is based on incorrect cognition (*viparyaya jñāna*). All incorrect cognitions come from treating the non-Self as if it were the Self. Therefore, the purpose of the afflictions is to bring about the experiences of all individuals in a state of ignorance (*avidyā*).

The paradox of the *kleśhas* being both the cause of worldly experiences and the primary obstacles to *samādhi* is at the crux of *yoga* practice in general and Kriyā Yoga in particular. The desires in the mind that motivate people to expand themselves and their worlds are based on the *kleśhas*. This motivation is an activating force in the mind, which disrupts concentration. So long as the urge to generate more and greater experiences is active in the mind, one-pointed concentration is not possible. It is for this reason that Kriyā Yoga is introduced to reduce the *kleśhas* and to attain one-pointed concentration or *samādhi*.

Note

In this *sūtra*, the five afflictions are introduced. From the perspective of the *yogi* trying to achieve and perfect *samādhi*, all activity in the mind is considered an obstacle. Since the five forces of ignorance, egoism, attraction, repulsion, and clinging are the primary fuels for thought, they are considered afflictions (*kleśhas*) or impediments to *yoga*.

All experiences of life are known through the mind. No matter what happens, if the mind doesn't register it, it can't be considered an experience. For example, consider a near-miss car accident. A person is driving down a road during a storm when a large branch falls from a tree, just missing the car. If the driver sees the branch falling, the experience will probably be anxiety, then relief and high levels of adrenaline in the bloodstream. If the driver doesn't see the branch falling, nothing additional would happen to the driver's emotional state and adrenaline levels. In both scenarios, the tree falls in exactly the same way, but the experience is completely different. Experiences occur in the mind or not at all.

We can see the force of all five afflictions in every experience of life. For example, take the desire for food, which includes the experience of hunger. It starts in the mind as the notion, "I am hungry." The "I" in the sentence is the conscious individual with characteristics, which is the manifestation of ignorance and egoism. Hunger is a feeling of discomfort that reminds the mind, however obliquely, of death. The mind is instantly engaged in pursuing the pleasure of eating. This pursuit includes the last three afflictions. It is seeking pleasure (attraction), avoiding the discomfort of hunger (aversion), and delaying death (clinging to life).

The five afflictions generate tremendous momentum in the mind. Every moment of wakefulness is spent defining our individuality, seeking pleasure, avoiding pain, and delaying death. We see it in a wide variety of forms, but especially in dwelling in the past and anxiety over the future. The mind spends very little time in the simple experiences of the present.

This is a substantial problem for meditation. Everything the five afflictions create is an obstacle to *yoga*. When the afflictions are in their active state, no concentration is possible. They must be weakened to the point of dormancy before one-pointed concentration and *samādhi* can be attained. This is the purpose of Kriyā Yoga.

In the next *sūtra*, the four states of the afflictions are described.

Bells placed by pilgrims at the temple in Bhowali, Kumaon.

Sūtra 4   अविद्याक्षेत्रमुत्तरेषां प्रसुप्ततनुविच्छिन्नोदाराणाम् ॥४॥

avidyā–kṣhetram–uttareṣhāṁ prasupta–tanu–vichchhinnodārāṇām

Ignorance is the field for the other [*kleśhas*], which can appear as dormant, weak, interrupted, or operative.

अविद्या	*avidyā*	ignorance, nescience
क्षेत्रम्	*kṣhetram*	field
उत्तरेषाम्	*uttareṣhām*	for the others, for the following
प्रसुप्त	*prasupta*	dormant
तनु	*tanu*	weak
विच्छिन्न	*vichchhinna*	interrupted, alternated, overpowered
उदाराणाम्	*udārāṇām*	operative, expanded

Ignorance (*avidyā*) is the root cause of the other four afflictions (*kleśhas*): egoism (*asmitā*), attraction (*rāga*), aversion (*dveṣha*), and fear of death (*abhiniveśha*). Ignorance, in fact, exists in all four of these afflictions. Just as apple seeds sown in the proper soil will germinate, grow into trees, and give fruit in time, the seeds of the afflictions germinate in the soil of ignorance (*avidyā*) and bind the self (*jīvātma*) in ignorance. Therefore, if ignorance is destroyed, the other four afflictions automatically disappear from the mind (*chitta*).

The afflictions appear in four stages: dormant (*prasupta*), weak (*tanu*), interrupted (*vichchhinna*), and operative (*udāra*). The purpose of the afflictions in these four states is to promote the development of the world. By creating obstructions in the process of achieving Self-knowledge (*ātma jñāna*), the afflictions impel people to seek satisfaction of their cravings through outer means, causing expansion of their worldly activities.

1. **Dormant (*prasupta*).** When dormant, the afflictions in the mind field (*chitta*) are not active, but they have the potential to become active when the proper time, space, cause and effect, or the person's maturity match the needs of the affliction. For example, the desire for sex exists in babies only in potential form, remaining dormant until puberty.

   The dormant state can also be achieved as a result of dispassion. When the mind has been purified of worldly desires and attachments, the afflictions are rendered dormant until they are either destroyed completely in *asamprajñāta samādhi* (super-consciousness beyond all knowledge) or reactivated due to *vyutthāna saṁskāras* (worldly mindedness).

2. **Weak (*tanu*).** The afflictions become weak when they are suppressed by the *yogi* practicing Kriyā Yoga. The indication of a weakened affliction is that it does not become active in the presence of objects, even though it continues to exist in the mind in a subtle form. Weak afflictions can be rendered dormant through continued effort of Kriyā Yoga.

   One method of weakening the afflictions is the practice of contemplating their opposites:

a. The affliction of ignorance (*avidyā kleśha*) is weakened by achieving knowledge of the truth.
b. The affliction of egoism (*asmitā kleśha*) is weakened by developing discrimination.
c. The afflictions of attraction and aversion (*rāga kleśha* and *dveṣha kleśha*) are weakened by developing neutrality.
d. The affliction of the fear of death (*abhiniveśha kleśha*) is weakened by developing non-attachment.
e. All the afflictions are weakened by developing *saṁyama*, which is practicing concentration (*dhāraṇā*), meditation (*dhyāna*), and super-consciousness (*samādhi*) simultaneously on one object.

The weakened state can also apply to an immature desire that is just beginning to sprout. Unless effort is made to control it, this type of weakened desire will naturally develop into the fully operative state (*udāra*).

3. **Interrupted or alternating (*vichchhinna*).** In the interrupted or alternating state of the afflictions, the same condition appears and disappears repeatedly. The afflictions in this state alternate between being active and inactive. For example, anger may be temporarily suppressed by thoughts of compassion or pleasurable memories, but then reappear at the slightest provocation. The interrupted state can also appear in the initial stages of dispassion as the mind alternates between one-pointedness (*ekāgratā*) and worldly preoccupation (*vyutthāna*).

4. **Operative (*udāra*).** Afflictions that are actively functioning in the present are called operative. In most people, whose minds are directed to worldly objects and their achievements (*vyutthāna*), all the afflictions are operative. The worldly preoccupation of most people is comparable to a child's total fixation on a new toy; the fixation is unbreakable except by another toy.

These are the four states of the afflictions. There is a fifth state in which the afflictions are completely inoperative, and the mental impressions (*saṁskāras*) caused by the afflictions become like roasted seeds (*dagdha bīja*) and cannot germinate. This is different from the dormant state because dormant afflictions still have the potential to awaken. In the case of a person who has perfected discriminative wisdom (*viveka khyāti*), the seeds of affliction will not sprout even if all the necessary conditions for germination are present. The afflictions have become permanently inoperative because they were roasted by the fire of discriminative wisdom (*prasaṅkhyāna*) and cannot germinate. The wise person whose afflictions are thus vanquished is freed from the cycle of birth and death.

Patañjali doesn't mention this inoperative state because it works contrary to the other states of the afflictions. This *sūtra* is speaking about the four states of the afflictions that bind the soul in ignorance, whereas the fifth or inoperative state results in liberating the soul from ignorance. Sūtras II:3 – 9 describe the active states of the *kleśhas*, which are the obstacles to liberation.

Patañjali also never mentions the phrase *dagdha bīja* (roasted seed) specifically. But, in the fourth book, *Kaivalya Pāda*, he talks about the inactivity of the *kleśhas*. The inactivity of the *kleśhas* is known as liberation, the state beyond all obstacles and all practices, and therefore outside the scope of *Sādhana Pāda* (On Practice). Vyāsa, on the other hand, does confirm the relevance of the fifth state to this *sūtra* in his commentary. The four states of the *kleśhas* do bind the soul in ignorance. However, there is a way that they can be disabled, so they are not eternally present nor eternally potent. Because discriminative wisdom removes the potency of ignorance (*avidyā*) and the other afflictions, there must be a state beyond these four (see Sūtra II:10).

Note

In the previous *sūtra*, the five afflictions were introduced. Now, in this *sūtra*, ignorance is established as the cause of the other four afflictions, and the four states of the afflictions are explained. Afflictions can be dormant, weak, fluctuating, or fully active. Ignorance (*avidyā*) as the cause of the other four afflictions is described in the previous two *sūtras*. The other afflictions, and all experiences of life for that matter, require consciousness and matter to be united. *Avidyā* is the functioning of the mind that joins them, so without it, nothing is possible.

Understanding the four states of the afflictions is key to understanding how both the mind and the process of purification work. When we begin the spiritual path, all the afflictions are active. The mind is not under our control as it swings from one emotional state to another. Gradually, through the practices of *yoga*, the afflictions are weakened and rendered dormant. If we continue our efforts all the way to discriminative wisdom (*viveka khyāti*), the dormant afflictions get "roasted" or permanently disabled. This cycle is true for the afflictions as a whole, but it can also be understood in the context of a single emotion, bad habit or addiction, or any obstacle to peace.

The fully active state (*udāra*) is obvious; the emotion, urge, addiction, or affliction controls the mind and feels like it will never end. It is like a tidal wave in that once it starts, all we can do is ride it out with as little damage as possible. But everything in the mind changes, and when the wave is over, we have an opportunity to do something about it. All the practices of *yoga* are for this.

In the alternating state (*vichchhinna*), the afflictions or urges come and go strongly. This state is slightly better than fully active because there are respites, but otherwise their force is just as strong. For example, a person craving a cigarette may temporarily forget the craving during a conversation, but as soon as it is over, the craving comes back as strong as it was before. For the *yogi*, these temporary breaks are opportunities to bring the mind back to its aim of peace and to exercise some form of alternative that weakens the affliction.

When the aspirant has made some progress in his or her practices, the afflictions, urges, and addictions are weakened (*tanu*). This means that the mind has gained a substantial level of control over its urges. The conscious will or intention has been strengthened through persistent practice, and has become more powerful than the urges, at least some of the time. The urges continue to arise, but now the mind is capable of ignoring them, even though significant effort is still required.

With continued practice over time, the weakened afflictions can be made dormant (*prasupta*). Dormant means that urges don't arise even when an opportunity does. The difference between weak and dormant is that in one the urge is noticed but not acted upon, while in the second, the urge isn't even felt. An example could be a recovering alcholic walking past a bar. In the weakened stage, the alcholic may feel the urge to go inside but resists. In the dormant stage, he or she walks on by without even a thought to enter.

Dormant, though, does not mean roasted (*dagdha bīja*). Roasted means they have completely lost their potential to germinate at any time. Dormant desires do not arise in the present, but they do have the potential to become active in the future. Just because the recovering alcholic walked past the bar this time, it does not mean that the desire to drink will never arise again. Mistaking a dormant desire for roasted has caused many people to fall.

To understand how people fall back to old habits or vices, we need to understand what makes desires or the afflictions dormant. The afflictions and desires are potential energies like seeds; they sprout only in the right soil. In the beginning, the mind is fertile for all the weeds of vice and barren for the flowers of virtue. The practices of *yoga* change the soil of the mind. The dormant state is when the mind is barren for the afflictions. No matter how many apple seeds you may throw into desert sand, no trees will grow. In other words, success in *yoga* comes from an internal change in the mind, and not from a physical separation from the objects of the world.

The reason why some people who have attained success in *yoga* fall back to their old habits is because they allow their mind to return to its previous condition. The effort still required for someone with dormant afflictions is to maintain the purity of the mind. The urges may feel like they have disappeared forever, but they haven't. They are gone only so long as the mind remains pure. Once soil fertile for the afflictions is returned to the mind, all the old seeds can grow again.

Technically, the roasted state of the afflictions comes only at the perfection of discriminative wisdom (*viveka khyāti*) and final liberation (*kaivalya*). Until that point, all the afflictions retain the potential to germinate once again.

This description relates to the reduction of the afflictions through *yoga*. These states, as explained in the commentary, also apply to the development of previously unseen afflictions. They begin dormant and gradually become weak and active if they are not opposed by some contrary force (*yoga*).

In the next *sūtra*, the affliction of ignorance is described in detail.

Sūtra 5 अनित्याशुचिदुःखानात्मसु नित्यशुचिसुखात्मख्यातिरविद्या ॥५॥

anity–āśhuchi–duḥkh–ānātmasu nitya–śhuchi–sukh–ātma–khyātir–
avidyā

Ignorance consists of seeing permanence in the impermanent, purity in the impure, pleasure in pain, and the Self in the non-Self.

अनित्य	*anitya*	non-eternal, impermanent
अशुचि	*aśhuchi*	impure
दुःख	*duḥkha*	painful
अनात्मसु	*anātmasu*	non-Self
नित्य	*nitya*	eternal, permanent
शुचि	*śhuchi*	pure
सुख	*sukha*	pleasurable
आत्म	*ātma*	Self
ख्यातिः	*khyātiḥ*	knowledge, taking to be
अविद्या	*avidyā*	ignorance

Ignorance (*avidyā*) appears in four forms. It is the root cause of all afflictions, and it is contrary to correct cognition.

1. **Seeing permanence in the impermanent**. The mind veiled by ignorance does not recognize the ephemeral nature of manifest objects. The whole universe and all its evolutes, including the sun, moon, and stars, are impermanent and perishable. Ignorance is seeing them as permanent and imperishable.

2. **Seeing purity in the impure**. The mind veiled by ignorance does not recognize the flaws inherent in manifest objects. The body is filled with all kinds of impurities, such as urine, sweat, phlegm, and toxins, but it is considered pure, beautiful, and attractive by the ignorant mind. Money earned by unjust means, stealing, or violence is impure, but it is considered pure and legitimate by many. The mind filled with violent, lustful, and evil thoughts is impure, but it is considered pure and justified when veiled by ignorance.

3. **Seeing pleasure in pain**. The mind veiled by ignorance does not recognize the pain that necessarily follows pleasure. All worldly objects are sources of pain, but they are considered sources of pleasure. This phenomenon is described in detail in Sūtra II:15.

4. **Seeing the Self in the non-Self**. The mind veiled by ignorance does not recognize the unconscious nature of the mind and body. The mind, body, and senses are the non-Self (unconscious), as they are evolutes of *prakṛiti* (matter), but they are seen as if they were the Self (conscious).

This *avidyā* (ignorance or nescience) is the cause of bondage of the soul. It is characterized by these four misconceptions, it appears in the four states of dormant to operative as mentioned in the previous *sūtra*, and it forms the basis for the remaining afflictions. Thus, ignorance is the cause of all afflictive experiences.

How does this ignorance arise? Nature (*prakṛiti*) is comprised of the three constituent qualities (*guṇas*). Before creation manifests, the *guṇas* exist in a state of equilibrium, in which there is balanced and mutual opposition. There is no interaction among the three *guṇas*, and consciousness (*puruṣha*) is completely isolated from them. But when the power of consciousness is reflected in the *guṇas*, this equilibrium is disturbed. The first evolute (*mahat*) arises, in which *sattva* (purity, sentience) predominates with *rajas* (activity) simply activating and *tamas* (inertia) simply stabilizing.

This evolute is the cosmic intellect (*mahat*), the first union of *puruṣha* (consciousness) and *prakṛiti* (matter). It is beyond all subject and object relationships even though all the potentialities of manifest creation exist within it. It is a vast ocean of cosmic consciousness, which is why it is called *mahat* (the great). The difference between *mahat* and *puruṣha* is that *mahat* has qualities (*guṇas*)—and thus the potential to manifest the entire creation—while *puruṣha* does not.

This first evolute of nature (*mahat*) has the nature of "I-sense" (*asmitā*). It means that *mahat* has an awareness of existence in the form of "I exist." This notion of existence has qualities, and it results from confusing the characteristics of consciousness and matter, and it is the cause of the remaining afflictions.

How does this happen? In the pure state of *buddhi* (intellect),[1] the light of *puruṣha* (pure consciousness) reflects. This reflection assumes the qualities of *puruṣha* just as a mirror in which the sun is reflected assumes the qualities of heat and light. The intellect is not conscious by itself, but gets its consciousness only from *puruṣha*. It is a predominantly *sāttvika* combination of the three *guṇas* activated by consciousness. But when *tamas guṇa* (delusion) becomes active in *buddhi*, the veiling power of ignorance causes *buddhi* to believe that it is *puruṣha* itself.

This is what is meant by seeing the Self in the non-Self, as mentioned above. It is the basis for the second affliction, known as *asmitā*. The remaining three forms of ignorance follow this misconception and all together they constitute *avidyā kleśha* (the affliction of ignorance).

Note

Mahat is the union of spirit and matter based on ignorance. Creation begins at *mahat*, which is the result of two prior causes (spirit and matter), therefore creation is impermanent. But because spirit and matter cannot be separately identified within creation, they are assumed to be permanently together.

One analogy that is used to explain the union of spirit and matter is the projection of film. Within the projector, the white light (spirit) and the colored film (matter) are distinct and separate. On the screen, however, the light is colored and the color is luminous; they cannot be separated. This means that the light

---

1   The term *buddhi* is used to denote the individualized intellect, while the term *mahat* is used for the universal or cosmic intellect. *Buddhi* is the term used when the intellect functions with the energy of individualization (*ahaṁkāra*).

and color are always separate (in the projector) and always together (on the screen). The Vedāntins use the term *māyā* to describe this phenomenon because it literally means, "It is and it is not." Ignorance is only seeing their union on the screen, while wisdom is also knowing the truth about their separation within the projector.

The phrase, "Seeing purity in the impure," also refers on an absolute level to the union and separation of spirit and matter. Spirit is absolutely pure, without any modification, qualification, or tainting of any kind. Matter is only qualification itself without any purity (light or consciousness). All consciousness within creation, e.g. in the intellect, is tainted by the qualities and is impure. Ignorance is the false notion that the consciousness within beings—even *buddhi sattva*—is absolutely pure. Even though *sattva* is pure like a crystal, compared to the absolute purity of spirit, *sattva* is impure.[2]

Seeing the Self in the non-Self means confusing the relative, individualized "I-sense" of creation with the absolute, universal "I" known as the spirit or Self. The Self is pure consciousness alone without any modification or qualification of any kind. The ignorant mind believes that the Self is limited to the mind-body complex.

Finally, seeing the Self in the non-Self means thinking that the mind and intellect are conscious. The ignorant mind believes that consciousness is its inherent quality when it thinks, "I am conscious."

All animate beings appear to be conscious. Both humans and animals pursue pleasure and react to stimuli. Humans can contemplate their fate and determine the cause of their pain. Does this not prove that consciousness is in us? No. A solar car runs by the energy of the sun, but that does not prove that the sun is within the solar car.

A subtler level of seeing the Self in the non-Self occurs in the lower states of *samādhi*. These are very profound experiences that can dramatically transform anyone who has them. A meditator may become merged into the subtle aspects of their object of concentration, or a devotee may have a vision of God. A feeling of seeing the Self may follow, but so long as the notion "I have seen the Self" exists, the "I" and the "Self" are still identified as different, which is ignorance.

So how is the ignorance of seeing the Self in the non-Self different from egoism? Egoism is the false notion in *buddhi* that the "I-sense" with qualities is actually the Self, whereas pure ignorance is simply seeing consciousness in matter.

In the next *sūtra*, the second affliction, egoism (*asmitā*), is described.

---

2 *Sattva* is like a crystal-clear window; the objects on the other side of the window can be seen without any noticeable distortion. But on an absolute level, no matter how pure and clean the window may be, it is not as pure as seeing the object directly, not through the window.

Mūrti of Lord Śhiva at the Gaṅgā River.

Sūtra 6   दृग्दर्शनशक्त्योरेकात्मतेवाऽस्मिता ॥६ ॥

dṛig–darśhana–śhaktyor–ekātmatevā–'smitā

Egoism (*asmitā*) is identifying the power of cognition (*buddhi*) as if it were the power of consciousness (*puruṣha*).

दृग	*dṛiga*	the subjective, seer
दर्शन	*darśhana*	the instrumental power of seeing, seen (*buddhi*)
शक्त्यो:	*śhaktyoḥ*	power of
एकात्मता	*ekātmatā*	identity, of one and the same nature
इव	*iva*	as it were, appearance
अस्मिता	*asmitā*	I-sense, egoism

In the previous *sūtra*, the first affliction, ignorance (*avidyā*), was described in detail. Now, in this *sūtra*, the second affliction, known as egoism (*asmitā*), is explained. The seer (*puruṣha*) is the subjective power of consciousness. The intellect (*buddhi*) is the instrumental power of seeing. The seer (*puruṣha*) is conscious, whereas the intellect (*buddhi*) is an evolute of nature (*prakṛiti*) and thus unconscious. *Puruṣha* is actionless, whereas *buddhi* is always active. *Puruṣha* is the pure conscious principle only, devoid of qualities, whereas *buddhi* is comprised of the three *guṇas*.

In these ways, *puruṣha* and *buddhi* are two completely different powers; but when the mind is veiled by ignorance they appear as if they were identical. The individualized power of perception is born, and there is an experience of separate existence. Therefore, the affliction of egoism (*asmitā kleśha*), which arises out of ignorance (*avidyā*), is the non-discrimination of *puruṣha* and *buddhi* with the corresponding notion of an independent existence.

As Pañcha-śhikh-āchārya said, "When one fails to see that *puruṣha* is different from *buddhi*, by virtue of its immaculateness, immutability, and universal consciousness, one regards *buddhi* as the true Self through delusion." In other words, when consciousness is not recognized as distinct and separate from the ability to know (*buddhi*), it is seen as if it were a part of *buddhi*. This is egoism based on ignorance. Knowledge is a modification of *buddhi*, while pure consciousness is beyond modification.

In summary, the appearance of the non-Self as the Self is *avidyā* (ignorance, nescience). The reflection of the *puruṣha* (conscious principle) on the pure *buddhi* (intellect or mind) produces *asmitā* or "I-sense." When *buddhi* acts as the *puruṣha*, it is known as *asmitā kleśha* (the affliction of egoism). In a practical sense, there can be no separation between *avidyā* and *asmitā*. Without *avidyā*, "I-sense" is not possible, and without "I-sense," there is no place for ignorance to exist.

Asmitā kleśha is called the knot of the heart (*hṛidaya granthi*) in the Muṇḍaka Upaniṣhad 2:2-8:

> The knot of the heart is broken, all doubts resolved, and all works
> cease to bear fruit, when He is beheld who is both high and low.

Note

If egoism is essential for life, and life is both pleasure and pain, then why is egoism only called an affliction and not also a boon? The primary answer is that egoism is an obstacle to perfection in *yoga*. It perpetuates life in the world. Furthermore, egoism is the basis for experience and experience is suffering. Therefore, it is an affliction. As was explained in the previous *sūtra* and in Sūtra II:15, pleasure cannot exist without suffering, so the very notion that egoism could be a boon because it leads to pleasure is wrong.

The activities of the body are linked to the Self through egoism. Without egoism, the activities of the body would continue, but without being linked to the Self. All of the practices of *yoga* are ultimately for the purpose of identifying the Self as separate from, and independent of, the mind and body. When this happens, the body may continue to function, but anything that happens within it or to it is not attributed to the "I" or the Self. The body may become rich and famous, but the "I" is unaffected. The body may get cancer, but the "I" is untouched. It is only because of egoism that the activities of the world are linked to the "I."

Where does this linking occur? It occurs in the intellect (*buddhi*). Egoism is the nature of the intellect—all the activity of the intellect is based on the fact that it considers itself to be an independent being. The intellect functions in order to bring the world to the Self for the dual purpose of experience and liberation.

Under the influence of egoism and ignorance, the Self appears to be linked to the intellect so the intellect functions as if it were the Self. All beings are seen acting for their own benefit, pursuing various forms of pleasure and avoiding pain. Their behaviors are modified according to the results of their actions in the hopes of becoming more efficient and more effective. Underlying it all is the great hope that somehow "I will experience more pleasure than pain."

People only believe that the experiences called pleasure are theirs (related to their self) because of egoism. Without egoism, the experience would simply be a momentary contact of the senses with their objects that would not motivate them to change their future behavior, nor would it affect their understanding of the Self or bring any form of attachment to the world.

In a practical sense, ignorance and egoism are always together. If egoism is removed, there is no ignorance.

Based on ignorance, egoism provides the seed for the remaining three afflictions, attraction (*rāga*), aversion (*dveṣha*), and clinging (*abhiniveśha*), which are described in the next three *sūtras*.

Sūtra 7 सुखानुशयी रागः ॥ ७ ॥

sukhānuśhayī rāgaḥ

Attachment is that which accompanies [the remembrance of] pleasure.

सुख	*sukha*	pleasure
अनुशयी	*anuśhayī*	accompanying, resulting (from), following
रागः	*rāgaḥ*	attraction, attachment, desire to possess

Ignorance (*avidyā*) is the cause of egoism (*asmitā kleśha*), and egoism gives rise to attachment (*rāga kleśha*). How does attachment arise? After a pleasurable experience involving an object of the senses, the mind stores the memory of pleasure and desires another experience of the same pleasure. This is attachment, which is called *rāga kleśha*.

Memory is required for attachment. One who has not experienced an object will not carry its memory. Pleasure is remembered only because attachment has already developed from prior experiences of enjoyment. Attachment is therefore a cognitive desire to possess or achieve pleasure.

When some experience or thing is known to give pleasure, it is stored in the mind as a cause of pleasure. The mind then infers that repeating it will cause the same physical, mental, or emotional pleasure as before. For example, one eats chocolate and experiences pleasure. The mind develops attachment to chocolate as a means of experiencing pleasurable taste and sensation.

The term *anuśhayī* (accompanying) implies that attachment exists in the mind as a latent impression (*saṁskāra*). Attachment (*rāga*) is a latent impression of desire. As long as ignorance and egoism are present, these latent impressions will germinate whenever proper conditions arise. The experiences of pleasure will in turn create more and deeper latent impressions as the cycle of *saṁsāra* (worldly life) continues. In the state of ignorance, it is quite natural for a person to get attached to those external objects that provide any type of pleasure. Since the mind had already lost its inner peace and happiness because of the bondage caused by ignorance and egoism, it naturally searches for happiness and fulfillment through external means.

The search for happiness and fulfillment through external means is known as worldly experience (*bhoga*). Without the desire for experience (*bhoga*), the creation would cease to exist. However, when one understands the afflictive nature of *bhoga*, dispassion develops, which leads to liberation (*apavarga*). This is the search for happiness and fulfillment through internal means (*yoga*).

This is similarly stated in the *Bhagavad Gītā* (III:34):

> Aversion for the objects of the senses abide in the senses. Let none come under their sway, for they are one's foes.

Note

Verses XVIII:36–39 of the *Bhagavad Gītā* describe three kinds of pleasure according to the predominance of the *guṇas*. *Tāmasika* pleasure is generally when the gross senses contact their objects in such a way that the ego is gratified, such as consuming alcohol and drugs, or excessive food and sex. Ego gratification comes when its notion of itself is reinforced. All sense pleasures reinforce the identity of the ego with the gross body. These pleasures are of a short duration and they affect the mind by making it denser, duller, and more attached to the physical world.

Rājasika pleasure is achievement oriented, such as getting a promotion or bonus at work, and winning at sports. The human ego longs to be recognized for its achievements, so it sets goals and works hard to achieve them. Whether it is financial compensation, recognition for achievement, or victory in competition, the ego derives great pleasure. Because effort is required, and because the pleasure is not based on a momentary sense experience, this pleasure lasts longer than *tāmasika* pleasure. It affects the mind by making it more restless, more passionate, and more attached to fame and power.

Finally, *sāttvika* pleasure is selfless service or *sādhana* oriented, such as caring for the sick or needy. When the ego sets aside its immediate self-interest and works for the benefit of others, a sense of well-being may arise. It makes the mind calmer, sharper, and more attached to love, happiness, and service.

Pleasure continues to bind the soul to experience for as long as the affliction of egoism controls the mind. When the mind is completely purified of egoism, there is no longer any identification of the world with the Self. In this case, there can be no binding or attachment of any kind.

What is this experience of pleasure that affects us so profoundly? Pleasure is the momentary reduction of mental effort that comes when an object of desire is attained. Desire is *rajas guṇa* (passion or restlessness), which activates the mind to achieve its desired object. All desires are *rajas*; the desire for sense pleasure is *rajas* mixed with *tamas*, and the desire to serve is *rajas* mixed with *sattva*. This activity or restlessness is known as pain because it is a state of discomfort and anxiety. If and when the desired object is attained, the mind temporarily relaxes its effort because it no longer needs to pursue it. Because this relaxation of effort can never be permanent, insecurity quickly develops, which is itself another form of pain.

It is very important to understand that the object is not the source of the pleasure because the same object may cause pleasure at one time and not another. For example, hearing your favorite song on the radio brings pleasure. But if you were to hear it thirty times in a row, hearing it again would not bring pleasure. The song has not changed, only your mind has changed. If the pleasure were in the song, then hearing it over and over would only be pleasurable.

But the common mind doesn't recognize this and associates the pleasure with the object. This association is known as attraction or attachment. So long as the mind believes that the feeling of pleasure comes from the object, it will always seek satisfaction outside itself.

The problem with seeking pleasure is that the pain of the seeking is as great as the pleasure derived from the object. Even if a pleasurable object is attained unsought, the attachment that forms from that experience will bring the pain of seeking in the future.

The practices of *yoga*, on the other hand, bring about the same relaxation of mental activity for a very different reason. In *yoga*, the mind is calmed by removing desires from the mind instead of fulfilling them. The anxiety of seeking is stopped, not because the object of desire is attained, but because the desire no longer exists.

The mind now recognizes that it has the power to achieve peace by abandoning the pursuit of desires, so dispassion arises for outer objects. This dispassion allows the mind to abandon other worldly desires, and the mind's activity is further reduced. In this way, the practices of *yoga* reinforce the removal of desires from the mind, and the removal of desires in the mind reinforces the practices of *yoga*.

In the next *sūtra*, the aversion that results from pain is explained.

A third generation pūjari performs evening arati at the Hairakhan Bābā temple in Katghariyā.

Sūtra 8　　　दुःखानुशयी द्वेषः ॥८॥

duḥkhānuśhayī dveṣhaḥ

Repulsion or aversion is that which accompanies pain.

दुःख	*duḥkha*	pain
अनुशयी	*anuśhayī*	accompanying, resulting (from), following
द्वेषः	*dveṣhaḥ*	repulsion, aversion

Attachment (*rāga*) and aversion (*dveṣha*) are opposites like light and dark, and cannot exist together. Just as darkness vanishes when the sun comes up, aversion is not experienced when the mind is filled with attachment. The reverse is also true; in the presence of aversion, attachment is not experienced.

Aversion is a feeling of repulsion, anxiety, or anger toward any object that causes pain. Furthermore, the mind can even develop aversion toward the means that once brought pleasure and happiness if they no longer bring the same. This is called *dveṣha kleśha* (the affliction of aversion).

Aversion develops after attachment and therefore is placed fourth among the *kleśhas*. Aversion is the same as attachment, only negative. It is the negative form of the ego's relationship to worldly objects. Both of these afflictions have the same effect on the mind. For example, the mind dwells equally on a hated person as on a loved person. The only difference is that in aversion there is a feeling of anger, whereas in attachment there is a feeling of pleasure.

Attachment and aversion bind the soul to the lower level of consciousness by creating desires for worldly objects. Thus, attachment and aversion are responsible for all human miseries. In a state of *vairāgya* (dispassion), not only is attachment eliminated, but aversion is also eliminated. This is because *rāga* is the breeder of *dveṣha*, and the two, as pairs of opposites, are transcended by dispassion for all worldly experience.

Note

Pain is described in the *Bhagavad Gītā* as having three forms. The first is injury or illness related to the gross body (*tāmasika*). Examples of this pain are rashes, broken bones, and any form of cancer.

Rājasika pain has several types of manifestation, all related to desire and aversion. One comes from not attaining or not maintaining a desirable experience, such as not winning a contest. Another is from attaining or maintaining an undesirable experience, such as sitting next to a crying baby on a long airplane flight. A third is the anxiety and restlessness that inevitably comes from seeking objects of desire.

Sāttvika pain also has several types of manifestation. The first is longing for, or separation from, God. The *gopis* of Kṛishṇa felt this pain strongly. The second is feeling the pain of existence for all creatures. One whose selfish ego is weakened has the capacity to empathize with the suffering of others. The third type comes from feelings of love and attachment for others. Finally, the pleasure that comes from serving others becomes addictive, and the mind longs to serve more and more. This longing is a form of pain.

In the next *sūtra*, the power of the fear of death is explained.

Sūtra 9 स्वरसवाही विदुषोऽपि तथारूढोऽभिनिवेशः ॥ ९ ॥

svarasa–vāhī vidusho–'pi tathā–rūdho–'bhiniveshah

The love of life—or the great fear of death—flows by its own potency, and is similarly established in all, even the wise.

स्व रस	*sva rasa*	by its own potency
वाही	*vāhī*	flowing
विदुषः	*vidushah*	in the wise
अपि	*api*	even
तथा	*tathā*	all the same
रूढः	*rūdhah*	established
अभिनिवेशः	*abhiniveshah*	love of life, great fear of death

Abhiniveśha kleśha (love of life) appears in all beings equally, no matter whether they are a worm or a human being, or whether the human being is foolish or wise. In this *sūtra*, the word *vidushah* (the wise) is used for those who have scriptural knowledge but are not yet freed from all worldly attachments.

The mental concept, "I am this mind-body complex," is a universal notion in all human beings. The first four afflictions strengthen the concept of individual identity so much that everyone becomes very attached to life. They remain constantly active in seeking the welfare of the body. In spite of all evidence to the contrary, one thinks, "Perhaps death will not happen to me. I might be able to exist forever," and, "May I never be separated from the sensual objects that provide such pleasure."

This strong attachment for life creates the fear of death. The latent impression in the mind (*samskāra*) of the fear of death is known as *abhiniveśha kleśha*. Because this latent impression is in every mind, all beings perform actions that feed their own self-interest in the hope of somehow defeating death.

This desire to live or fear of death is a universal fact because everyone carries the latencies (*samskāras*) of death. The desire to live manifested the very moment the conscious principle (*purusha*) and the matter principle (*prakriti*) united.

The Self is eternal and unchanging, but due to ignorance (*avidyā*, or the notion, "I am this mind-body complex"), there is always the fear of its extinction. So long as ignorance (*avidyā*) is not removed by achieving Self-knowledge (*ātma jñāna*), the fear of death will exist in some form. If the "I" believes it is the mind-body complex, then it thinks "I" will die when the body dies. But the "I" is actually the eternal Self, so it cannot be affected by any changes to the mind or body.

The five afflictions develop in a cause and effect series starting with ignorance (*avidyā*) and ending with the fear of death (*abhiniveśha*). The fear of death or the love of life is the final development of the afflictions. It springs naturally from the accumulated latent impressions of attachment (*rāga*) and aversion (*dveṣha*). This is why it is called *svarasa-vāhī* (flowing by its own potency).

Note

Clinging and fear are two sides of the same coin. Whenever there is clinging to any object, there is also fear that it will go away. The core clinging is to life, so the core fear is of death. The *sutra* says that this affects even the wise, referring to those individuals who have cultivated a deep knowledge of life and the scriptures, but who have not removed the affliction of egoism.

The phrase, "flowing by its own potency," means that clinging is built into the normal functioning of the mind. It is not an add-on or a flaw to healthy living, but rather it is inherent in being a person. Ultimately, clinging can only be completely removed by transcending the identification with being an individual.

In the next two *sutras*, the process of destroying the afflictions is described.

Sūtra 10 ते प्रतिप्रसवहेयाः सूक्ष्माः ॥१०॥

te pratiprasavaheyāḥ sūkshmāḥ

The subtle forms of these [afflictions] are destroyed by resolving them back into their cause.

ते	*te*	these
प्रति प्रसव	*prati prasava*	resolving back into their cause
हेयाः	*heyāḥ*	that are destroyed, abandoned
सूक्ष्माः	*sūkshmāḥ*	subtle, potential

In Sūtras II:3–9, Patañjali described the five afflictions (*kleśhas*) with their four states of existence. The afflictions are ignorance (*avidyā*), "I-amness" (*asmitā*), attraction (*rāga*), aversion (*dveṣha*), and fear of death (*abhiniveśha*). The states of existence are dormant (*prasupta*), attenuated (*tanu*), overpowered (*vichchhinna*), and fully active (*udāra*).

How are the afflictions overcome? First they are weakened by the practices of Kriyā Yoga (austerity, self-study, and surrender to God) and/or *samprajñāta samādhi* (super-consciousness with complete knowledge of duality). The afflictions are thereby reduced to their subtle or seed state, which means they are inactive but can germinate whenever the conditions are favorable. Those seeds, which are the subtle forms of affliction, lose the potential even to germinate when they are roasted in the fire of discriminative wisdom (*viveka khyāti* or *prasaṅkhyāna*).

The term *prasava* means to give birth or the process of evolution. *Pratiprasava* is the reverse, which means re-absorption or involution. To remove the subtle state of the afflictions, the aspirant must reverse the process of evolution for the five afflictions and their four states.

In the process of involution, each effect absorbs into its immediate cause. For example, the fear of death (*abhiniveśha*) absorbs into its immediate cause, attraction and aversion (*rāga* and *dveṣha*). Attraction and aversion absorb into their immediate cause, "I-amness" (*asmitā*), and "I-amness" absorbs into its immediate cause, ignorance (*avidyā*). Ultimately, ignorance is removed by enlightenment just as darkness is removed by sunlight.

By the word *sūkshma* (subtle), the *sutra* indicates that reducing active afflictions to their subtle or dormant state is a prerequisite to the further resolution of the afflictions. Then the dormant or subtle afflictions are made unproductive—like roasted seeds—by resolving them back into their causes. The seeds keep the same form but lose their potential to germinate.

Since the afflictions are rooted in ignorance, they cannot be destroyed (*heya*) until ignorance is removed. This means as long as the mind (*chitta*) exists, the afflictions will exist in at least one of the four states. Ignorance (*avidyā*) is the opposite of discriminative wisdom (*viveka khyāti*). Ignorance is the breeding ground of the afflictions. The removal of ignorance is the final step in the process of resolving the afflictions back into their cause.

Ignorance is removed when discriminative wisdom (*viveka khyāti*) and supreme dispassion (*paravairāgya*) reinforce each other and bring *dharma megha samādhi* (literally "cloud-pouring virtue"). Then freedom from the afflictions (*kleśha*) and from action (*karma*) is attained (see Sūtra IV:30). The mind (*chitta*), along with the roasted seeds of the afflictions, resolves back into its cause, *mūla prakṛiti* (the matter principle), and ceases to exist as a separate entity. This leaves *puruṣha* (the pure conscious principle) completely isolated from all contact with nature, and the *yogi* is established in the state of *kaivalya* (absolute freedom or non-dual reality).

Note

Weak afflictions are those that are known, but that don't overpower the mind. For example, a weak desire to gamble would be a fleeting thought that arises when in the presence of a casino, "Perhaps it would be fun to play a hand or two." This thought can be easily dismissed with little effort. So long as the desire is felt in any form, it is weak and not dormant.

In the above example, a dormant desire would not be perceived. The person would walk past or even through the casino without ever considering playing. The only way to know for sure if the desire existed in a dormant form would be if it were to become active in the future. In the present moment, there is no perceptible difference between a dormant and a roasted desire (one that will never sprout in the future).

This apparently minor distinction between dormant and roasted is actually very significant to the aspiring *yogi*. Desires are rendered dormant through regular practice (*abhyāsa*) and dispassion (*vairāgya*); they are destroyed by *samādhi*. A dormant desire remains dormant only so long as the practices are maintained and/or the right conditions do not arise. Roasted desires, on the other hand, have lost their ability to sprout under any conditions. If the desires for wealth and excitement have been roasted, the desire to gamble will never arise.

Even though each affliction can be resolved back into its cause, as long as the primal cause (ignorance) remains in any form, the potential remains for all the afflictions to evolve back into their fully active states. This means that until discriminative wisdom (*viveka khyāti*) is fully established and destroys primal ignorance (*avidyā*), the *yogi* is not free.

Discriminative wisdom is not the final state because it is not permanent. The process of stabilizing discriminative wisdom is known as *dharma megha samādhi*. *Dharma megha samādhi* brings supreme dispassion (*paravairāgya*) and *asamprajñāta samādhi* (*samādhi* beyond all knowledge and all modifications of the mind). The perfection of *asamprajñāta samādhi* is final liberation (*kaivalya*), which is complete and permanent freedom from the afflictions.

This process of resolving the afflictions back into their cause can also be applied to everyday life. Nearly all of the desires we experience on a daily basis are modifications or outgrowths of a few core desires. The outgrowths are like leaves on a tree, while the core desires are like the branches, and the afflictions are the roots and trunk. The leaves are numerous; the branches are few. Furthermore, cutting off a branch automatically cuts off the leaves, while removing the leaves alone keeps the branch intact.

In the next *sūtra*, the role of meditation is explained.

Ānanda Mayi Mā, 20th century Bengali saint. Her Mahā Samādhi is in Kaṅkhal near Haridwār.

Sūtra 11   ध्यान हेयास्तद्वृत्तयः ॥११॥

dhyāna heyās–tad–vrittayaḥ

Mental modifications based on the afflictions are destroyed by meditation.

ध्यान	*dhyāna*	by meditation
हेयाः	*heyāḥ*	they are destroyed
तद्	*tad*	their, of the *kleśhas* (afflictions)
वृत्तयः	*vrittayaḥ*	mental modifications

The modifications (*vrittis*) of the afflictions (*kleśhas*) are destroyed (*heyā*) by meditation (*dhyāna*). The seeds of the afflictions that exist in the mind (*chitta*) and that have the ability to become operative (*udāra*), are weakened by the practices of austerity (*tapaḥ*), self-study (*svādhyāya*), and surrender to God (*Īśhvara pranidhāna*). These weakened afflictions are further reduced and finally destroyed by the practice of meditation (*dhyāna*). In this case, the term meditation (*dhyāna*) includes *samādhi*, which results in the development of discriminative knowledge (*viveka khyāti*).

Nevertheless, all thoughts are based in the *kleśhas*. The notion of the existence of the mind as a separate entity is based on ignorance (*avidyā*). Every thought that occurs in that mind is an expression of "I-sense" (*asmitā kleśha*). Gross thoughts are an expression of self-preservation (*abhiniveśha kleśha*), and they are colored by attraction and aversion (*rāga* and *dveṣha kleśha*). Meditation (*dhyāna*) is the prescribed method for removing thoughts in their gross and subtle forms. When meditation deepens (*samādhi*), profound knowledge (*prajñā*) of the reality appears, greatly weakening the *kleśhas*, which are the cause of thoughts.

This *sutra* completes Patañjali's explanation of the removal of the afflictions. The sequence of their removal is as follows:

1. The afflictions in their active form (*udāra*) are in a gross state in the mind (*chitta*). They are attenuated (*tanu kāraṇa*) by the practice of Kriyā Yoga (Sūtra II:2). This is comparable to shaking the excess dirt from a piece of cloth.

2. The attenuated afflictions (*tanu kleśha*) are further reduced by meditation on self-discernment (*viveka khyāti*) until they become dormant (*prasupta*) and finally unproductive (*dagdha bīja*) (Sūtra II:11). This is comparable to washing the cloth in water.

3. The afflictions in their unproductive state (*dagdha bīja*) are removed by resolving them backward into their cause (*pratiprasava*), which is primordial matter (*mūla prakriti*, see Sūtra II:10). The unproductive afflictions (*dagdha bīja*) exist in the mind (*chitta*) until the complete dissolution of the mind in *asamprajñāta samādhi* (super-consciousness beyond all knowledge). This is comparable to dissolving the cloth into its elements.

Note

Meditation, in this *sūtra*, means turning the mind away from the flow of the world and focusing it on one internal object. As the concentration is perfected, the *kleśhas* are weakened, made dormant, rendered unproductive, and finally removed in the highest *samādhi* (*asamprajñāta*). The purpose of the *kleśhas* is *vyut-thāna*, which means they impel the mind outward toward experience of the world. Meditation is the opposite; it is the effort to retain the mind within the mind. The absolute perfection of this opposing effort is the complete and permanent removal of the afflictions.

In the higher states of *samprajñāta samādhi*, the lower three *kleśhas* are dormant and resting only as potential within the purified "I-sense" (*asmitā*). Then, as discriminative wisdom (*viveka khyāti*) dawns, the purified "I-sense," which is a result of ignorance, is recognized as a false cognition. *Asmitā* is the universal sense of "I am." *Viveka khyāti* is the understanding "I am not" (*nāsmi*). This knowledge resolves *asmitā* back into its cause (ignorance or *avidyā*), and renders ignorance dormant. But *viveka khyāti* is not stable at first and ignorance returns to a weakened, attenuated, or even fully active state. Therefore, the initial presence of discriminative wisdom does not destroy the afflictions.

The process of stabilizing discriminative wisdom is known as *dharma megha samādhi*. In this process, the dormant affliction of ignorance, which also contains the potential forms of all the other afflictions, is roasted in the fire of knowledge. This roasted affliction of ignorance is completely and permanently destroyed by the highest level of *samādhi* known as *asamprajñāta* (complete cessation of mind or the *samādhi* beyond all knowledge of duality). The result of *asamprajñāta samādhi* is *kaivalya* (complete isolation or liberation).

This is the literal or absolute meaning of the *sūtra*. For the aspirant in the early stages of *yoga*, meditation is the best austerity. At first, the mind is difficult to concentrate; it jumps like an excited monkey from limb to limb. But this does not mean that the effort performed in trying is wasted. Actually, it is quite the contrary. Every effort made to concentrate, calm, or stabilize the mind weakens the afflictions. In fact, all the other practices of *yoga* are designed exclusively to improve the practice of meditation.

Yoga practices can be done anywhere at any time. The mind can be turned inward, its motives examined, its nature explored. Every such effort performed throughout the day improves the mind's ability to concentrate itself during daily *sādhana* (practice). Then, the knowledge gained by improved concentration allows the aspirant to watch the mind more effectively throughout the day. This back and forth process feeds on itself and gradually weakens the five afflictions. The weaker the five afflictions get, the more profound the meditation is. The more profound the meditation, the weaker the afflictions. Finally, the afflictions are resolved back into their cause (ignorance), and ignorance is roasted and finally removed through the highest *samādhis*.

In the next *sūtra*, the role of the afflictions in causing birth and rebirth is described.

Sūtra 12   क्लेशमूलः कर्माशयो दृष्टादृष्टजन्म वेदनीयः ॥ १२ ॥

kleśhamūlaḥ karmāśhayo dṛishṭādṛishṭajanma vedanīyaḥ

Latent impressions of action (*karmāśhaya*) have their origin in the afflictions, and are experienced in the present and future births.

क्लेश	*kleśha*	affliction
मूल	*mūla*	origin
कर्म	*karma*	of action
आशयः	*āśhayaḥ*	the storehouse, resting place, vehicle, seat, abode, heart
दृष्ट	*dṛishṭa*	visible, seen (present)
अदृष्ट	*adṛishṭa*	invisible, unseen (future)
जन्म	*janma*	in births
वेदनीयः	*vedanīyaḥ*	to be experienced

This *sutra* explains the term *karmāśhaya* (latent impressions of action), its cause (the afflictions), and its fruit (present and future births).

The afflictions (*kleśhas*) are the underlying cause of action (*karma*). The direct cause of all thoughts, words, and deeds is the desire to perform action (*karma vāsanā*). The latent impressions of action (*karmāśhaya*) stored in the mind (*chitta*) force a person to act for their own happiness and enjoyment. Then these actions create new latent impressions (*saṁskāras*), which collectively constitute the *karmāśhaya*. This whole cycle of cause and effect, in which latent impressions cause and are caused by virtuous and non-virtuous actions, is both supported by and supportive of the afflictions.

The *karmāśhaya* (storehouse of *karmas*) that is experienced in the present birth is seen and known in this life (*dṛishṭa janma vedanīya*). The *karmāśhaya* that is unseen and not experienced here and now will be experienced in the future births (*adṛishṭa janma vedanīya*). Sūtra II:13 explains in greater detail how the *karmāśhaya* affects present and future births.

The effects of the *karmāśhaya* will be of the same nature as the cause. Latent impressions of action caused by meritorious acts give the experience of higher births, such as that of celestial beings. Latent impressions of action caused by unmeritorious acts produce the experience of lower beings like animals. Latent impressions of action caused by a mixture of meritorious and unmeritorious acts give rise to the experiences of human beings.

The individual and collective creation can be understood in terms of the three *guṇas*, which are the qualities of sentience or purity (*sattva*), will or activity (*rajas*), and matter or inertia (*tamas*). Without *rajas guṇa* there cannot be any activity. When *rajas guṇa* acts with *sattva guṇa*, the mind develops the inclination toward knowledge (*jñāna*), merit (*dharma*), dispassion (*vairāgya*), and prosperity (*aiśhvarya*). These four qualities are the inherent qualities of the intellect (*buddhi*) that manifest when *sattva guṇa* predominates.

When *rajas* acts with *tamas guṇa*, the mind develops the inclination toward the opposite four traits: i.e. ignorance (*ajñāna*), demerit (*adharma*), passion (*rāga*), and failure (*anaiśhvarya*). These four are also inherent in the intellect, and they manifest when *tamas guṇa* predominates.

These two kinds of actions are called white actions (*śhukla karma*) and black actions (*kṛiṣhṇa karma*). When *rajas guṇa* works equally with *sattva guṇa* and *tamas guṇa*, the mind develops the inclination for both white and black actions (*śhukla kṛiṣhṇa karma*). These three types of actions necessarily create latent impressions of action (*karmāśhaya*).

So long as latent impressions of action are rooted in the five afflictions, the cycle goes on and on. When the afflictions are weakened by the practices of meditation and Kriyā Yoga, then naturally the latent impressions of *karmāśhaya* caused by the cycle of action get weaker and weaker. The weakened *karmāśhaya* gradually becomes unproductive (*dagdha bīja*) as described in the previous two *sūtras*.

The *yogis* who have attained *nirbīja samādhi* (seedless *samādhi*) have eliminated afflictions and their actions become desireless. Their actions are neither white nor black (*aśhukla akṛiṣhṇa karma*), and these actions do not create latent impressions as they are not based on the afflictions (*kleśha*).[1]

Note

Actions are thoughts, spoken words, and deeds. All actions have their causes, and these causes are the *karma vāsanā* (drives or urges to act) residing in the *karmāśhaya*. The *vāsanā* are the middle step between dormant *saṁskāras* and the actions themselves. Every experience we have gets stored in the mind as an impression (*saṁskāra*). This impression is dormant, like a seed waiting for fertile soil. When that fertile soil is found, the seed sprouts as a desire or an urge to act. Depending on the nature of the seed, the urge will be stronger or weaker. This urge matures into action of some form. Even the decision not to act on the urge would itself be an action of restraint.

These new actions are then stored in the mind as new impressions. This is how habits and addictions are created. In gambling, for example, the original desire exists in some form. After placing the first bet, the original desire is there along with the impression of acting on that desire. Then, every time a bet is

---

1 The question of how one who is established in the non-dual reality (*kaivalya*) continues to act in the world is much debated. As there is no vestige of individual identity, these actions are necessarily reflecting universal nature and are spontaneous (or from a theistic point of view, one could say "God's will"). Though *prārabdha karma* (past *karmas* coming into fruition now) continues to support the mind-body complex of the *yogi*, no new impressions of *karma* (*saṁskāras*) are created. In order for a *saṁskāra* to be created, there has to be an identification with the action, which is not the case for a liberated being. This breaks the cycle of birth and death (*saṁsāra*) based on the *kleśhas* (afflictions). From the outside, the *yogi* will appear to function as any other person and is able to answer questions, work, etc., but the effects of these actions will not belong to the *yogi*.

placed, a new impression is added, which makes the next urge to gamble stronger. Furthermore, the seeds of restraint atrophy from not being exercised. Later, if the person decides to give up gambling, they will find it very difficult because the urge to gamble is much stronger than the urge of restraint. This pattern is true for all positive and negative actions in the world.

As *sattva* increases, discriminative wisdom develops. This leads to the highest *samādhi* (*nirbīja* or *asamprajñāta*) which destroys primal ignorance (*avidyā*) and all the other afflictions. At this point, the *puruṣha* is isolated (*kevalam*) from any identification with matter (the three *guṇas*). Whether the body continues to function in the world depends solely on the *prārabdha karma* (actions previously begun but not yet completed). As there is no spirit identified with the body, all such functioning would leave no impression and create no future *karma*. Therefore, such actions have been called neither white nor black (*aśhukla-akṛiṣhṇa karma*). There is no cause for future births, which means the cycle of *karmāśhaya* is finished.

In the next *sūtra*, the relationship of *karmāśhaya* to birth, span of life, and experiences is described.

Gaṇeśh and Pārvati Mā

Sūtra 13   सति मूले तद्विपाको जात्यायुर्भोगाः ॥ १३ ॥

sati mūle tadvipāko jātyāyurbhogāḥ

As long as the root [afflictions] exist, the [*karmāśhaya*] ripens into birth, span of life, and experience.

सति	*sati*	of existing
मूले	*mūle*	of the root
तद्	*tad*	of it
विपाकः	*vipākaḥ*	ripening
जाति	*jāti*	class, species
आयुः	*āyuḥ*	span of life
भोगाः	*bhogāḥ*	experience

That part of the collective pool of latent impressions of action (*karma saṁskāras*) that will come to fruition in one birth is called *karmāśhaya*. This *karmāśhaya* is the direct cause of birth in a particular species, span of life, and the nature of the experiences in that birth, but only when the afflictions (*kleśhas*) are active. If the afflictions are cut by the axe of discriminative wisdom (*viveka khyāti*) and the seeds of latent impressions (*saṁskāra*) are parched in the fire of the highest wisdom (*prasaṅkhyāna*), the *karmāśhaya* will not create any action and the cycle of birth and death will be finished.

When *karmāśhaya* becomes operative due to the existence of the afflictions it brings three kinds of results, known as *trivipāka* (triple fruition): life state or species (*jāti*), span of life (*āyu*), and life experience (*bhoga*).

1. **Life state (*jāti*)**: Birth within human, animal, bird, or other species is created by the *karmāśhaya*. The form of the species itself is determined according to the needs of nature; the individual variations within that species are determined according to the unique *karmāśhaya* of each *jīvātma* (embodied soul or self). The *karmāśhaya* is generated by the thoughts, desires, and actions of the past birth. All beings go through many births. In each birth, they work out the *karmas* of the past and also generate new *karmas*, which will ripen into fruit in future births.[1]

2. **Span of life (*āyu*)**: The association of the *jīvātma* with one body between the period of birth and death is called the span of life. Within the span of life, the *saṁskāras* coming to fruition are experienced.

3) **Life experience (*bhoga*)**: The contact of the sense organs with their objects—along with the preexisting condition of the mind, intellect, and ego—creates the experience of pleasure and pain. The experience of life is different for all species. The experience of each species is according to the capacities and limitations of their sense organs. Pleasure and pain are experienced by all, but those species with a more highly evolved intelligence will experience a wider

---

1 The *karma saṁskāras* are carried in the subtle body through multiple births.

range of pleasure and pain than less evolved species. Because the final determination of an experience is based on the condition of the mind and intellect, the extent of an individual's pleasurable and painful experience in life is determined by one's *karmāshaya*.

There are two kinds of *karma saṁskāras* (latent impressions) within the *karmāshaya*. The strongly operative are called *pradhāna* (primary), and the loosely operative are called *upasarjana* (secondary). The primary *karmāshaya* determines birth in a particular species, life span, and experience, as described in this *sūtra*, and it is called determined fruition (*niyata vipāka*). Determined fruition corresponds to *dṛshṭa janma vedanīya*, or the *karmāshaya* that is experienced (seen in the present as mentioned in Sūtra II:12). The secondary fruition (*upasarjana karmāshaya*) are those *saṁskāras* that will be experienced in the future. Their result is not yet determined, so they are called undetermined fruition (*aniyata vipāka*). In Sūtra II:12, they are called *adṛshṭa janma vedanīya* (the unseen result that will be experienced in future births).

The secondary *karmāshaya* remain dormant in the present birth; their potency is for a future birth. There are three possible outcomes for the secondary *karmāshaya*: It may be destroyed without fruition, it may become merged with the primary *karmāshaya* as a subordinate element, or it may be overpowered by the primary *karmāshaya* and remain dormant for many births.

Note

In the previous *sūtra*, the term *karmāshaya* was introduced. In this *sūtra*, its nature is further explained. There is a pool of *karma saṁskāras* that contains all the impressions accumulated from all births for a particular individual (*jīvātma*). This all-encompassing pool can be divided into two categories: the primary *karmāshaya* and the secondary *karmāshaya*. The primary *karmāshaya* gives rise to birth in a particular species (*jāti*), for a particular length of time (*āyuḥ*), with particular experiences of pleasure and pain (*bhoga*). The secondary *karmāshaya* remains dormant in the current birth with the potential for arising in future births.

The purpose of this *sūtra* is not to prove the theory of reincarnation, nor to give the aspirant tools to discover their previous lives. Instead, the purpose is to show four things:

1. Without the afflictions in their active state, the *karmāshaya* has no purpose and cannot cause anything.
2. When supported by the afflictions, the *karmāshaya* blossoms into the species, span of life, and experiences of the birth.
3. The *karmāshaya* functions according to the natural order, in which *karmas* become either dominant or subordinate in the primary *karmāshaya*, or dormant in the secondary *karmāshaya*, depending on their strength.

4. All actions, whether they are good or evil, selfless or selfish, have their effects in the present or future births.

In Vyāsa's commentary, a thorough explanation of cause and effect as it relates to *karma* is given. The first component is that the afflictions (*kleśhas*) are the field in which the *karmāśhaya* bear fruit. In other words, without ignorance, egoism, and the other afflictions, the *karmāśhayas* have no purpose. Therefore, the same methods of removing the afflictions described in Sūtras II:10 – 11 will also remove the potency of *karmas* to create further births.

This *sūtra* states that the primary *karmāśhaya* gives rise to birth, span of life, and experiences. How? The answer is that the impressions generated from all the actions performed in one life—including thoughts, words, and deeds—gather together in a pool called *karmāśhaya*. This pool is the direct cause for the next birth.

The process by which the impressions of past actions cause present and future actions is obviously complex. In general, we can think of *karma* in terms of a crop. What flourishes depends on two things: the seeds and the soil. Sowing more seeds of a particular plant leads to a greater abundance of that plant. But if the soil is not fertile for that kind of plant, then it doesn't matter how many seeds are present because they won't grow. Another complicating factor is that sometimes the seeds of one plant are overpowered by other plants, so they can't grow as they normally would.

Every action performed in this birth adds to that person's general pool of *karma saṁskāras*. Most of them become part of the primary *karmāśhaya* that creates the next birth. Some actions can bring an immediate consequence and, depending on the present actions, be worked out completely in this life without affecting future births. Some actions are overpowered by opposing actions and become subordinate aspects of the primary *karmāśhaya*, which means they remain dormant in the next birth unless awakened by similar actions in that birth. And, some actions will be substantially overpowered by opposing actions, becoming part of the secondary *karmāśhaya* that does not become active in the next birth at all.

Some people have claimed that this theory of *karma* proves that people get what they deserve because of their past actions. They say that people with birth defects or those born into poverty or horrific circumstances are "punished" for being "bad" in a previous life. This is a misunderstanding.

The conditions of the present birth are simply the ones most appropriate to play out the dominant *karmas*. Wealth, poverty, sickness, and health are only playing fields. All experiences cause suffering of some kind (Sūtra II:15), so it is impossible to say what is a blessing and what is a curse.

To facilitate an understanding of the different ways in which *karma* works, a few oversimplified examples follow. An example of a dominant *karma* manifesting could be a person who is dedicated to his or her spiritual practices in one life, and then is born into a devotional family in the next birth. The new family is fertile ground for the actions of the previous birth to be continued in the next birth.

An example of a *karma* that gets worked out in the present birth is the sage Valmiki. Valmiki began life as a selfish person and even became a thief as a young adult. When he realized the consequences of his actions, he engaged himself in tremendous austerities. The story is that he sat so still repeating God's name for so long that an ant hill grew up around him. His mind became purified such that when he emerged from the ant hill, all his negative *karmas* were burned away and only virtuous *karmas* remained.

An example of a *karma* that becomes subordinate in the next birth might be a worldly person who is married to a devotional person. The worldly person might be exposed to many devotional rituals and may hear God's name being repeated constantly. But without actively participating, he or she will not have strong devotional momentum in the next birth. However, if devotional *samskāras* are otherwise awakened in that birth, the subordinate *karmas* from the previous birth can act as a support in that birth.

Finally, an example of a *karma* that becomes part of the secondary *karmāshaya* might be living on a farm in a foreign land for a few months as a child. If that person lived the rest of his or her life in big cities, the farming *karmas* would be relegated to the secondary *karmāshaya* and may not manifest for many lifetimes.

Now the question arises, how does the primary *karmāshaya* result in birth in a particular species, span of life, and experiences? Each species on the planet serves two functions: to support the natural development of the world order, and to serve as a vehicle for each individual to play out his or her *karmas*.

Death is the initiator of the next *karmāshaya*. This new *karmāshaya* has dominant and subordinate *karmas* that seek to get played out. The qualities of the *karmāshaya* are like a multidimensional puzzle piece. When this piece "fits" somewhere in the natural development of the world, it manifests as a new birth. The general qualities of the species are predetermined by nature, such as wings instead of fins, or two arms and two legs instead of four legs. Then, the specific qualities within that species are determined by the individual *karmas* of that being. This would affect everything from hair color and texture to facial features, body size, and any physical abnormalities.

At the same time, the span of life is also determined. Depending on the number and types of *karmas* present, the length of time needed to work out the *karmas* in that body varies. Sometimes, a very long time is required to work out all the *karmas* related to a particular body, and at other times, only a short while is needed. This explains why a healthy person may be killed in an accident; all of his or her *karmas* related to that body were finished. Now, a new body is required to continue working out *karmas*.

Furthermore, the *karmāshaya* determines the condition of the mind, which directly affects the experiences of the *jīva*. For example, a calm and virtuous person will enjoy the natural beauty of the world much more readily than an agitated and vicious person. Also, a person filled with greed and jealousy will experience a friend's successful career differently compared to how a loving and compassionate person will experience it. Even direct sense experiences are affected by the *karmāśhaya* and the condition of the mind. A stable mind can perceive subtle differences among objects of creation, thereby developing a truer understanding of the world. An unstable mind cannot perceive these differences and remains confused in life.

Another important component to understand about *karmas* is the principle that like produces like and that opposites balance each other. For example, spiritual practices done with faith and devotion always lead toward peace. Selfish actions performed with cruelty and malice always lead toward misery. Furthermore, spiritual practices performed now with the same or even greater intensity as previous selfish actions counteract the effects of those selfish actions.

In the next *sūtra*, the cause and effect relationship between the type of actions performed and the nature of the experiences generated is explored.

Sankaṭ Mochan Hanumān Mandir, Mount Madonna Center, California

Sūtra 14   ते ह्लादपरिताप फलाः पुण्यापुण्य हेतुत्वात् ॥ १४ ॥

te hlādaparitāpa phalāḥ puṇyāpuṇya hetutvāt

Pleasure and pain are the fruits of them (birth, span of life, and experience) according to merit and demerit.

ते	*te*	they
ह्लाद	*hlāda*	joy, pleasure
परिताप	*paritāpa*	pain, sorrow
फलाः	*phalāḥ*	fruits
पुण्य	*puṇya*	virtue, merit
अपुण्य	*apuṇya*	vice, demerit
हेतुत्वात्	*hetutvāt*	their causes

In the previous *sūtra*, it was explained that the primary *karmāshaya* results in birth, span of life, and life experience. These three can be divided into two broad categories: joyful experiences caused by virtuous thoughts, feelings, and actions, and painful experiences caused by non-virtuous thoughts, feelings, and actions.

Virtuous actions (*puṇya*) are those actions that weaken the five afflictions and bring joy in life's experiences. Non-virtuous actions (*apuṇya*) are those actions that support the five afflictions and bring misery in life's experiences.

The effect is directly related to its cause. If the cause is based on virtuous action, then naturally the effect is experienced as joy, which is the quality of the cause. Contrary to this, the effects of non-virtuous action will be experienced as pain.

For an average person, painful experiences are undesirable and joyful experiences are desirable. But for a *yogi*, even joyful experiences are undesirable because eventually they too will cause pain, as described in the next *sūtra*.

Note

In the previous *sūtra*, the general mechanics of *karmāshaya* were explained. Now, in this *sūtra*, the specifics of cause and effect are given. Virtuous actions bring pleasure, and vicious actions bring pain.

An objection arises. Nothing in life is this simple. For example, we see that some vicious people are happy and some virtuous people are sad. On what basis does the *sūtra* make this statement?

The *sūtra* is simply making the philosophical statement that like produces like. Virtuous actions are those based on the predominance of *sattva guṇa* (quality of purity). The consequence of these actions is the strengthening of *sattva* in the mind. The experience in the mind that corresponds to the strengthening of *sattva* is called joy or pleasure.

In contrast, vicious actions are those based on the predominance of *tamas guṇa* (quality of dullness) in the mind. The consequence of *tāmasika* actions is the strengthening of *tamas* in the mind. The experience in the mind that corresponds to the strengthening of *tamas* is called pain. In the same way, actions that are based on a combination of *sattva* and *tamas* result in a mixture of pleasure and pain.

All three *guṇas* are present in every aspect of every object and experience within creation. Therefore, there is no possibility that one could live only in *sattva* without any influence of *tamas*. Instead, it is a continuum in which the more *sattva* predominates, the more the experiences will be joyful, and the more *tamas* predominates, the more the experiences will be painful.

In the next *sūtra*, the inevitability of pain in all the experiences of the world is explained.

Sūtra 15　परिणाम ताप संस्कारदुःखैर्गुणवृत्तिविरोधाच्च दुःखमेव सर्वं विवेकिनः ॥ १५ ॥

pariṇāma tāpa samskāra–duḥkhair–guṇa–vṛitti–virodhāch–cha
duḥkham–eva sarvam vivekinaḥ

For a person with discrimination everything is painful. Even pleasurable experiences bring pain because everything changes, because of acute suffering, because of the [perpetuation of] latent tendencies, and because of the opposing nature of the *guṇas* (qualities of creation).

परिणाम	*pariṇāma*	change, consequence
ताप	*tāpa*	acute suffering, anxiety
संस्कार	*samskāra*	tendencies, habituation
दुःखैः	*duḥkhaiḥ*	by reason of the pains
गुण	*guṇa*	of the qualities
वृत्ति	*vṛitti*	modification of the mind
विरोधात्	*virodhāt*	by reason of opposing, contrary nature
च	*cha*	and
दुःखम्	*duḥkham*	painful
एव	*eva*	only, indeed
सर्वम्	*sarvam*	all
विवेकिनः	*vivekinaḥ*	to the discriminating, enlightened

In the previous *sutra*, it was explained that virtuous actions lead to pleasure and non-virtuous actions lead to pain. Any experience of the world that is predominantly *sāttvika* (pure) brings the feeling of pleasure, and any experience that is predominantly *tāmasika* (dull) brings the feeling of pain.

Now, in this *sutra*, it is explained that even these experiences of pleasure are considered painful by the wise. Four reasons are given: pain is the consequence of pleasure (because of attachment and the nature of change), the pursuit of pleasure itself is suffering, pleasure reinforces latent tendencies (*vāsanā*), and the changing nature of the three *guṇas* guarantees that pleasure cannot last.

Happiness comes from pleasure, which is experienced because of attachment (*moha*) and desire (*rāga*) to sentient beings or insentient objects. Only a desired object can create pleasure; the same object does not bring pleasure when it is not desired. Because pleasure is based on attachment and desire, its experience reinforces *karmāśhaya* (the storehouse of *karmas* that results in birth, span of life, and experiences). *Karmāśhaya* is based on the afflictions, which are the source of all suffering. Therefore, the perpetuation of *karmāśhaya* in any form is the perpetuation of suffering.

When the attainment of a desired object is obstructed in any way, it gives rise to aversion. Aversion causes delusion, and together they reinforce *karmāśhaya*. Therefore, whenever there is attachment and desire, *karmāśhaya* and its associated suffering result, either from attainment (pleasure) or from obstruction (aversion and delusion). As such, it has been said, "Enjoyment is not possible without causing pain to beings." Violence always comes to the enjoyer because of the continuation of the *karmāshaya* as described above, and when pleasure is derived from the consumption of objects, violence also comes to the object.

The enjoyment of pleasure is insatiable. The more it is experienced, the more desire (*vāsanā*) develops. The stronger and broader the desires are, the more obstructions are experienced. These greater obstructions bring greater aversion. Therefore, desire brings pain in both the enjoyment of pleasure and in the obstruction of pleasure.

For a wise person, all experiences of pleasure in the world that are achieved by action (*karma*) are full of pain, either directly or indirectly. The *sutra* mentions four specific reasons: pain as a result of attachment, pain due to afflictive circumstances, pain due to latent tendencies, and pain due to the contrary nature of the *guṇas*.

1. *Pariṇāma duḥkha* (**pain as a consequence of attachment**). Any object, sentient being, or insentient thing that gives pleasure to the senses creates attachment in the mind of the enjoyer. The consequence of attachment is desire (*vāsanā*), which creates greed and dissatisfaction. The more the mind gets attached to pleasure, the more greed develops. The result is more pain. Furthermore, the sense organs are weakened by the enjoyment of sense objects because *tamas guṇa* (quality of dullness) increases. Therefore, the senses are less able to enjoy their objects, even though the desires to enjoy them remain the same or even increase. Again, the consequence is more pain.

   This idea is also expressed in other scriptures. In Manusmṛiti (II/94) it is said, "Desire is never extinguished by enjoyment of desired objects; it only grows stronger like a fire fed with clarified butter." Verse V:22 of *Shrīmad Bhagavad Gītā* explains it as, "The enjoyments that are born of contacts (of the senses and objects) are only generators of pain, for they have a beginning and an end. O son of Kunti, the wise do not rejoice in them."

2. *Tāpa duḥkha* (**pain due to acute suffering**). Everyone feels pain when they are motivated to pursue or avoid objects because of aversion in the mind. To remove this afflictive pain, people seek pleasure, using their mind, body, and speech as their vehicle of action. In doing so, they favor certain objects over others, and accumulate further *karmāshaya* of virtue and vice. The *karmāshaya* of vice results directly in painful experiences. But even enjoying the results of the *karmāshaya* of virtue is painful because there is always fear of losing that enjoyment. The fear of losing pleasure is the result of greed and delusion, and it brings acute pain. All of these are known as acute suffering.

3. *Saṁskāra duḥkha* (**pain due to latent impressions of action**). The latent impressions (*saṁskāra*) of experience (*bhoga*) that are gathered in the mind (*chitta*) are the cause of attachment (*rāga*) and aversion (*dveṣha*). Attachment and aversion in the mind give rise to the experiences of the pairs of opposites

including pleasure, pain, love, anger, fear, and hate. The imprints of these feelings, thoughts, words, and actions in the mind become *karmāshaya*, and impel the person toward virtue and vice, which again create latent impressions in the mind. In this way, an eternal cycle of suffering takes place from birth to death to rebirth.

This eternal stream of miseries (*samsāra*) causes distress to a wise person. Ordinary people, who are living in ignorance, are merged in worldly desires (*vāsanā*) and are totally occupied in their selfish motives. They don't see the true nature of suffering and continue to take birth again and again. On the other hand, the wise person, whose mind has become as sensitive to suffering as an eyeball is to a thread of cotton, becomes aware of the cause of all suffering, and understands the true nature of *samsāra* (the cycle of rebirth). The wise, therefore, take refuge in right knowledge, which is the cause of the destruction of all suffering, and become liberated from the cycle of birth and death.

4. ***Guṇa vṛitti virodha duḥkha*** **(pain due to the contrary nature of the *guṇas*).** According to the *Sāmkhya Yoga Darshana* of Kapila Dev, the material cause of the universe is *prakṛiti* (the matter principle), which has the nature of the three *guṇas* (qualities). These three—*sattva, rajas,* and *tamas*—have the qualities of knowledge, activity, and stability, respectively.

   The evolutes (*tattvas*) of *prakṛiti*, which are all the myriad aspects of creation, carry these three qualities. The *guṇas* are always changing. At any given moment, one of the *guṇas* is predominant, suppressing the other two, but then it weakens and another takes its place. When *sattva guṇa* predominates, there is peace, but the mind is pulled by *rajas* and *tamas guṇas*. When *rajas guṇa* predominates, there is pain and passion, but the mind is pulled by *sattva* and *tamas guṇas*. When *tamas guṇa* predominates, there is delusion, but the mind is pulled by *sattva* and *rajas guṇas*.

   The thought waves (*vṛitti*) in the mind also have the nature of the *guṇas*, and they are experienced by the *buddhi* (intellect) as pleasure (*sukha*), pain (*duḥkha*), and attachment (*moha*) according to the predominance of *sattva, rajas,* and *tamas* respectively. Because these three *guṇas* are constantly subject to modification, the mind also has the nature of change. The fluctuation of the *guṇas* brings about the notions of pleasure, pain, and delusion by each subverting the others. For this reason, a discriminating person sees that everything is full of miseries due to the fluctuation and contradictory nature of the *guṇas*.

The main point of this *sūtra* is stated simply in the *Sāmkhya Darshana*:[1] "Is there anyone who is happy? Any happiness found is mixed with miseries. Therefore, the person of discrimination considers happiness to be pain."

The science and philosophy of the *Yoga Sūtras* can be compared to the science and philosophy of medicine. The latter analyzes disease according to four fac-

---

1 From *Sāmkhya Kārikā* by Kapila Dev.

tors: the disease, the cause of the disease, health or the absence of disease, and the means for removing the disease.

The science of liberation can also be understood according to these four factors. Pain (*duḥkha*), which is the cycle of birth and death, is the disease to be avoided (*heya*, see Sūtra II:16). The association of *puruṣha* and *prakṛiti* based on ignorance is the cause of pain (*heya hetu*, see Sūtra II:17). The continual separation (*hāna*) of *puruṣha* and *prakṛiti*, which is *kaivalya* (liberation, see Sūtra II:25) is health, or the absence of disease in the form of pain. Finally, discriminative wisdom or knowledge (*viveka khyāti*, see Sūtra II:26) is the means of removing pain (*hānopāya*) and attaining *kaivalya*.

In other words, ignorance, which is the cause of pain, is destroyed by knowledge of the Self. Therefore, all of the practices (*sādhana*) of *yoga* are designed for the sole purpose of removing ignorance and establishing knowledge of the Self. The next *sūtra* explains that it is the pain of the future that is to be avoided.

Note

The *sūtra* explains that for a *yogi* with discrimination, even pleasurable experiences are considered painful. This one concept is the cornerstone of *yoga* philosophy because if it were not true, there would be no reason to attain liberation, and the practices and philosophies of *yoga* would be superfluous.

Every living being wants to be happy. Most people pursue happiness through gratification of the senses. We see that their greatest efforts are performed in order to secure physical comfort, delicious food, and sexual pleasure. When they get these things, they are happy; when they are obstructed, they are not.

Some people, however, do not pursue happiness only through sense gratification. They may work hard to achieve their goals, sacrificing personal comfort until their aim is reached. Most of these people seek their happiness in different types of ego gratification such as wealth, power, and fame. When they get these things, they are happy; when they are obstructed, they are not.

There is also a rare group of people who seek their happiness by serving others. These people are satisfied by the help that they bring to others, by the suffering alleviated by their efforts, and/or by feeling that they are doing good. When they are able to serve others and see beneficial results, they are happy; when they are obstructed, they are not.

All of these efforts to attain happiness are flawed because they are not complete and not permanent. They all can bring temporary happiness, and sometimes the happiness lasts for a long time. But in the end, they all result in pain and misery due to the four inevitable reasons described in the *sūtra*: pain is the consequence of pleasure (because of attachment), the pursuit of pleasure is itself suffering, pleasure reinforces latent tendencies (*vāsanā*), and the changing nature of the three *guṇas* guarantees that pleasure cannot last.

The essence of this *sūtra*, then, is that the cycle can only be broken by abandoning the pursuit of ego-based pleasure. Since the individual ego can do nothing but pursue pleasure and avoid pain, the only way to abandon the pursuit of pleasure is to control, abandon, or transcend the individual ego. And, ultimately, the only way to transcend the individual ego is to realize the truth about the eternal and infinite Self. This is known as discriminative wisdom and liberation, and these will be discussed in detail in Sūtras II:25 – 26.

In the classical commentaries, the *yogi's* acute sensitivity to pain and its causes are compared to the eye's sensitivity to cotton. In other words, if a cotton ball is rubbed against the skin of the arm, it will feel soft and comforting. But if that same cotton ball is rubbed against the eyeball, it will feel irritating and extremely painful.

In the same way, the average person experiences a delicious meal or a consensual act of romantic passion as delightful and deeply satisfying, while the *yogi* with discrimination sees pain, attachment, and the deepening of the cycle of suffering. The physical sensations are perceived the same way, but their interpretations in the mind and intellect are very different.

Everyone tries to avoid pain. Most people pursue pleasure, but if the *sūtra* is correct, then pursuing pleasure only brings more pain. What then is the opposite of pain? The opposite of pain is the absence of pain, which only arises when the *yogi* realizes the true nature of the Self in discriminative wisdom. The Self is isolated from the mind-body complex and no experience of pain is possible. This has been called eternal bliss by some, however, it is very different from pleasure.

A question arises. How, then, does the *yogi* relate to experience? Obviously, they continue to act in the world, but what motivates them if they see everything as pain? Why don't they just abandon the body?

The answer is that the *yogi's* actions are performed as a duty, or say as a natural expression of the *guṇas* interacting with each other. Both pleasure and pain come of their own accord no matter what people do, so the wise say that neither is to be sought and neither is to be avoided. Instead, the mind is to be controlled so as to remove ego, attachment, and desires. When the three are completely removed, the nature and content of gross experiences become irrelevant to the enlightened *yogi*.

The next *sūtra* explains that it is the pain of the future that is to be avoided.

*Devprayāg, the Saṅgam (confluence) of Bāgirathi and Alaknanda Gaṅgā;
beginning of Gaṅgā (Ganges) proper.*

Sūtra 16   हेयं दुःखमनागतम् ॥ १६ ॥

heyaṁ duḥkhamanāgatam

The pain of the future is avoidable.

हेयम्	*heyam*	the avoidable, not keeping in the mind
दुःखम्	*duḥkham*	pain
अनागतम्	*anāgatam*	not yet come

In the previous *sūtra*, it was explained that all experiences are painful for those wise people who have discrimination. Now, in this *sūtra*, it explains which pain is to be removed.

The pain that has already passed cannot be avoided. The pain of the present moment is already being experienced, so it cannot be avoided. Therefore, only the pain that will appear in the future is considered avoidable pain. This pain that has yet to be experienced troubles the *yogi* who perceives the true nature of experience in the world.

Others who are engrossed in worldliness will not be troubled by the pain of the future. The *yogi*, who is as sensitive to pain as an eyeball is to a thread of cotton, will seek to avoid the pain that has not yet come.

Note

What is pain? Pain, according to the *yogi* with discrimination, is any form of individualized experience. Therefore, the ending of pain must be the ending of all individualized experiences, which can only occur through discriminative wisdom and liberation. This means that the more clearly one realizes the truth about worldly experiences, the more intent they will become on attaining liberation.

Pain is the single greatest motivator on the path of *yoga*. People experience pain all their lives, but not everyone practices *yoga*. Most people try to alleviate their pain by obvious means: if they are hungry, they eat; tired, they sleep; sick, they see a doctor. But these obvious means cannot completely or permanently remove the experience of pain (see Kārikās 1 & 2 of the *Sāṁkhya Kārikā*). Therefore, a categorically different type of solution is required.

This solution is discriminative wisdom (*viveka khyāti*) or liberation from individualized existence. It is attained by the perfection of the practices of *yoga* in the present, and it removes the pain of the future by removing all identification with the experiences of the world. This does not mean that the mind-body complex ceases to function; instead it means that the activities of the mind-body complex are not identified with the indwelling spirit (*puruṣa*).

In order for there to be suffering, there has to be an "I" that suffers. The "I" that suffers is the association of the *puruṣa* with the intellect. Discriminative wisdom is the ending of all such identification, so it must also be the ending of all suffering.

In the next *sūtra*, the cause of pain is explained.

Worship of Śhiva Liṅgam, Jāgeshwar Temple.

Sūtra 17   द्रष्टृदृश्ययोः संयोगो हेयहेतुः ॥ १७ ॥

drashtridrishyayoḥ samyogo heyahetuḥ

The conjunction of the knower and the knowable is the cause of the avoidable pain.

द्रष्टृ	*drashtri*	of the knower, the seer
दृश्ययोः	*dṛishyayoḥ*	and of the knowable, the seen
संयोगः	*samyogaḥ*	conjunction, union
हेय	*heya*	of the avoidable (pain)
हेतुः	*hetuḥ*	the cause

In the previous *sūtra*, Patañjali stated that the pain yet to come is avoidable. Now he explains the cause of that avoidable pain, which is the conjunction of the knower and the knowable.

The knower (*drashtri*) is the conscious *purusha*, who sees the *sattva buddhi* (pure mind) by being its master.[1] The knowable (*dṛishya*) is the *buddhi* (intellect or discriminative faculty), which becomes the vehicle by which the rest of creation is known. In *sattva buddhi*, which is also known as *chitta*, the transformation of the *guṇas* (three aspects or qualities of *prakriti*) is seen, so anything seen through the *buddhi* also becomes knowable or seen (*dṛishya*).

The word *samyoga* indicates the union of *purusha* (conscious principle) and *buddhi* (*prakriti* or matter principle), which is based on ignorance and attachment. This union creates the feeling of being an enjoyer of the experiences of creation. This is also called *asmitā kleśha* (affliction of egoism rooted in *avidyā* or ignorance). This union of *purusha* and *buddhi* is the source of all pain.

The relationship between *purusha* and *buddhi* can be understood from several different angles. The first is that *purusha* gives the power of cognizing to *buddhi*, which is the instrument of all cognition. In other words, the conscious principle in *buddhi* is the knower (*drashtri* or *purusha*). It can also be said that *purusha*, which appears to take the form of *buddhi*, goes through *buddhi* for all experiences. At the same time, the known (*dṛishya*) is also in *buddhi*. Although the known (*prakriti*) has its own independent existence, it serves the purpose of *purusha* by being dependent on *purusha* (the knower).

The beginningless union of *purusha* and *prakriti* (consciousness and matter), which manifests in the relationship of master and servant, enjoyer and enjoyed, is the cause of all miseries. These miseries can be avoided (*heya*) by removing their cause.

As Pañchaśhikāchārya says, "By giving up the cause of the union with *buddhi*, this absolute remedy of affliction can be effected." The pain yet to come can be avoided by understanding who is susceptible to afflictions, who is the afflicter, and by what means the removal of afflictions can be effected.

---

1   *Purusha* is the master of *buddhi* for two reasons: it shines on *buddhi*, making it active, and *buddhi* only functions for the sake of *purusha*.

Vyāsa, in his classical commentary, uses an analogy to further explain how the pain of the future can be avoided. The sole of the foot is susceptible to damage from thorns, but the afflictive power of the thorn can be avoided either by not stepping on a thorn or by wearing shoes. In the same way, the mind (*sattva buddhi*) is susceptible to affliction or disturbance. *Rajas guṇa* (the energy of action) has the afflictive power to disturb *sattva* and create pain. Therefore, if the effect of *rajas guṇa* is avoided in the present through discriminative wisdom, future pain will not manifest.

The experience of pain must reside in some entity, which is the objectified mind (*sattva buddhi*) alone. Pain cannot live in the subjective *puruṣha*, since it is the unchanging, actionless knower of experience.

Puruṣha is seated in *sattva buddhi*, so when *buddhi* is subjected to pain, *puruṣha* is also pained by association. The removal of pain is effected by discriminative wisdom (*viveka khyāti*) through which the ignorance regarding the association of *puruṣha* and *buddhi* is removed (see Sūtra II:25).

Note

In order to understand the *sūtra*, each term must be clearly defined. The first term is *drashtri* (the knower). *Drashtri* refers to the pure conscious principle (*puruṣha*) and not to the individualized I-sense in the intellect (*buddhi*), even though this I-sense is what we identify as the knower in everyday life.

Instead, the intellect and ego are *dṛishya* (knowable or seen), the second term in the *sūtra*. Immediately, a question arises. In everyday experiences, the ego and intellect are the subject, while the gross elements are the objects. How can it be that the subject or knower of everyday experiences becomes the object or becomes known?

Discriminative wisdom is of a nature categorically different from worldly wisdom. In everyday experiences, the ego and intellect are the subjective knower. The objects of creation are experienced as the known. But this is the worldly experience that ultimately produces nothing but pain. If we are to remove that pain in any lasting way, we have to remove the very mechanism that produces it.

In everyday experiences, the ego and intellect appear to be conscious. Indeed, worldly consciousness is their predominant characteristic. But now we have to go deeper and look at just what the intellect is. For this, we turn to classical Sāmkhya philosophy.

The intellect (*buddhi* or *mahat*) is the first evolute or combination of the three *guṇas* with consciousness. The three *guṇas* are *sattva* (sentience), *rajas* (activity), and *tamas* (inertia). They have two categorically different conditions: active, in which case the universe is manifest, and inactive, in which case nothing is manifest (not unlike the state before the Big Bang). When consciousness is reflected in the three *guṇas*, they are active, and when consciousness is not reflected in them, they are dormant.

The dormant state of the *guṇas* is the great unmanifest (*pradhāna*). It is the state of pure potential; there is no manifest creation, universe, or activity. But it is out of this great, potent unmanifest that everything arises.

Something cannot come from nothing. The universe must have a cause. The ultimate cause of the universe is *pradhāna*, the dormant state of the *guṇas* when consciousness is not reflected.

Somehow, consciousness does get reflected in the *guṇas*, at which point they become unbalanced and intermixed. This intermixture combines and recombines to form all the myriad aspects of creation.

The first manifestation of the *guṇas*—once consciousness is reflected in them—is the cosmic intellect (*mahat*). The nature of *mahat* is universal existence, the notion of pure "I-sense" (*asmitā*), and it is the basis for all of creation. Individualized existence (*ahaṁkāra*) is a modification of *mahat*, as are all the animate and inanimate beings. Everything flows from *mahat*.

Returning to the terms of the *sūtra*, the conjunction (*saṁyogaḥ*) of the knower (consciousness) and the knowable (the three *guṇas*) is the cause (*hetuḥ*) of experience and hence, suffering. *Mahat* is that first conjunction, and everything flows from it. Therefore, all of creation and all experiences within creation are simply modifications of this primal conjunction. The separation of consciousness from the *guṇas* isolates the knower, removing the possibility of further experience and further suffering. In other words, because experience and suffering are the results of a cause, and because that cause can be removed, suffering is avoidable (*heya*).

The details of this union and the process of separation are described in detail in the next eight *sūtras*.

Mūrti of Lord Kṛṣṇa playing his flute.

Sūtra 18   प्रकाशक्रियास्थितिशीलं भूतेन्द्रियात्मकं भोगापवर्गार्थं दृश्यम् ॥१८॥

prakāsha–kriyā–sthiti–shīlaṁ bhūt–endriy–ātmakaṁ
bhog–āpavarg–ārtham dṛishyam

The knowable (*prakṛiti*) is by nature knowledge (*sattva*), activity (*rajas*), and stability (*tamas*). The elements and sense organs are its form, and experience and liberation are its purpose.

प्रकाश	*prakāsha*	of illumination, cognition, consciousness of
क्रिया	*kriyā*	of activity
स्थिति	*sthiti*	inertia, stability
शीलं	*shīlaṁ*	nature, qualities
भूत	*bhūta*	the elements
इन्द्रिय	*indriya*	the power of sensations, sense organs
आत्मकम्	*ātmakam*	consisting of
भोग	*bhoga*	experience
अपवर्ग	*apavarga*	emancipation, liberation
अर्थम्	*artham*	object, for the sake of
दृश्यम्	*dṛishyam*	knowable, the seen

In Sūtras II:3 – 14, Patañjali described the *kleśhas* (afflictions) and *karmāśhaya* (the storehouse of past actions). In Sūtra II:15 – 17, the painful nature of this creation (*samsāra*) was explained along with the cause of the pain. Now, in this *sutra*, Patañjali gives a complete definition of nature (*prakṛiti*) and the purpose of creation in terms of the *guṇa*s (qualities of *prakṛiti*), the elements (*bhūtas*), and the senses (*indriyas*).

The unmanifest (*avyakta*) is the cause (*kāraṇa*) of manifestation. Before manifestation, *prakṛiti* (the matter principle) is dormant. In this unmanifest, primordial energy of creation, also called *mūla prakṛiti* (literally root or origin of matter), the three *guṇas*—*sattva* (sentience), *rajas* (activity) and *tamas* (inertia)—are equal, balanced, and unmixed. They are collectively known as *pradhāna* (the chief or principal energy), and within their dynamic equilibrium is the potential for manifestation.[1]

The *sutra* describes the characteristics of the *guṇa*s. *Sattva guṇa* has the nature of illumination (*prakāsha*), cognition, and consciousness or knowledge. The word *sattva* means "it is" or "existence." *Rajas guṇa* is the energy of activity. *Rajas* literally means "dust." Just as dust covers the form of an object, *rajas guṇa* has the power to color everything. *Tamas guṇa* has the nature of stability or inertia. *Tamas* literally means "darkness." In the dark, objects remain obscure and undifferentiated.

1　In *mūla prakṛiti*, the three *guṇa*s are inferred to be active or potent within themselves but not interacting with one another. It is potential energy that only manifests when the *guṇa*s reflect the influence of pervasive consciousness (*puruṣha*).

In their active form, the three *guṇas* are always transforming amongst themselves. Ignorance of the separateness of *puruṣha* perpetuates the momentum of the *guṇas*, and the three cooperate to produce the manifest forms of creation. Thus, the *guṇas* remain in an unequal state, with one *guṇa* in predominance and the other two acting as subsidiary energies. Knowledge of the separateness of *puruṣha*, or the identification of the conscious principle as independent of matter, causes the *guṇas* to become balanced, unmixed, and inactive.

In creation, the *guṇas* always work together in a mixed state like three strands of a rope, yet they still retain their separate qualities. There is no state of creation that is exclusively *sāttvika*, exclusively *rājasika*, or exclusively *tāmasika*. In every aspect of creation, one *guṇa* is predominant and the other two are subordinate. Each aspect of creation (object or state of mind) appears as if it were a single, unified entity with unique characteristics, though in reality it is comprised of three *guṇas*, with one *guṇa* predominant.

The three *guṇas* function by balancing each other. When one *guṇa* predominates, the other two operate to balance the effect of the dominant *guṇa* with their opposing natures. However, in manifestation, the opposition of the two subordinate *guṇas* is reduced to the point that they become supportive. For example, in a meditative state, *sattva guṇa* predominates in the mind. This *sāttvika* state is supported by *rajas guṇa* in its activity and by *tamas guṇa* in its stability. Similarly, when *rajas* or *tamas guṇa* predominates, the other two assist by balancing with their opposing natures.

Each level of creation is characterized by a ratio of the three *guṇas*. The mind, senses, and the objects of the senses are nothing but combinations of *guṇas*. As matter transforms from causal to subtle to perceptible states of being, the ratio changes and becomes increasingly *tāmasika*.

The entire objective, manifest creation (*dṛiśhya*) is a product of the activity of the three *guṇas*. According to yoga philosophy, the *guṇas* create the world through twenty-four principles: the five gross elements (*mahābhūtas*), the five subtle elements (*tanmātras*), the five organs of perception (*jñānendriyas*), the five organs of action (*karmendriyas*), mind (*manas*), ego (*ahaṁkāra*), intellect (*buddhi*), and the field of consciousness (*chitta*).[2]

Created beings, from the highest of the divine to the lowest forms of life, are all characterized according to the predominance of the different *guṇas*. In the creation of divine beings, *sattva guṇa* predominates with *rajas* and *tamas* assisting. In the creation of human beings, *rajas guṇa* predominates with *sattva* and *tamas guṇas* assisting. In the creation of lower beings such as animals, *tamas guṇa* predominates with *rajas* and *sattva guṇas* assisting.

---

2 Sāṁkhya Philosophy, upon which the philosophy of the *Sūtras* is based, recognizes only twenty-three manifest principles. The *Sūtras* have added *chitta* (field of consciousness) as an additional manifest principle. In Sāṁkhya, the concept of *chitta* is contained within *mahat* (cosmic intellect), which is the universal aspect of *buddhi* (individualized intellect). In both systems, *puruṣha* and *pradhāna* exist as separate, additional principles.

The *guṇas'* natural cooperation, opposition, and transformation occur only when the *puruṣha* (consciousness) is reflected in them. In fact, the *guṇas* function only for the dual purpose of *puruṣha* (*puruṣhārtha*), which is experience (*bhoga*) and liberation (*apavarga*). Without this dual purpose, the *guṇas* would have no purpose and no reason to manifest as they do. A conscious knower is required for all experiences; indeed, without the potential to be known, an object or experience has no meaning.

Actually, *puruṣha* simply witnesses the two states of experience and liberation, which both take place in the *buddhi* (intellect). The *guṇas* become active in the presence of *puruṣha* just as iron filings are pulled by the proximity of a magnet, with no effort on the part of the magnet. When the *guṇas* are not in the proximity of *puruṣha*, they remain dormant, unmixed, and unmanifest.[3]

This *sūtra* covers both the seen (*dṛiśhya*) and the seer (*draṣhṭa*). It begins by describing the nature of the seen and concludes by giving the purpose of this creation, which is the experience (*bhoga*) and liberation (*apavarga*) of *puruṣha*.

Bhoga (experience) occurs only in ignorance of the true nature of the seer and the seen. In reality, the seer and the seen are completely separate, but in ignorance, they appear to be identical. The apparent identity of these two principles (the subjective and the objective) is necessary for phenomenal experience.[4] This experience appears in desirable and undesirable forms.

For a *yogi* (one desiring liberation), the undesirable experiences of creation take the forms of the afflictions (*kleśhas*), past impressions and desires (*samskāras*), and attachments. It has the purpose of binding the *puruṣha* in ignorance. This state of bondage in ignorance is what creates the potential for the liberation of *puruṣha* (for without bondage there can be no liberation).

The desirable experience of creation is the acquisition of knowledge of *prakṛiti* and of the modifications of the *guṇas*, which is achieved through *samprajñāta samādhi* (super-consciousness with perfect knowledge). *Samprajñāta samādhi* leads to *asamprajñāta samādhi* (super-consciousness beyond all knowledge) through which the *puruṣha* is liberated and established in its own essential nature.

Experience (*bhoga*) and emancipation (*apavarga*) are actually both characteristics of *buddhi*, but they are ascribed to *puruṣha* just as the victory and defeat of two armies are ascribed to their kings. Experience and liberation are states of

---

3 There is no adequate language for discussing the phenomena of the unmanifest. Time and space do not exist in the unmanifest, so terms like presence and proximity are misleading. Somehow, the reflection of consciousness is not registered in the unmanifest *guṇas*, and somehow it is registered in the manifest state of the *guṇas*. If both states were not possible, then the dual functions of experience and liberation would not be possible.

4 In this case, the seer is the pure, undifferentiated consciousness (*puruṣha*) and the seen is the intellect (*buddhi*), through which all experiences are known. In everyday experiences, the seer is the intellect, ego, mind, and senses, while the seen are the manifest objects of creation. The fact that this everyday seer is the conjunction of the *puruṣha* and the *buddhi* is the very point of this section of the *Sūtras*.

mind, which are attributed to *puruṣha* because consciousness pervades the whole creation. Specifically, there are six functions of *buddhi* that get attributed to *puruṣha*:

1. Cognition (*grahana*), which is the perception of an object by the ten senses and five *prāṇas*,
2. Retention (*dhāraṇa*), which is storing an experience in memory,
3. Recollection (*ūha*), which is activating a stored experience in memory,
4. Elimination (*apoha*), which is dismissing certain ideas while retaining others,
5. Conception (*tattva jñāna*), which is the secular or spiritual knowledge generated from the process of recollection and elimination, and
6. Determination (*abhiniveśha*), the clinging to life which is expressed in the final resolution to accept or reject, to act or to abstain.

These six functions are performed by the mind and senses jointly, but they are ignorantly ascribed to *puruṣha* because *puruṣha* is the master of *buddhi*. These six functions are present in all activities of *buddhi*, including one-pointedness (*samādhi*). It is only when the activities of the mind are completely arrested that these six stop.

Within the experienced creation, the mind appears to be conscious, just as an electric fan appears to have the ability to rotate. But in reality, the fan only functions due to the flow of electricity, which is completely separate from the fan itself. When the fan is powered by electricity, it rotates. When it is separate from electricity, it is incapable of rotating.

Similarly, all people believe that they are capable of intelligent functioning. But the mind, which is a modification of the three *gunas*, is inert and insentient by itself; all intelligence comes from the reflection or pervasiveness of consciousness. In ignorance, consciousness and matter are united as one entity (the living being). In wisdom, consciousness is seen as separate from all matter, which gets active and appears to be alive due to consciousness.

Emancipation (*apavarga*) is the ascertainment of the true nature of the *puruṣha*, which is separate and ever free from the modifications of *prakṛiti*.

Note

In the previous *sūtra*, it was explained that the conjunction of the knower and knowable (*puruṣha* or *draṣhṭri*, the seer, and *prakṛiti* or *buddhi*) is the cause of all pain. Now, in Sūtras II:18 and 19, the knowable (*prakṛiti*) is explained in detail. The knower (*puruṣha*) is explained in Sūtra II:20.

First and foremost, the knowable is the three *gunas*—*sattva* (sentience), *rajas* (activity), and *tamas* (retention or inertia). This means that everything in creation is simply a combination of these three qualities. Every object, every aspect of every person, and every component of every experience, is nothing but the three *gunas*.

An objection arises. Where is the proof of the theory of three *guṇas*? No surgeon has ever found the *guṇas* in any patient. No scientist has ever found the *guṇas* in any rock or in outer space; nor any chef in any food, nor any lover in any beloved. And yet, the philosophy says that nothing exists in reality except these three invisible energies.

The answer is in experience. Nothing exists for us except that which is known. Nothing will ever exist for us except that which has the potential to be known. Therefore, the ability to be known (perceived or recognized) is a prerequisite for existence. This is called *sattva*.

Change or activity is also required for any experience. In fact, every thought, emotion, perception, breath, word, or action is a modification of creation. Every tick of the clock is change. This is called *rajas*.

Finally, at least one aspect of the following is also required for experience: substance, retention, cohesion, stability, and/or ignorance. The physical reality perceived by the senses; the retained impressions of past actions; words, perceptions, and thoughts required for contemplation; the cohesion of disparate elements, energies, or ideas into a common whole; the relative stability of objects that creates the illusion of permanence; and the ignorant conjunction of the conscious knower and the material known are all required for experience. This is known as *tamas*.

It is true that the three *guṇas* have never been isolated and directly perceived by the senses. That is not their nature. Instead, they work together in combination and opposition to create the perceptible objects. An analogy that resembles the workings of the *guṇas* is the technology of color printing.

Almost every mass-produced full color magazine, catalog, book, postcard, and newspaper is printed using the same basic technology. Tiny dots of yellow, red, and blue are combined to create the illusion of the millions of subtle colors we see on paper. Perhaps not coincidentally, these are the three colors used to represent the three *guṇas* (*sattva* is yellow, *rajas* is red, and *tamas* is blue).

In other words, when we look at a color ad for a vacation resort in some tropical paradise, the thousands of subtle colors in the sand, plants, water, and sky are simply illusory combinations of yellow, red, and blue dots. Somehow, it is a trick of the eye to recognize the variations in dots as distinct colors. The average person never acknowledges the dots and only sees the picture.

Basically, the same thing is true with the three *guṇas* and the experience of the world. It is a trick of the mind to take the same three *guṇas* and to create the countless varieties of objects and experiences in the world. And, no matter how much they combine in the objects themselves, each *guṇa* never takes on the characteristics of the other two. To understand how all of creation, and all experiences within creation are nothing but combinations of the *guṇas*, we can start from the outside in.

The *sūtra* says that the elements and the sense organs are the forms of the knowable *prakṛiti*. If we start with the objects of creation, we can see that all objects are combinations of five basic principles or elements: solidity, liquidity, visibility, movement, and space. The various relationships of these five create all the differences in the objects. For example, a tree has more solidity than ice cream, and a cloud has more movement than a rock. Of course, no botanist has ever opened a tree to find solidity existing as a separate substance inside, but its existence is no less real.

In the same way, these five elements are themselves combinations of five subtler elements, which are the abilities to be smelled, tasted, seen, felt, and heard, respectively. These are called the *tanmātras* in yoga philosophy, and they combine to form the gross elements. These subtle abilities are not perceptible to the gross senses; they can only be intuited or inferred by the concentrated mind.

But even these five are not the subtlest aspect of creation. They are modifications of individuality (*ahaṁkāra*). Again, this cannot be perceived by the senses, only inferred by the mind. How? Actually, it is quite simple.

What can possibly have the ability to be perceived? It has to be the characteristic of an individualized object or being. The opposite, universality, is undifferentiated by definition, so it cannot have specific characteristics. In other words, in order for an object to have any distinguishing characteristics, it must be individualized.

For example, a wave in the ocean is individualized. It starts somewhere and ends somewhere else. We see many waves, and even though they are not separate from the ocean, they are separate from each other. If the entire ocean were one big wave, there would be no way to distinguish the wave from the ocean. Therefore, individuality (*ahaṁkāra*) must be the predecessor or cause of the five subtle elements (*tanmātras*).

Going further, just as the individual wave cannot exist without the ocean, so individuality cannot exist without universal existence (*mahat* or *chitta*). This universal existence is the first conjunction of spirit and matter, consciousness and the *guṇas*. This state is an awareness of existence contrasting with non-existence, the first step of duality. Consciousness (*puruṣha*) brings the awareness, and the *guṇas* bring duality (existence vs. non-existence).

Taking the ocean analogy one step further, the universal ocean of existence is both the substratum for, and the substance of, each individual wave. Every aspect of the wave is nothing but ocean, including the swell, the crest, the white caps, the tube, the foam, and the spray. In the same way, every aspect of creation, from mind and senses to the elements and the animate and inanimate beings, is nothing but the *guṇas*.

Practically, the play of the *guṇas* can be understood in a variety of ways. In gross sense perception, such as looking at a flower, the eyes contact the visual substance of the flower (*tamas*) and present it to the mind. This momentary increase in *tamas* is immediately balanced by an increase in *sattva*, which produces awareness of the flower. The change is caused by the activity of *rajas*.

The mind, also comprised of the three *guṇas*, is characterized by their relative strengths. When the mind is *sattva* predominant, sense perceptions will be accurate, inferences will be clear and correct, and actions will be appropriate and balanced. When the mind is *rajas* predominant, sense perceptions will be colored by desire, inferences will be self-interested, and actions will be passionate and excessive. When the mind is *tamas* predominant, sense perceptions will be inaccurate, inferences will be deluded and incorrect, and actions will be misdirected and harmful. All of the practices of *yoga* are designed to make the mind more *sāttvika*.

It should be clearly understood that a *sattva* predominant mind also contains both *rajas* and *tamas*. In this case, the characteristics of *rajas* (passion and restlessness) and *tamas* (confusion and laziness) are overpowered by the strength of *sattva* (clarity and determination). The same dynamic is true of the *rājasika* and *tāmasika* minds.

Because the *guṇas* are constantly changing in an effort to balance themselves, our every action, word, and thought affects the relative strength of the *guṇas* in the mind. *Sāttvika* actions, such as meditation, worship, and serving the needy, increase the strength of *sattva* in the mind. *Rājasika* actions, such as competition, romance, and self-promotion, increase the strength of *rajas* in the mind. *Tāmasika* actions, such as overeating, idleness, and taking drugs and alcohol, increase the strength of *tamas* in the mind.

The *sūtra* says that experience and liberation are the purposes of the knowable (*prakṛti* or the three *guṇas*). Experience is the conjunction of the knower and the knowable, while liberation is knowledge of their separation. In this sense, experience and liberation are characteristics of the intellect, though they are attributed to the spirit by association. Experience requires consciousness to be linked to the *guṇas* in the form of "I am this mind-body complex," and "All these experiences are happening to me." Liberation is the knowledge that "The 'I' is not associated with the activities of the mind, body, or world in any way," and "Pleasure and pain happen to the mind-body complex and not to me."

But because experience is the conjunction of spirit and matter, we must also speak of bondage and liberation of the spirit. The individualized spirit is bound within the subtle body until liberation, just as the air within a balloon is trapped until the balloon pops. Neither the spirit nor the air is affected by its bondage, but that doesn't make the bondage any less real.

In the previous *sūtra*, it was explained that the conjunction of the knower and the known is the cause of all suffering. Discriminative wisdom (*viveka khyāti*) is the disjunction of the knower and the known—in the form of the knowledge, "I am not related to the objects and activities of creation in any way"—and so the cause of suffering is removed.

In the next *sūtra*, the states of the *guṇas* are categorized into four levels according to their production and characteristics.

Sūtra 19 विशेषाविशेषलिङ्गमात्रालिङ्गानि गुणपर्वाणि ॥ १९ ॥

viśheṣhāviśheṣha–liṅgamātrāliṅgāni guṇa–parvāṇi

The states of the *guṇas* (qualities of *prakṛiti*) are specialized, unspecialized, indicator only, and that which is without indication.

विशेष	*viśheṣha*	specific, specialized, diversified
अविशेष	*aviśheṣha*	non-specific, unspecialized, undiversified
लिङ्गमात्र	*liṅgamātra*	a mere mark, undifferentiated phenomena, indicator only
अलिङ्गानि	*aliṅgāni*	without mark, without indication
गुण	*guṇa*	qualities
पर्वाणि	*parvāṇi*	states, stages

In the previous *sūtra*, it was explained that the knowable (*prakṛiti*) is the three *guṇas*, which take the form of the senses and their objects for the purpose of experience and liberation. Now, in this *sūtra*, Patañjali categorizes the *guṇas* into four states according to their function and production.

Purity (*sattva*), activity (*rajas*), and inertia (*tamas*) are the three qualities of nature (*prakṛiti*) that appear in four states: specialized (*viśheṣha*), unspecialized (*aviśheṣha*), indicator alone (*liṅga mātra*), and without indicator (*aliṅga*).

The first three stages—*viśheṣha*, *aviśheṣha*, and *liṅga mātra*—are the evolutes or manifest states of the three *guṇas*. They serve the dual purpose of *puruṣha*. In the fourth state, "that which is without indication" (*aliṅga*), also known as the unmanifest state (*pradhāna*), the three *guṇas* are in perfect balance and in equilibrium.

This last state is the one into which all manifest objects merge during the final dissolution of creation. However, the three *guṇas* themselves do not dissolve in that state. The *guṇas* are eternal. They have no preceding cause, so they do not arise out of a cause and disappear back into that cause. In the *aliṅga* state, the *guṇas* simply remain dormant, unmixed, and unproductive.

The sequence of *prakṛiti's* evolution according to these stages is from the one *aliṅga* to the one *liṅga mātra* to the six *aviśheṣhas* to the sixteen *viśheṣhas*. No further transformation is caused by the sixteen *viśheṣhas*, as all perceptible phenomena are merely combinations of these principles.[1] The sequence of involution or dissolution is the reverse order of the sequence of evolution (*viśheṣha* to *aviśheṣha* to *liṅga mātra* to *aliṅga*).

1. Sixteen *Viśheṣhas* (diversified) are the grossest principles that form the building blocks of the physical creation. They are the five gross elements (*bhūtas*), the five energies of perception (*jñānendriyas*), the five energies of action (*karmendriyas*), and the mind (*manas*).

---

1 The same sequence of evolution described according to the principles (*tattvas*) is from the unmanifest *pradhāna* to *mahat* (cosmic intellect) to *ahaṁkāra* (ego) to the five *tanmātras* (subtle elements) and eleven senses, and from the *tanmātras* to the five gross elements.

The five gross elements are space (*ākāsha*), air (*vāyu*), fire (*agni*), water (*āp*), and earth (*kshiti*). The five energies of perception are hearing (*śhrota*), touch (*tvachā*), sight (*chakshu*), taste (*rasanā*), and smell (*nāsikā*). The five energies of action are speaking (*vānī*), grasping (*hasta*), locomotion (*pāda*), excretion (*pāyu*), and procreation (*upastha*). *Manas* is that part of the mind that works with the senses, directing, recording, and presenting their activities to the ego and intellect. *Manas* also has the ability to ponder, which means to fill in gaps in perceived information with memory, inference, and imagination.

These sixteen are the diversified principles of the three *guṇas*. They do not cause any further modifications as they are the final modification of the *guṇas* in the evolution of the matter principle. All physical objects and sensual experiences are merely combinations of these energies. The inherent characteristics of the three *guṇas*—pleasure, pain, and delusion—exist in them in the form of pleasant, unpleasant, and stuporous experiences.

2. Six *Avisheshas* (**undiversified**), which are the subtle causes of the sixteen diversified principles, are the ego (*ahaṁkāra*) and the five subtle elements (*tanmātras*). The five *tanmātras* are the subtle energies of sound (*śhabda*), touch (*sparśha*), light (*rūpa*), taste (*rasa*), and smell (*gandha*). The undiversified ego (*ahaṁkāra*) is the cause of the eleven senses and the *tanmātras*. In the process of evolution, *ahaṁkāra* is the agency or principle of individualization.

These six, being the undiversified capacities of sensation and feeling, cannot produce specific experiences of pleasure, pain, and delusion by themselves. It is only when they modify further into the sixteen diversified principles that this capacity arises. Therefore, the eleven senses and five gross elements are required for worldly experiences.

3. One *Liṅga Mātra* (**indicator only**) is called *mahat* (cosmic intellect). *Mahat* is the indicator of both the Self (*puruṣha*) and the unmanifest (*mūla prakṛiti*), which is why it is called indicator only (*liṅga mātra*). Though the senses are also indicators, they only indicate external objects and their immediate cause (*ahaṁkāra*). *Mahat* is the direct indicator of *puruṣha* and *prakṛiti* because it is the first evolute, the purest union of consciousness reflected in the *guṇas*. *Mahat* means "the greatest." It is the causal level of creation—cosmic consciousness—with the nature of pure "I-sense" (*asmitā*).

4. One *Aliṅga* (**non-indicator**) is the unmanifest state of the *guṇas* known as *mūla prakṛiti*. It is not the indicator of anything because it can never be known directly. It is that state of the three *guṇas* in which the *guṇas* are balanced, unmixed, and unproductive, so it is without phenomenal existence.

This *pradhāna* is considered non-existing (*asat*) because of its unmanifest state, but it is also considered existing (*sat*) because it has the potential for creating and thus being the object of *puruṣha*. Therefore, it is neither existing (*sat*) nor non-existing (*asat*). Everything that exists does so only for the sake of *puruṣha*, thereby directly or indirectly indicating the existence of *puruṣha*. But the unmanifest state of the *guṇas* (*pradhāna*) does not serve the purpose of *puruṣha*, so it is termed as non-indicator (*aliṅga*).

This *sūtra* explains how each level of creation directly indicates its immediate cause and indirectly indicates *puruṣha*. The next *sūtra* explains how the functions of consciousness and matter are falsely attributed to each other, causing matter to appear to be conscious and consciousness to appear mutable.

Note
In the previous *sūtra*, it was explained that *prakṛiti* is the three *guṇas*—*sattva*, *rajas*, and *tamas*—which take the forms of the senses and their objects for the dual purpose of experience and liberation. The *guṇas* by themselves are unconscious, but they become active when the presence of *puruṣha* is reflected in them. All objects and experiences of creation are nothing but modifications of the *guṇas* in which consciousness is reflected.

Now, in this *sūtra*, the three *guṇas* are categorized into four states according to their function and to cause and effect. Going in order of gross to subtle, these four categories are *viśheṣha* (specialized or diversified), which are effects only, *aviśheṣha* (general or undiversified), which are both causes and effects, *liṅga mātra* (indicator only), which is also a cause and an effect, and *aliṅga* (non-indicator), which is a cause only.

There are several reasons why the sage Patañjali uses this system of classification. For one, it explains the sequence of evolution and involution of creation and the mind. In this way, it supports the sequence of *samprajñāta samādhis* described in Sūtra I:17. Furthermore, classifying nature in this way aids in the development of discrimination.

Before the aspirant has gained the profound wisdom of the *samprajñāta samādhis*, all knowledge is gained through sensory information. Sensory information is only on the specialized (*viśheṣha*) level. Of course, all the principles of the mind are used to generate this knowledge, but their separateness is not known to the aspirant. Because this knowledge is limited to the *viśheṣhas*, there arises doubt as to the reality of the subtler levels.

In all sense perceptions, the outer objects are recreated in *manas* for presentation to the ego and intellect. The intellect identifies and discriminates the object while the ego establishes a relationship to it. Because the ego and intellect are the sources of the worldly sense of "I," this means that the "I" never sees the outer world; it only sees the recreated objects in *manas*. But by some great mysterious force, these internal objects are experienced as if they were outside.

Of course, the question arises how it is possible that external objects can be recreated in *manas* with such realism that they appear to be the actual objects. The only plausible explanation is that there is a subtler level of creation that is shared between the mind and all the objects of creation. This is the *aviśheṣha* (general or undiversified) level of *ahaṁkāra* and the subtle elements. These six principles are in both the mind and in the objects themselves. The mind uses the subtle elements to recreate the external image.

Then a question arises about the field or substratum in which these subject-object interactions occur. The ego and intellect are interacting with the objects created in *manas*. But where does this interaction take place? What is the basis for individualized experience?

Upon deep reflection, it can be determined that pure, universal existence must be the basis for all individual experiences. This is the level of *mahat* (cosmic intelligence), known in this *sūtra* as *liṅga mātra* (indicator only).

This sense of universal existence (*mahat*) is called "indicator only" because it is so undiversified that it simply indicates the presence of consciousness and of the qualities. Even the sense of individual existence is not differentiated in *mahat*, so no subject-object relationship is possible. There is only a sense of pure existence. This is still duality because it is contrasted to non-existence, but no other cognitions or experiences arise.

Another question arises. Isn't this "God the Creator"? Isn't this the highest state possible, for what could be more subtle than pure, undiversified, universal consciousness, the cause and substratum of all creation?

The answer is yes and no. This is the level of "God the Creator," but because it is duality (existence vs. non-existence), it must come from somewhere. Anything that manifests must at some point return to the unmanifest state. When the mind is so completely purified of self-interest and even of the notion of individuality, it dwells in this state of universal existence only. When even this awareness is stabilized, the intellect is capable of recognizing that the conscious "I," that has been the subject of every experience it has ever known, is separate from all qualities and cognitions. In other words, consciousness and the *guṇas* are separate and distinct.

This universal existence is the subtlest manifestation of creation in which both consciousness and the qualities (*guṇas*) are known. Therefore, it must indicate the great unmanifest (*mūla prakṛiti* or *pradhāna*), and it must also indicate unadulterated consciousness (*puruṣha*). For this reason, it is called "indicator only."

The great unmanifest, therefore, is that which is indicated by *mahat*. But because it is unmanifest, it cannot be the indicator of anything, so it is called *aliṅga* (non-indicator). Something cannot come from nothing, and since *mahat* is something, it must come from something else. But since *mahat* is the subtlest aspect of creation, it cannot come from anything else in creation. Therefore, it must come from something unmanifest (the *pradhāna*). In this way, the entire creation is described, from a blade of grass up to the unmanifest cause.

There is another very important reason for understanding these four stages. All experiences of the world are known as pleasurable, painful, or deluding, or as a combination of these three. All beings seek pleasure and happiness while avoiding pain and unhappiness, but due to attachment and delusion, their efforts are often misguided. The wise seek their happiness through *sāttvika* means, such as meditation, devotional activities, and service to others. Worldly-minded people seek their happiness through *rājasika* means, such as wealth, fame, power, and recognition. Fools seek their happiness through *tāmasika* means, such as physical pleasure, drugs, and alcohol.

But a question arises. If all gross experiences are simply modifications of the subtle elements and the ego, and since both of them are in the mind, why do we need bodies at all? Why can't we just experience everything directly through the mind without the need for an external world at all?

The answer is that the subtle elements and ego are undiversified, which means that they don't have the ability to generate experiences of pleasure, pain, and delusion. The sixteen diversified principles are absolutely necessary for the experience of creation. Without them, the dual purpose of experience and liberation is not possible.

For example, *shabda tanmātra* is the subtle energy of sound, or the ability to be heard. This same ability is present in a drum, a bell, and a baby's voice, but the sounds produced by these three are very different. The uniqueness of each sound is not present in *shabda tanmātra* alone; it only arises from the mixture of the subtle and gross elements.

Even in dreams, in which the entire world may be recreated in the mind, the diversified senses and objects are present. We are aware of ourselves having all sorts of perceptions and performing all types of actions; all of these require the diversified principles. Knowledge of all four stages of *prakṛiti* gives a complete understanding of both experience and liberation.

In the next *sūtra*, both the seer (*puruṣha*) and the relationship between the seer and the seen are explained.

Sun reflecting on the holy Gaṅgā river.

Sūtra 20   द्रष्टा दृशिमात्रः शुद्धोऽपि प्रत्ययानुपश्यः ॥ २० ॥

drashtā drishimātrah śhuddho–'pi pratyayānupashyah

The seer is consciousness only, and though entirely pure, appears to know the content of *buddhi*.

द्रष्टा	*drashtā*	the seer
दृशिमात्रः	*drishimātrah*	consciousness only
शुद्धः	*śhuddhah*	pure
अपि	*api*	even though
प्रत्यय	*pratyaya*	by imitation, concept through the mind, content
अनुपश्यः	*anupashyah*	cognizing ideas, appears as if seeing

What is the nature of the seer (*drashtā*)? The *sutra* states, "The seer is consciousness only." The seer is an immutable knower (*drishimātrah*) or consciousness in itself (*purusha*). The seer is that power of becoming conscious and is beyond the *gunas* (qualities) of *prakriti* (the matter principle).

The seer functions in creation by reflecting in *buddhi* (an evolute of *prakriti*). In cognition, the seer is neither quite similar nor quite dissimilar to *buddhi*. The *buddhi* is only capable of cognition or knowledge when *purusha* is reflected in it. *Purusha* is different from *buddhi* in that *purusha* doesn't go through any modifications, whereas *buddhi* is constantly modifying. In *buddhi*, external objects are either known or not. This mutative nature of *buddhi* is further identified by its taking the form of objects like a cow or a pitcher, which are sequentially known or unknown. *Buddhi*, which is the activity of the *gunas* in which the *purusha* reflects, assumes the form of the object in the mind producing cognition.

Purusha's knowledge, on the other hand, is simply of the modifications of *buddhi*, and thus it is always present and unchanging. In other words, the knowing principle is never absent in *buddhi* as it goes through the process of cognition.

The determinative energy of all objective phenomena is based on the qualities (*gunas*), which are purity (*sattva*), activity (*rajas*), and inertia (*tamas*). *Purusha* is consciousness itself and is without qualities (*gunas*). The *purusha*, however, is the seer of the qualities, and it is due to the reflection of *purusha* that the *gunas* become active and the creation become manifest.

The *buddhi*, as an evolute of *prakriti*, is unconscious by itself. The *buddhi*, illumined by pure consciousness, becomes conscious, manifesting as the discriminative intellect. *Purusha*, though distinct from *buddhi*, remains united with *buddhi* for the purpose of cognition. This is the meaning of the statement in the *sutra*, "And though entirely pure, appears to know the content of *buddhi*."

Pañchaśhikhāchārya comments, "The power of the enjoyer is certainly unchangeable, and it does not run after every object. In connection with a changeful object (*buddhi*), it appears as if it is being transferred to every object and imitates its modification." Here *purusha* is called "the enjoyer" because the whole creation happens in the presence of *purusha*. In the next *sutra*, it is said that this creation is only for the dual purpose of the experience and liberation of *puruṣa* (*puruṣārtha*). Thus the *puruṣa*, rooted in *buddhi*, imitates the functions of *buddhi* and appears as if it were an aspect of *buddhi*. In reality, *puruṣa* is separate and distinct. Only in the state of ignorance does *puruṣa* appear as *buddhi* and *buddhi* like *puruṣa*.

Puruṣa is conscious in two ways: As a seer (*draṣṭā*), *puruṣa* is by itself in all circumstances, and as a knower (*grahītā*), it is together with *buddhi*. This distinction is known only through discriminative wisdom (*viveka khyāti*).

Note

Sūtra II:17 stated that the conjunction of the knower and the knowable is the cause of all pain. In Sūtras II:18–19, the knowable was described as the three *guṇas*, which take the form of the senses and their objects, and which can be categorized into four different stages. Now, in this *sūtra*, the knower is described as pure consciousness only, even though it appears to modify with every cognition.

The purpose of these *sūtras* is to explain the underlying truth about experience. People appear to be conscious beings. They walk, talk, think, adapt, evolve, and make decisions. If we try to determine exactly which part of us is conscious, we discover that consciousness is centered in the intellect, though consciousness also appears in the ego, mind, and senses. From the perspective of worldly experience, this is correct.

But this *sūtra* is telling us that the consciousness of the intellect is actually borrowed from another. The intellect (*buddhi*) is indeed conscious, but not because of its own inherent capabilities. Just as an electric fan does not have the power to rotate without electricity, so the intellect does not have the power to cognize without *puruṣa* (pure consciousness).

All knowledge of the world comes as a modification of *buddhi*. All perceptions, thoughts, emotions, dreams, and fantasies are known as modifications of *buddhi*. When a cow or a vase is seen, it is known because the *buddhi* temporarily takes the form of that cow or that vase. Specifically, the cognition in the mind forms as, "I see the cow." Therefore, *buddhi* is mutable.

On the other hand, *puruṣa* is immutable. While worldly consciousness in the form of *buddhi* is constantly changing—"I see the cow; now I don't see the cow, I see the vase; now I don't see the vase"—the *puruṣa* is the unchanging awareness of these modifications. There must be something that knows that "I see the cow," and this could be said as, "I know that I see the cow, and now I know that I don't see the cow, but see the vase instead." This type of "knowing" is called pure and immutable.

An analogy is a person watching television; they see all the changes on the screen and all the different programs without moving or becoming part of any of the shows. And yet, without the viewer, there would be no purpose for the television set or its content. Furthermore, though the viewer is the sole reason why the television and its content exist, the viewer has nothing to do with creating the television or its content. In the same way, without the *puruṣha*, there would be no purpose for creation or its modifications and experiences. And, even though the entire creation is for the purpose of *puruṣha*, the *puruṣha* has nothing to do with the form of creation nor its experiences.

Therefore, the *puruṣha* is both similar and dissimilar to *buddhi*. From a worldly perspective, they are identical; indeed the two are merged and cannot be separated. Together, they are the knower of the world. But in the underlying reality, they are opposite; *puruṣha* is the unchanging consciousness that witnesses all the unconscious changes in *buddhi*.

The ego is the vehicle by which the knower and knowable are joined. The ego is the "I-sense" that exists as conscious existence. In all beings, the ego is the notion, "I am an individual." In *mahat*, the ego is simply "I exist." But in all its forms, the ego always links consciousness and matter (*puruṣha* and *buddhi*). Once these two are linked, the ego functions as a seamless whole just as when hydrogen and oxygen atoms are linked, they function as water (in which the two cease their separate existence).

The next *sūtra* explains that *prakṛiti* (nature) exists only for the sake of *puruṣha*.

Mūrti of Goddess Gaṅgā riding on crocodile.

Sūtra 21 तदर्थ एव दृश्यस्यात्मा ॥ २१ ॥

tad–artha eva dṛiśhyasyātmā

Prakṛiti (manifest nature) exists for the sake of that (*puruṣha*) alone.

तद्	*tad*	that, his, of the *puruṣha*
अर्थे	*artha*	purpose, sake, object
एव	*eva*	alone
दृश्यस्य	*dṛiśhyasya*	of the knowable (*prakṛiti*)
आत्मा	*ātmā*	being

In Sūtra II:18, the nature and purpose of *prakṛiti* were explained. In this *sūtra*, Patañjali states that *prakṛiti*, from *mahat* (cosmic intellect) down to the *bhūtas* (gross elements), is only a vehicle to serve the purpose of *puruṣha*. The phrase *"tad artha"* means that *prakṛiti* exists to fulfill the dual purpose of *puruṣha*: *bhoga* (experience) and *apavarga* (liberation).

All knowables, in terms of color, form, cognition, and feelings, are seen by *puruṣha* through the modifications of the intellect, mind, and senses. This includes all exercises of the will. But when the mind becomes completely purified of its outgoing nature, there are no more objects to be experienced by *puruṣha*. At this point, it is said that *puruṣha* becomes isolated within itself, which is known as liberation.

The nature of the knowable (*prakṛiti*) is to be known through consciousness (*puruṣha*). All objects exist only to be experienced (known or seen) by *puruṣha*. When the object is not experienced by someone, then it does not exist as an object for that person. This does not mean, though, that the object disappears for other *puruṣhas* (see Sūtra II:22).

Prakṛiti has no self-interest, which means that it does not exist for its own purposes. All of its interactions are simply for the experience and liberation of the *puruṣha*. When liberation is attained, *prakṛiti* ceases to exist for that individual *puruṣha* because it is not witnessed by that *puruṣha*. It does not cease entirely because of the witnessing of the other *puruṣhas*.

Note

In the previous *sūtra*, it was explained that *puruṣha* is the unchanging seer of all the modifications of *buddhi* (intellect). The intellect, empowered by the reflected presence of *puruṣha*, is the individualized and changing seer and experiencer of the inner and outer worlds. Now, in this *sūtra*, it is explained that all of *prakṛiti* (nature), including the intellect, ego, mind, senses, gross and subtle elements, and all the myriad objects of creation, exists only for the sake of *puruṣha*. It simply means that without the ability to be known or experienced, creation has no meaning or purpose.

This is actually a logical and irrefutable statement. Creation without intelligence or consciousness is unimaginable, primarily because imagination is based on consciousness. What would happen in a creation without knowledge? Who would be there and why?

Life is experience. All beings experience life according to their nature and capacity. A plant experiences growth and decay, lightness and darkness, wetness and dryness. An animal experiences birth, growth, and death; lightness and darkness; wetness and dryness; companionship and separateness; hunger and satiety; fear and comfort. Human beings have all these, plus a much more diverse set of experiences because the capacity of our intellect allows us to conceive multiple layers of cause and effect (thus giving rise to complex emotions).

Everything in manifest creation is either known or it has the potential to be known. Said differently, everything in manifest creation exists for the sake of sentient beings.

Humans are part of creation, so our bodies and our experiences exist for the sake of the knower (*puruṣha*) and not for our own sake, just as a bed exists for the sake of the sleeper and not for its own purpose. Our bodies, senses, minds, and intellects are all combinations of the three *guṇas* that come together as they do for the sake of experience and liberation.

It is crucial to understand how the unchanging *puruṣha* "knows" creation. All it "does" is witness the modifications of *buddhi* (intellect). *Buddhi* is highly mutable; it takes the form of every cognition. For example, when we look at a sunset, the *buddhi* is simultaneously taking the form of the setting sun, the landscape between us and the sun, our physical bodies, and all the thoughts and emotions we may have about it. It is one of the great miracles of life that these modifications of *buddhi* are experienced as if they were spatially located within and without the body.

This one point is extremely important to all students of yoga philosophy. Without understanding it, a clear grasp of the rest of the philosophy is impossible. Everything we experience is a creation of *buddhi*, nothing more, nothing less. This does not mean that the world has no reality; but it does mean that our experiences of the world occur entirely in the mind.

Therefore, the universe is not created for the sake of humans. Humans, as a part of the universe, are created for the sake of the embodied *puruṣha*. This is the central point of these *sūtras*. The experiences of the world are modifications of *buddhi*, which is empowered by the reflection of *puruṣha*. This activity of *buddhi* is known as worldly consciousness, which is of a nature categorically different from the pure, immutable consciousness (*puruṣha*). The consciousness in *buddhi* creates the sense of "I" that is the subject of all experiences.

Much debate has occurred over the term *artha* in this *sūtra*. It is often translated as *puruṣha's* purpose, which, to some people, gives the incorrect notion of agency to *puruṣha*. Humans have purposes for all their actions because they are combinations of both consciousness and matter. They exist in a body with desires, and they can make decisions based on the knowledge they have. Every action they perform has a purpose, which is to increase pleasure and to decrease pain.

But none of these characteristics apply to *puruṣha*. There are no desires, no limitations, no needs, and no aspirations in *puruṣha*. All of these terms can be applied to manifest *prakṛiti* alone. Instead, the term *artha* can be understood correctly as the object to be known by *puruṣha*. Nature exists because it can be known. If it couldn't be known, it wouldn't exist.

There is a relationship between *puruṣha* and the *guṇas*. *Puruṣha* has the ability to know and the *guṇas* have the ability to be known. When the knower is "present," the *guṇas* become active and create the knowable universe. When the knower is "absent," the *guṇas* remain inactive and nothing manifests.

Both *puruṣha* and the three *guṇas* are eternal and uncaused. Their unmanifest existence is not co-dependent. But, because they are compatible, a relationship forms between them in which the *guṇas* become active for the sake of being known. There are no needs being met by this relationship; neither the *guṇas* nor *puruṣha* are greater or lesser, better or worse, during their conjunction or during the isolation; the *guṇas* remain the *guṇas* and *puruṣha* is simply *puruṣha*.

There are benefits and drawbacks for all beings within creation. The benefits are that they get to experience the world and play out their desires. The primary drawback, as seen in Sūtra II:15, is that all experiences ultimately result in suffering. The profound recognition of this suffering greatly reduces desire for further experiences. When all such desires are removed, the individualized *jīva* merges back into the undifferentiated *puruṣha*, fulfilling the second aspect of nature's purpose, liberation (*kaivalya*).

In the next *sutra*, the effect of one *jīva's* liberation on the rest of creation is described.

View of Gaṅgā waterfront at Haridwār with tridents, the symbol of Lord Śhiva, and bell.

Sūtra 22   कृतार्थं प्रति नष्टमप्यनष्टं तदन्यसाधारणत्वात् ॥ २२ ॥

kritārtham prati nashtam–apy–anashtam tad–anya–sādhāranatvāt

Although *prakriti* ceases to exist for one whose purpose has been fulfilled, it is not destroyed for others because of its communal use [by all].

कृतार्थं	*kritārtham*	whose objects have been achieved
प्रति	*prati*	to him, toward
नष्टम्	*nashtam*	destroyed
अपि	*api*	although
अनष्टम्	*anashtam*	not destroyed
तद्	*tad*	from that
अन्य	*anya*	to others
साधारणत्वात्	*sādhāranatvāt*	being common, owing to commonness

In Sūtra II:18, it was explained that the dual purpose of *prakriti* is to serve the *purusha* through experience (*bhoga*) and liberation (*apavarga*). Now, this *sūtra* explains that the whole manifest universe is for the experience and liberation of all individual souls (*jīvātma*) and not just for one particular *jīvātma*.

Unimpaired discriminative wisdom is the culmination of experience. When it becomes firmly established (see Sūtra II:26), the *jīvātma* has achieved its final purpose (liberation). For that *jīvātma* alone, *prakriti* ceases to exist. For others, who are not yet liberated, it continues to exist and is shared for the two purposes of experiencing the various objects of creation and then finally achieving liberation from all experience.

Sūtra II:18 also stated that *prakriti* is constituted by the three *gunas*, *sattva* (illumination), *rajas* (activity), and *tamas* (inertia), which are active in manifest creation and dormant in the unmanifest state. This *sūtra* says that *prakriti* "ceases to exist," meaning that the *gunas* merge back into their cause, primordial nature (*mūla prakriti*). This is the case for that one particular *jīvātma*, which becomes separated from, and independent of, *prakriti* or *buddhi* through discriminative wisdom (*viveka khyāti*) and supreme dispassion (*paravairāgya*). Such a *jīvātma* is called liberated (*jīvan mukta*).

In the individual or microcosmic level, *prakriti* works as *buddhi* (intellect), providing the *purusha* with the whole spectrum of experiences in the form of *vrittis* (modifications of the mind). In Sūtra I:2, *yoga* was defined as the control of all *vrittis* in the mind. For one who has achieved Self-realization, all worldly thought waves (*vrittis*) subside. In the absence of thought waves, *prakriti* in the form of the *buddhi* (mind) also ceases to exist. For that individual, the function of *prakriti* as a vehicle of experience and liberation is finished, but for others, *prakriti* continues to exist in a natural way, i.e. for the experience and liberation of those *jīvātmas* still bound by ignorance.

The question arises, "Would creation disappear entirely if all the embodied souls (*jīvātmas*) were liberated?" Such a situation is not possible, because souls are innumerable. No number added to or subtracted from an innumerable quantity affects it because there remains an innumerable quantity. Therefore, it is not possible that all *jīvas* would get liberated, so there can't be an end of creation as a whole.

On the macrocosmic level, the union of *puruṣha* (the seer) and *prakṛiti* (the seen) is without beginning. This union is caused by ignorance. Therefore, the ignorance that keeps this union eternally together must also be beginningless.

Pañchaśhikhāchārya says, "As the three *guṇas* have been allied with *puruṣha* from time without beginning, so too have their modifications been associated with him from time without beginning." This means that the *guṇas* are in eternal conjunction with the embodied soul (*puruṣha* or *jīvātma*) and thus the spirit's conjunction with *prakṛiti*, in the forms of *mahat*, *buddhi*, mind, and the senses and their objects, is also eternal.

On the individual level, however, the conjunction of the embodied soul (*jīvātma*) with *prakṛiti*, in the form of *buddhi* and the other evolutes does have an end. Each individual goes through the myriad forms of experience, and eventually develops knowledge and dispassion. When the highest knowledge and the most supreme dispassion are attained, the primal ignorance that binds the soul to the mind and body is dispelled. At this point, the individual spirit returns to its infinite nature just as a bucket of ocean water is poured back into the ocean.

In the next *sūtra*, it is explained that the conjunction of *puruṣha* with *prakṛiti* brings about the potential for both worldly knowledge based on ignorance and discriminative knowledge based on wisdom.

Note

The previous *sūtra* stated that the manifest *prakṛiti* exists solely to fulfill the purpose of *puruṣha*. Now, in this *sūtra*, it is explained that this *prakṛiti* ceases to exist after liberation for that *puruṣha* only; for everyone else, creation remains the same. This is a fairly simple concept by itself, but the implications of it are significant. It means that there are both individual and common (shared) aspects to creation, and that there is a way out.

The phrase *sādhāraṇatvāt* refers to *prakṛiti*. This means that we all live in the same universe. Our experiences of this universe, though, are unique to each of us. Imagine twenty people riding on a bus. They will all hit the same bumps and all be subject to the same forces of gravitation and acceleration. And yet, their experiences of that bus ride will all be unique. Some will be hungry and thinking about food, others will be full or satisfied. A pregnant woman may notice every bump, while a drunk man might not even realize he is on the bus at all. But, if the bus were to get into an accident, everyone would acknowledge that shared experience.

This simple concept actually distinguishes Sāṃkhya and Yoga philosophies from many others. The universe is not created and dissolved for each person with every thought as some philosophies say. If that were the case, then there would be no requirement for everyone on the same bus to experience the same accident. Some people simply wouldn't manifest the accident in their thoughts. Instead, the physical reality is shared, while the mental response to—and thus the experience of—that shared reality is unique.

This also means that we cannot all be one, as suggested by some other philosophies. In order for us to have unique experiences, the subject or "I" must also be unique. If there were only one *puruṣha* embodied in all beings, then there would be no possibility for diversity of experience. If there were only one "I," then when one person was happy, everyone would be happy. But, of course, this is not the case. Therefore, we can safely conclude that each person's consciousness and individual identity is distinct and separate from everyone else's. When one person fulfills the dual purpose of experience and liberation, creation ceases to exist for him or her. For everyone else, creation functions without interruption.

We can understand this with an analogy. Individualized or embodied consciousness is contained within the subtle body just as air is contained within a balloon. So long as the balloon remains intact, the air inside the balloon is separated from the air outside. But, when the balloon is popped, the air inside is merged back into the ambient air. In the same way, individualized consciousness is merged into the absolute consciousness when the container of the subtle body is dissolved during *dharma megha samādhi* (the *samādhi* that accompanies the perfection of discriminative wisdom).

There is a paradox in this analogy. The air inside the balloon is both different and the same as the ambient air. It is the same in that they come from the same source and when the balloon pops they are merged back into an undistinguishable whole. It is different in that whatever happens to the air in the balloon does not change the ambient air. This is homologous to the individual and absolute *puruṣhas*. They are from the same source and they merge at final liberation. But, none of the experiences associated with that embodied consciousness affect the absolute consciousness.

Taking the analogy one step further, if one balloon pops, the air inside it is freed, but the air inside every other balloon remains trapped. In the same way, when one *yogi* attains liberation, the *puruṣha* in that subtle body reunites with the absolute *puruṣha* without affecting any of the other *puruṣhas*.

The *sūtra* says that *prakṛiti* ceases to exist for the liberated one. This concept follows directly from Sūtras 18 & 21. Manifest *prakṛiti* exists only for the sake of the experience and liberation of *puruṣha*. When experience and liberation are complete, the cause of manifest *prakṛiti* is fulfilled and thus removed. Then, *prakṛiti* ceases to manifest. Without the cause, the effect ceases to be. But, since the cause is removed only for the one liberated *puruṣha*, the effect continues to manifest for all the other *puruṣhas*.

The principle of cause and effect can also be understood with an analogy. Rain and smoke are examples of effects, while clouds and fire are examples of causes. If the clouds and fire are removed, there can be no rain or smoke. While it may be argued that you can have clouds without rain and fire without smoke, you cannot have rain without clouds and smoke without fire. In the same way, *prakṛti* cannot manifest without the experience and liberation of *puruṣha*.

A question arises. What exactly is *puruṣha*? The term *puruṣha* is used in different ways in different places in the philosophy. The absolute *puruṣha* is undifferentiated consciousness that never changes; it simply reflects on, and thus activates, the three *guṇas* of *prakṛti*. It is the Self, the original source of the "I" in the mind, and the reason why the cosmos develops.

The term *puruṣha* is also used to mean person, soul, or embodied consciousness (*jīva*). While there is only one absolute *puruṣha*, there are numberless embodied *puruṣhas*. The embodied consciousness exists as the core of the subtle body, accompanying it through all the various trials, tribulations, and incarnations.

There has been, however, a debate about the multiplicity of *puruṣha* on the absolute level. Though several great commentators have claimed that the multiplicity of *puruṣha* is permanent and absolute, such a position is inconceivable to us. The absolute, eternal, unchanging *puruṣha* can only be one. So many different rivers flow into the ocean, but the ocean is only one (even though it may have different names in different areas). Furthermore, once the river water has entered the ocean, it is the ocean and not the river.

The *sūtra* speaks to another debate in Yoga philosophy. At which moment does the *puruṣha* actually become liberated from its bondage? Bondage is the conjunction of *puruṣha* and *prakṛti*, so bondage is relevant to them both. It is clear that the bondage of *prakṛti* ends with discriminative wisdom because the primal ignorance that had pervaded every modification of *buddhi* in the form of "I am this mind-body complex" is completely removed. After discriminative wisdom, the *buddhi* continues to function so long as the body continues to function, only without ignorantly linking the "I" to the activities of the intellect. In other words, the intellect continues to recognize bodily sensations such as hunger, heat, and cold, but the ego no longer creates the feeling that these sensations are happening to "me." This is the liberation of *prakṛti*.

When the *puruṣha* gets liberated is less clear. Some argue that the perfection of discriminative wisdom is also the liberation of the *puruṣha*, while others say that so long as the body continues to function, the *puruṣha* must still be bound within the subtle body, energizing the thoughts, words, and actions. The unchanging witness consciousness continues its normal function, the only difference being that it witnesses an intellect that is no longer ignorant and no longer suffering the delusions of bondage. In this latter case, complete liberation for that enlightened *yogi* would only occur at the death of the gross body.

Understanding the Sāṁkhya theory of the subtle body is helpful in evaluating this debate. The subtle body comprises eighteen principles (*tattvas*): intellect, ego, mind (*manas*), the ten senses, and the five subtle elements. This subtle body contains all the *karma saṁskāras* (impressions of past experiences) and *vāsanās* (tendencies and desires) of the individual. This subtle body transmigrates from gross body to gross body playing out old *saṁskāras* and generating new ones. It is this subtle body that is sometimes called the *soul* in the West.

Relating the subtle body back to the previous analogies, the subtle body is the balloon or the bucket that contains the air or the ocean water. Without the *puruṣa* trapped inside, there is no knower, so the subtle body has no function and thus no existence. All experiences are related to the subtle body, but only when the *puruṣa* is there. Liberation of the *puruṣa* occurs when the *puruṣa* is freed from the container of the subtle body. Some say that this happens at the perfection of discriminative wisdom. The embodied consciousness merges with the infinite and the gross body is activated by the absolute *puruṣa*. Others say that the embodied *puruṣa* is still contained within the subtle body until the death of the gross body. The difference is immaterial from the standpoint of suffering; after discriminative wisdom, the cause of suffering is removed so the embodied one must be freed from it.

The nature of the conjunction of *puruṣa* and *prakṛiti* is further explained in the next *sūtra*.

Inner Sanctum, Jāgeśhwar Temple

Sūtra 23   स्वस्वामिशक्त्योः स्वरूपोपलब्धिहेतुः संयोगः ॥ २३ ॥

sva–svāmi–shaktyoḥ svarūpopalabdhi–hetuḥ samyogaḥ

Conjunction is that which brings about the realization of the inherent capabilities of *purusha* and *prakriti*, which are owning and being owned, respectively.

स्व	*sva*	of being owned, of one's own (*prakriti*)
स्वामि	*svāmi*	of owning, master (*purusha*)
शक्त्योः	*shaktyoḥ*	of the powers of both
स्वरूप	*svarūpa*	of the natures, own form
उपलब्धिः	*upalabdhiḥ*	the recognition, realization
हेतुः	*hetuḥ*	that brings about, cause
संयोगः	*samyogaḥ*	conjunction, union

Starting with Sūtra II:17, the nature and characteristics of the union of *purusha* and *prakriti* were described. Now, this *sūtra* explains that the reason for their conjunction is the manifestation of their respective powers. *Purusha* is the power to own or to see, and *prakriti* is the power to be owned or to be seen.

All that is seen, including the primary mind (*chitta*) is unconscious *prakriti*. *Purusha* is only the conscious energy that "owns" or witnesses the knowable *prakriti*. *Purusha* and *prakriti* are both eternal and ever-present. The primary characteristic of *prakriti* is to be experienced (*bhogya*) and the primary characteristic of *purusha* is to experience (*bhokta*).

Experience manifests by the union (*samyoga*) of *purusha* and *prakriti*, which is caused by ignorance or wrong knowledge (*avidyā*). This union of *purusha* and *prakriti* is beginningless, but not endless as described in the previous *sūtra*. It exists only until *purusha* is known as separate from *buddhi* (*prakriti*). To remove this wrong knowledge, the alliance of *purusha* and *prakriti* is disunited (*viyoga*), which is called the liberation (*apavarga*) of *purusha*.

In various scriptures, this alliance of *purusha* and *prakriti* is described in different terms: the experiencer (*bhoktā*) and that which is experienced (*bhogya*); the seer (*drashṭā*) and that which is seen (*dṛishya*); the knower (*jñāta*) and that which is known (*jñeya*). In the *Bhagavad Gītā*, the seer, experiencer, and knower is called the owner of the field (*kshetrajña*) and the seen, experienced, and known is called the field (*kshetra*).

In verse XIII:26, the *Gītā* says:

> *yāvatsañjāyate kiñchitsattvam sthāvarajaṅgamam*
> *kshetrakshetrajña samyogāttadviddhi bharatarshabha*

> Oh, Arjuna, know that whatever is being born, whether unmoving or moving, that it is from the union of the field and the knower of the field.

Similarly, in verse 21 of the *Sāṁkhya Kārikā*, it is said:

> *puruṣasya darśanārtham kaivalyārtham tathā pradhānasya*
> *paṅgvandhavad–ubhayor–api samyogas–tatkṛitaḥ sargaḥ*

> The union of *puruṣa* and *pradhāna*, like that of a lame person and a blind person, is for the purpose of seeing the *pradhāna* and for the purpose of isolating the *puruṣa*. From this [association] creation proceeds.

Sūtra II:17 states, "The union of the seer with the seen is the cause of the avoidable pain." This union is actually the affliction of egoism (*asmitā kleśha*) described in Sūtra II:6, which states, "Egoism is the appearance of the identity of the seer (*puruṣa*) and the seen (*buddhi*)." The *puruṣa* (pure consciousness) is reflected in the *buddhi* giving rise to the notion of individual identity (*jīva bhava*).

This union of *puruṣa* and *prakṛiti* serves two purposes: It unfolds the powers latent in *prakṛiti* and *puruṣa*, which is experience (*bhoga*), and it establishes the Self (*jīvātma*) in its essential nature (*paramātma*), which is liberation (*apavarga*). The unfolding of *prakṛiti* is the manifestation of the 23 energies (*tattvas*) of creation, which arise out of the great unmanifest (*pradhāna*) when the reflection of *puruṣa* activates the three *guṇas*.

Non-discrimination (*adarśhana*) is the cause of the alliance of *puruṣa* and *prakṛiti* and thus the cause of experience. Right discrimination (*darśhana* or *viveka khyāti*) is the cause of the separation of *puruṣa* and *prakṛiti* and thus the cause of liberation. The sage Vyāsa, in his classical commentary on the *Yoga Sūtras*, cites eight different views on the origin of non-discrimination. The fourth view, which is most tenable, is that non-discrimination is a latent tendency (*saṁskāra*) that sprouts in the reflection of *puruṣa*. For a full description of all eight views, please reference any of the available translations of Vyāsa's commentary (such as Āraṇya or Bhāratī).

In the next *sūtra*, the cause of the conjunction is given.

Note

In this *sūtra*, the conjunction of *puruṣa* and *prakṛiti* is described again, this time as the means by which their respective powers are manifested. Sūtra II:6 explained that the affliction of egoism (*asmitā kleśha*) is the union of the seer and the seen. Sūtra II:17 then stated that this union is the cause of all pain.

At first, it may seem that this topic is getting excessive treatment. After all, it is said that the early Indian philosophers were so committed to brevity and efficiency of language that they would prefer to sell off their first born son rather than add a superfluous word to their text. So indeed we may conclude that this thorough coverage is warranted because it is the crux of the *yoga* philosophy.

This union is both the primal cause of life and the primary obstacle to liberation. The remainder of all the *sutras* were designed simply to help the aspirant identify the cause of the conjunction and to effect its removal. When the conjunction is present, there is experience, bondage, and suffering. When it is removed, there is liberation. Ultimately, nothing more needs to be understood, but since the true understanding of this core concept is so difficult to achieve, the rest of the philosophy is extensive in its explanations.

This *sutra* explains that the conjunction allows for the inherent powers of *puruṣha* and *prakṛiti* to become manifest. When conjunction does not occur, or say when *puruṣha* is isolated from the *guṇas*, there is nothing to know, see, enjoy, witness, or experience. *Puruṣha* is simply pure, unchanging, unadulterated, infinite consciousness. It is not aware of itself; it is not even aware of existence.

In this state of disjunction, *prakṛiti* is separated from the reflection of *puruṣha*, and the three *guṇas* are dormant, unmixed, inactive, and noncreative. Nothing is manifest; not time, space, or matter in any form, and no experience is possible. *Prakṛiti* is unconscious, so without the reflection of *puruṣha* there is no way for it to know or experience anything.

When the two are thus separate and isolated, their inherent powers of knowing and being known cannot be realized. It is only when they come together that they are manifested. But, this manifestation does not bring anything new to either *puruṣha* or *prakṛiti*; these powers always exist. Instead, the conjunction simply makes latent powers active. The conjunction is the field in which their inherent powers play.

Both powers manifest themselves directly through *buddhi*, and indirectly through the rest of creation. *Buddhi* is the vehicle through which all of creation, and all the experiences within creation, are known. It appears to be conscious, taking the forms of the inner and outer worlds for the sake of experience and liberation. In all experiences, *puruṣha* is the power of knowing within *buddhi*, and *prakṛiti* is *buddhi's* power of being known by *puruṣha*.

When the *buddhi* is confused, believing that it is inherently conscious, it is afflicted by the *kleśhas*, and thus bound to suffering. This is known as experience. When the *buddhi* is awakened to discriminative wisdom, it recognizes the separate functioning of consciousness and the *guṇas*. It realizes the true "I" that is unrelated to the mind-body complex, and thus beyond suffering. This is known as liberation. These two states are the complete purpose of the conjunction. When they are fulfilled, the cause of the conjunction is removed, and so the conjunction itself is removed.

The commentary cites the *Bhagavad Gītā* and the *Sāṁkhya Kārikā*. Both quotations state that all of creation arises from the union of *puruṣha* and *prakṛiti*. The *Kārikā* adds the analogy of the lame person and the blind person. The story in full is as follows:

Two groups are traveling through the forest. In one group there is a lame man and in the other group there is a blind man. Both groups are attacked by robbers. Everyone flees for their own safety, leaving the lame man and the blind man to fend for themselves. Through fate, they encounter each other. By themselves, they are incapable of fulfilling their purpose of getting out of the forest. But when the lame man gets on the shoulders of the blind man, he is able to direct the movements of the blind man. Thus, they are able to get out of the forest and reach the next village. When they arrive at their destination, the purpose of their union is completed and they separate.

The lame person in this analogy stands for the spirit. Sight represents consciousness, and lameness represents inactivity. The blind person is nature. Blindness represents unconsciousness, and mobility represents all the activities of the three *guṇas*. Without each other they cannot achieve anything. Together, they can reach the destination. This means that experience and liberation, which are the dual purpose of creation, cannot happen without the union of spirit and matter. Finally, once the destination is reached, which means that experience and liberation have both been fulfilled, the purpose of their union has been realized and they separate. This indicates the impermanence of the union of spirit and nature. In other words, when experience and liberation have been completed, spirit and nature return to their pristine states of unmanifest isolation.

A question arises about how this union comes about. If the premise is accepted that *puruṣa* and *prakṛiti* are the two eternal primordial energies, unmanifest in themselves and yet the cause of all manifestation, there is still a question how. How does something unmanifest become manifest?

The answer is given by Vyāsa, in his classical commentary, as *adarśhana* (non-discrimination). This is supported in the next *sūtra*, which says that *avidyā* (primal ignorance) is the cause. But where does this non-discrimination or primal ignorance come from? Vyāsa gives eight explanations that are found in various commentaries on different philosophies. Though the serious scholar may wish to evaluate the merits and weaknesses of all eight, we will be more efficient and describe only the most acceptable.

Non-discrimination or primal ignorance is a latency (*saṁskāra*). This means that it exists inherently in the three *guṇas*. In *pradhāna* (the unmanifest state of *prakṛiti* or the *guṇas*), ignorance is dormant, existing only as potential. In *mahat* (cosmic consciousness), which is the first manifestation of the conjunction, ignorance is present. Actually, the two cannot be separated. *Mahat* is the expression of ignorance, or say, the existence of *mahat* is the linking or identification of consciousness with qualities. One does not cause the other; they are two words for the same thing.

In the next *sūtra*, ignorance (*avidyā*) is explained as the cause and catalyst for this manifestation of the inherent powers of *puruṣa* and *prakṛiti*.

Sūtra 24 तस्य हेतुरविद्या ॥ २४ ॥

tasya heturavidyā

Ignorance is the cause [of this conjunction].

तस्य	*tasya*	it (the conjunction of *purusha* and *prakriti*)
हेतुः	*hetuḥ*	cause
अविद्या	*avidyā*	ignorance, nescience

In the previous *sūtra*, the purpose of the union of pure consciousness (*purusha*) and matter (*prakriti*) was explained as realizing the essential natures and powers of both principles. Now, this *sūtra* explains that the cause of the union of *purusha* and *prakriti* is ignorance or nescience (*avidyā*). This *avidyā*, which includes all knowledge based on non-discrimination (*adarśhana*), creates a false alliance between the discriminative function of the mind (*buddhi*) and pure consciousness (*purusha*). Due to this wrong identification, the discriminative mind and pure consciousness appear to be one and the same. Therefore, all the characteristics of the mind, such as happiness, sadness, pain, and attachment, are wrongly attributed to pure consciousness.

This concept is also found in other scriptures. In verse 20 of the *Sāṁkhya Kārikā*, it is said:

> *tasmāt–tatsaṁyogād–achetanaṁ chetanāvad–iva liṅgam*
> *guṇa–kartṛitve–'pi tathā karteva bhavaty–udāsīnaḥ*

By the union of *purusha* and *buddhi*, the unconscious *buddhi* appears conscious and the inactive *purusha* appears active.

And in verse III:27 of the *Shrīmad Bhagavad Gītā*, it is said:

> *prakṛiteḥ kriyamāṇāni guṇaiḥ karmāṇi sarvaśhaḥ*
> *ahaṁkāra–vimūḍhātmā kartā–'ham–iti manyate*

All actions are being performed by the modes of *prakriti*. The fool whose mind is deluded by egoism thinks, "I am the doer."

All the activities of the mind-body complex appear to be functions of the "I," but in reality, the relationship of the "I" to the body is ignorance (*avidyā*).

The latencies of *avidyā* formed in previous lifetimes are the cause of *adarśhana* (non-discrimination). When the *buddhi* is soaked in wrong knowledge (*viparyaya jñāna*), it neither develops fully nor does it achieve knowledge of the pure conscious principle (*purusha*). The mind's inherent nature is to constantly fluctuate, which perpetuates ignorance. As long as the mind remains veiled in ignorance, there is no break in the alliance between pure consciousness (*purusha*) and matter (*prakriti*).

However, when discriminative knowledge (*viveka khyāti*) is fully established, the mind completes its function, i.e. the dual purpose of experience and liberation (*bhoga* and *apavarga*) is fulfilled. Ignorance (*avidyā*), which is taking the non-Self for the Self, ceases to reappear. Therefore, since *avidyā* is that which opposes discriminative knowledge (*viveka khyāti*), and since the removal of *avidyā* removes the false association of consciousness and matter, it must be the cause of the alliance between the *buddhi* and *puruṣha*.

The sage Vyāsa introduces an objection in his classical commentary. All knowledge—including discriminative wisdom—is a modification of *buddhi* based on duality, so it cannot be liberation (the absence of duality). Saying that any form of knowledge brings liberation is like an impotent husband promising his wife a child after he dies.

This objection can be broken down into parts. The first part concerns the ability of a cause to generate an effect in time. A potent husband impregnates his wife in the present, not after he dies. Churning milk provides butter in the present, not after the milk has spoiled. But, since discriminative wisdom is an attribute of the *buddhi*, it cannot be liberation, which means that discriminative wisdom cannot cause liberation in the present. Instead, the philosophy promises that discriminative wisdom leads to liberation after it ceases. The objection claims that such a promise of liberation in the future is like the impotent husband's promise of children after he dies.

The objection is not correct. Wrong knowledge (*adarśhana* or *avidyā*) is the cause of bondage. Discriminative knowledge (*viveka khyāti* or *darśhana*) removes *avidyā*. When discriminative knowledge is established, supreme dispassion (*paravairāgya*) arises and wipes away any vestige of identification, including *viveka khyāti* itself. When even *viveka khyāti* is abandoned, the Self is established only in itself, which is liberation (*mokṣha*). This is explained more fully in the next *sūtra*.

Note

This *sūtra* explains the cause of the union of *puruṣha* and *prakṛiti*. The principle of cause and effect is called *satkāryavāda*, and it is an essential component of both Yoga and Sāṁkhya philosophies. There are three basic components of *satkāryavāda*: All effects have a cause, the effect is inherent in the cause, and if the cause is removed, the effect ceases to be. These are explained in detail in Kārikās 8 and 9, but only the third aspect is relevant to this *sūtra*.

Without fire, there can be no smoke; without clouds, there can be no rain; without ignorance, there can be no bondage. These first two are relatively easy to test. We can look at an empty fire pit and see that there is no fire and no smoke. But, if we collect and set fire to a pile of wood, smoke is created. Therefore, fire causes smoke.

A clear sky produces no rain. After some time, clouds come and it rains. While not all clouds produce rain, rain cannot be produced without clouds. Therefore, clouds are the cause of rain.

The third example, which is the essence of this *sūtra*, is more difficult to demonstrate because we cannot perceive anything without ignorance. The philosophy says that even though ignorance exists from time without beginning, it needn't always exist in the future. And, when ignorance is removed, the conjunction of *puruṣa* and *prakṛti* ceases.

The conjunction of *puruṣa* and *prakṛti* causes each to take on the characteristics of the other. The *puruṣa* appears active and the *prakṛti* appears conscious. This manifests as a single entity (*buddhi*) in which neither *puruṣa* nor *prakṛti* alone can be distinguished. In other words, *puruṣa* is not seen as pure consciousness, and *prakṛti* is not seen as the active qualities; instead, only the *buddhi* is seen, which appears to be both conscious and active.

The *buddhi* is a combination or mixture of consciousness and active qualities. It mutates, responds, and discriminates, all of which require the functioning of both *puruṣa* and the three *guṇas*. It is not possible to have any experience without this joint functioning, so we only see them together. In fact, even if we study the philosophy and say that consciousness and matter are distinct, we do not believe it nor fully understand it until we attain discriminative wisdom for ourselves. The purity of *sattva buddhi* is so refined that we cannot imagine how it can be based on ignorance. That is, we cannot imagine it until we experience it directly with discriminative wisdom.

Seeing only the conscious *buddhi* without differentiating *puruṣa* and the *guṇas* is called ignorance (*avidyā* or *adarśhana*). This means that everything we know and everything we experience is based on ignorance. Ignorance is the core thought, the basis upon which everything else is built. Inherent in this is the identification of the "I" with the *buddhi* and its content, which is called egoism (*asmitā*). The combination of egoism and ignorance is the foundation for all worldly experience. But where does it come from?

Ignorance is a latent tendency (*saṁskāra*), which means that it is inherited from before. Since ignorance is the cause of individuality, we cannot say that previous individual experiences caused ignorance. Some commentators say that the *saṁskāra* of ignorance is present from prior births. Even if we accept the notion that ignorance in the present birth comes from previous births, the question still remains about where the original ignorance comes from.

Most commentators say that primal ignorance has existed from time without beginning. This, of course, must be true because ignorance is the cause of time, but it still doesn't answer the question of what caused it. All that can be said for sure is that ignorance is a property of the mind, just as heat is a property of fire, but not like milk is a property of the cow. If we say that fire causes heat or that cows cause milk, we are correct. But the crucial difference is that you can find a cow that doesn't give milk, but you can't find fire that doesn't give heat. In the same way, you cannot know your mind without ignorance.

Getting rid of ignorance is like getting rid of heat; you have to put the fire out. When a fire burns up all its fuel, there is nothing left for it to do and it dies out.

When a mind plays out all its worldly desires, there is nothing left for it to do and it stops fluctuating. When the mind stops fluctuating, the *puruṣha* and the *guṇas* are recognized as the distinct sources of the *buddhi*, and this is known as discriminative wisdom.

Technically, this wisdom is still a part of the dualistic mind, and therefore not liberation. However, it completes the dual purpose of the mind, which annihilates all desires for further experience. Just as the dross burns up as it burns away the impurities of the gold, discriminative wisdom burns itself up with supreme dispassion and complete liberation. This is similar to a dying man who thinks, "I am dying," on his last breath. While he is thinking and exhaling his last breath, he is still alive, but as soon as that breath and that thought are complete, he is dead. So long as discriminative wisdom shines in the mind, there is still a mind and still bondage for the *puruṣha*, but as soon as it is complete, there is no more thought and the *puruṣha* is liberated.

This is the reason that the objection mentioned in the commentary is not correct. Discrimination does lead to liberation, so it is not like an impotent man promising results to his wife after he is dead. Instead, it would be like the relationship of conception to birth. The conscious effort is getting to conception; the rest happens as a matter of course.

The next *sūtra* further explains the process of liberation or isolating the *puruṣha*.

Sūtra 25 तदभावात्संयोगाभावो हानं तद्दृशेः कैवल्यम् ॥ २५ ॥

tad–abhāvāt–saṁyogābhāvo hānaṁ tad–dṛiśheḥ kaivalyam

From the absence of ignorance comes the absence of union (of *puruṣha* and *prakṛiti*). This avoidance is absolute freedom of the seer (*puruṣha*).

तद्	*tad*	its, that (ignorance)
अभावात्	*abhāvāt*	absence
संयोग	*saṁyoga*	union
अभावः	*abhāvaḥ*	disappearance, absence
हानम्	*hānam*	removal, avoidance, absence
तद्	*tad*	that
दृशेः	*dṛiśheḥ*	of the knower or seer (*puruṣha*)
कैवल्यम्	*kaivalyam*	absolute freedom

In the preceding *sutra*, it was explained that ignorance (*avidyā*) is the cause of *adarśhana*, which is the wrong identification of pure consciousness (*puruṣha*) and the discriminative faculty of the mind (*buddhi*). "I-consciousness" (*asmitā*) is in *buddhi* by the power of the reflection of consciousness. The veiling power of ignorance causes the "I-consciousness" in *buddhi* to be attributed to *puruṣha*.

Now, this *sutra* explains that ignorance is removed by discriminative knowledge (*viveka khyāti*). By discrimination, the wrong identification (*adarśhana*) ceases and the *buddhi* no longer identifies the pure consciousness principle with the "I-consciousness." With the cessation of wrong identification, there is automatically a separation of pure consciousness (*puruṣha*) and the discriminative faculty of the mind (*buddhi*).

The discriminative knowledge, which correctly identifies (*darśhana*) the essential and separate natures of *puruṣha* and *prakṛiti*, brings supreme dispassion (*para-vairāgya*). This supreme dispassion replaces all worldly tendencies with the *saṁskāras* of restraint (*nirodha saṁskāras*), which in turn remove all vestiges of identification including *viveka khyāti*. This removal (*hāna*) of the identification of pure consciousness with the mind is the absolute freedom (*kaivalya*) of the Seer (*puruṣha*), in which all afflictions and their causes cease to exist.

Note

This *sutra* is a continuation of the logic presented in the previous *sutra*. Ignorance is the cause of the conjunction of *puruṣha* and *prakṛiti*. Discriminative wisdom (*viveka khyāti*) removes ignorance, and since ignorance is the cause of conjunction, discriminative wisdom removes the conjunction also.

The fact that the logic is circular does not make it any less true. Ignorance is seeing the inactive consciousness as active and the unconscious *guṇas* as conscious. This misidentification takes the form of the intellect (*buddhi*), which functions as active consciousness. Said differently, ignorance is an attribute of *buddhi*, which appears as the notion, "I am conscious." This notion is the basis for, and essence of, every experience and every thought in the mind. This one notion is verily the identification of *puruṣha* and *prakṛiti*.

In everyday life, ignorance takes the form of *ahaṁkāra* (individual ego), which is the notion, "I am this mind-body complex." *Ahaṁkāra* is a modification of the core ignorance ("I am conscious") in which the "I" is completely identified with the body, personality, and mind. In the early stages of purifying the intellect, the identification of the "I" is broken from the body, though it remains with the mind, or at least with the notion of pure individualized existence. The pure notion, "I am conscious," is known as *sāsmitā samādhi* ("I-sense" alone). It is still a cognition, which means it is duality based on ignorance.

An objection arises. The *puruṣha* is pure consciousness, which is also the source of the "I" in the mind. Therefore, *puruṣha* must also be the undifferentiated "I" separate from all identifications. Why then is it ignorance to say that "I am conscious?"

The answer is that while the first two points of the objection are correct, the notion "I am conscious" is based on linking consciousness to the qualities. The pure, undifferentiated "I" is also the pure, undifferentiated consciousness. But this isolated *puruṣha* is free from all cognitions and all modifications, including the notion that it is conscious. The notion "I am conscious" can be contrasted to "I am unconscious," so it is a dualistic notion. The pure, undifferentiated consciousness is infinite and unmodified, so it cannot be contrasted to anything.

Every experience of life starts with "I" because each one of us is having the experience. If there were no "I" in the experience, then it couldn't be happening to us, so it wasn't our experience. But it is not the pure, undifferentiated "I" that experiences the world. It is the conscious "I" in *buddhi*, which is known as *ahaṁkāra*, that feels, thinks, and acts. All experiences of the world require the "I" (*puruṣha*) to be linked to the qualities (*guṇas*).

It seems like it should be fairly easy to realize this simple truth. But there is a very strong force that keeps us from knowing it. This force is desire. Desires are the armed sentries that guard the palace of knowledge. They are brilliant, cunning, and ruthless. No one enters that palace so long as even a single worldly desire remains.

It is for this reason that the philosophy of *yoga* cannot be separated from the practice of *yoga*. The practice of *yoga* is the purification of the mind of all desires, while the philosophy of *yoga* not only gives the roadmap, the techniques, and the obstacles to be avoided, it provides a detailed description of the palace itself, inspiring the *yogi* to practice. In other words, it answers the question, "How do we become free from egoism and from suffering?"

Because of ignorance, we desire worldly experiences. But all experiences cause suffering, as described in Sūtra II:15, so eventually we seek an end to them. Through practice, they become weaker and weaker, until we are able to progress through the various levels of *samprajñāta samādhi*. Eventually, through repeated practice and dispassion, the mind can be stabilized in *sāsmitā samādhi*, which is the pure notion, "I am conscious." This is the level of universal existence, the cosmic intellect (*mahat*).

This notion can also be expressed as "I exist," without any other qualifications. It is still duality because it is opposed to "I don't exist," but it is very subtle. At this point, when the pure, universal existence is stable, the intellect is capable of perceiving that the "I" is actually separate from the modifications. This is known as discriminative wisdom, and it takes the form of the notion, "I am not, nothing is mine, and I don't exist with qualities" (*nāsmi, name, nāham*, see Kārikā 64).

This threefold negation is still a cognition, but it blocks all other cognitions because it undermines their very basis. All experiences require the "I" to be linked with the qualities, and discriminative wisdom denies that very linkage.

But discriminative wisdom is not stable at first. It arises and then it disappears. It gets stronger each time it arises, which makes ignorance weaker and weaker. When this wisdom is completely and permanently established, the "I" separates from the three qualities in the sense that it no longer identifies with any of the cognitions in *buddhi*.

The mind and body may continue to exist and function in the world due to *prārabdha karma* (momentum) and the pervasiveness of consciousness, but there is no longer any confusion or ignorance that links the modifications of the *buddhi* with the "I." This is known as liberation.

In the next *sūtra*, the vehicle for removing ignorance is established.

Mūrti of Hairakhan Bābā, saint of Kumaon Region.

Sūtra 26   विवेकख्यातिरविप्लवा हानोपायः ॥ २६ ॥

viveka–khyātir–aviplavā hānopāyaḥ

Unwavering discriminative knowledge is the vehicle for removing [ignorance].

विवेक	*viveka*	of discrimination
ख्यातिः	*khyātiḥ*	knowledge
अविप्लवा	*aviplavā*	undisturbed, unfluctuating
हान	*hāna*	for the removal
उपायः	*upāyaḥ*	the means, vehicle

In the previous *sutra*, it was explained that ignorance is the cause of the conjunction of *puruṣha* and *prakṛti*. Now, in this *sutra*, the means for removing that ignorance is given as unwavering discriminative wisdom.

The knowledge (*khyāti*) that discriminates (*viveka*) the seer (*puruṣha*) separate from the seen (*prakṛti*), which takes the forms of the mind, intellect, senses, and body, is called discriminative wisdom (*viveka khyāti*). In discriminative wisdom, the knowledge is "I am not this mind-body complex, I am the Self," which eradicates the false notion, "I am this mind-body complex."

This discriminative knowledge can be attained through any of the three forms of correct knowledge described in Sūtra I:7. But two of them are indirect means, testimony (*āgama*), which can be either the teachings of a realized master or a true scripture, and inference (*anumāna*). These indirect means are not capable of completely wiping out the beginningless false knowledge (*anādi avidyā*).

Why? Because they are not capable of producing *unwavering* discriminative wisdom. In the beginning stages of discriminative wisdom, the latencies of worldly-mindedness (*vyutthāna saṁskāras*) still exist, giving rise to *rājasika* and *tāmasika* thought waves (*vṛittis*). This is called the fluctuating or disturbed state of discriminative wisdom (*viplavā viveka khyāti*). It is not the means of completely removing (*hāna*) ignorance (*avidyā*).

By regular practice of Kriyā Yoga and *samādhi*, the afflictions (*kleśhas*) caused by *rajas* and *tamas guṇas* are removed, and the light of *sattva guṇa* in the intellect (*buddhi*) is purified. When the *yogi* achieves the highest stage of renunciation (*vaśhīkāra saṁjñā*, see Sūtra I:15), the flow of discriminative wisdom is stabilized, free from all disturbances, and the latencies of false knowledge become unable to cause bondage, just as roasted seeds are unable to sprout. This pure and undisturbed discriminative wisdom (*aviplavā viveka khyāti*) is the means for removing the beginningless false knowledge (*anādi avidyā*).

In verse XIII:34 of the *Shrīmad Bhagavad Gītā*, it is said:

kṣhetrakṣhetrajñayor evamantaraṁ jñānachakṣhuṣha
bhūtaprakṛitimokṣhaṁ cha ye viduryānti te param

Those who thus perceive with the eye of wisdom (*viveka khyāti*) the difference between the field (*prakṛti*) and the knower of the field (*puruṣha*) and the phenomenon of liberation from *prakṛiti* with the evolutes, reach the supreme Brahman.

Note

In this *sūtra*, the means of removing the primal ignorance (*avidyā*) that causes the conjunction of pure consciousness (*puruṣha*) with the three *guṇas*[1] (energies of creation) and that results in the material universe, is described as unwavering discriminative wisdom. The term unwavering (*aviplavā*) is very significant.

When discriminative wisdom (*viveka khyāti*) first dawns, it is not stable. It is mixed with worldly tendencies (*vyutthāna saṁskāras*) that pull the mind back into ignorance. Even though *viveka khyāti* is a special kind of knowledge that counteracts all other knowledge, it does not do so instantly. There is a battle of sorts between them.

Every experience of the world starts with the notion of "I" as the subject of the experience. Normally, this "I" includes the mind, body, and senses, such as "I am reading this book." The mind, body, and senses are the subject, and some other thing is the object of the experience (the book). Sometimes, though, the "I" is limited to the mind, as in "I have blurry vision." In this case, the mind is the subject and the senses (eyes) are the object. But in all experiences, the "I" must be identified with some aspect of the mind and body.

Without the "I" linked to the activities of the mind and body, there is no one there to experience. All of yoga philosophy is based on the premise that the linking of the "I" to the body is a function of the mind and not an intrinsic fact. According to yoga and Sāṁkhya, the body is not the source of the "I," but rather, the body can only emerge when the "I" is present.

Discriminative wisdom is the knowledge, "I am not (linked to the mind and body in any way)." It counteracts all other types of knowledge, which are necessarily based on "I am (linked to the mind and body)." For this reason, discriminative wisdom is knowledge of a completely different category that ultimately removes the primal ignorance (*anādi avidyā*), which is the cause of bondage and all suffering.

The knowledge that "I am not," or that the "I" is not linked to the mind, body, or world in any real way, is considered the truest form of correct cognition (*pramāṇa*). There are three means to correct cognition, described in Sūtra I:7 as direct perception (*pratyakṣha*), inference (*anumāna*), and valid testimony (*āgama*). Correct cognition simply means that the notion in the mind is correct, whether or not it can be proved or repeated. In other words, if the idea arises in the mind that the "I" is not related to the body, it is considered correct, even if it was only

---

1 The three *guṇas* exist in potential form in *mūla prakṛiti* (the unmanifest state of *prakṛiti*). When activated by pervasive consciousness (*puruṣha*) they become the three cosmic energies of creation: *jñāna śhakti* (energy of knowledge), *icchā śhakti* (energy of will), and *kriyā śhakti* (energy of matter). In manifestation the *guṇas* are qualities.

the repetition of a teaching. But, this *sutra* explains that the ability of discriminative knowledge to completely remove ignorance depends on its being unwavering (*aviplavā*).

Unwavering means firmly established and uninterrupted. So long as the mind is not purified of all its worldly tendencies (*vyutthāna saṁskāras*), discriminative wisdom cannot be unwavering. In the above example of repeating the teaching, the discriminative wisdom did not arise out of the complete purification of the mind. Therefore, the aspirant still identifies the "I" with the mind. This identification is in direct conflict with the cognition of discriminative wisdom, which is "I am not identified with the mind." So long as this conflict remains, discriminative wisdom cannot be unwavering.

How does discriminative wisdom become uninterrupted? The mind must be completely purified of all worldly tendencies. Worldly tendencies include all desires and all identifications with any aspect of creation or the three *guṇas*.

In the mind and intellect, *sattva* takes the form of knowledge, power, virtue, and dispassion, while *tamas* takes the form of ignorance, weakness, vice, and passion. *Rajas guṇa* is the force that activates these eight aspects of mind. So long as *rajas* is activating *tamas*, the mind will be drawn toward worldly activities and discriminative wisdom will not be stable or even possible. The more that *rajas* activates *sattva*, the more the mind is drawn toward discriminative wisdom.

Rajas guṇa does not function the same when it works primarily with *tamas* as it does when it works primarily with *sattva*. *Rajas* and *tamas* reinforce each other, getting bigger and stronger like the wall of a fort that is constantly reinforced. When *rajas* begins to work primarily with *sattva*, it is like scraping away the walls of the fort. By repeated effort, the walls are completely removed, and there is nothing left to do. In other words, the purification of the mind, in the form of the gradual predominance of *sattva guṇa*, actually dissolves the mind because it results in unwavering discriminative wisdom.

The difference between the unwavering discriminative wisdom that arises in a purely *sattva* predominant mind and the fleeting wisdom that arises in a mind polluted by *rajas* and *tamas* is like the difference between fire and a picture of fire. The first has the ability to burn, the second only creates an idea of burning. Without the purification of the mind, discriminative wisdom is incapable of completely and permanently removing suffering.

The next *sūtra* explains the seven stages of discriminative wisdom by which all fluctuations are removed and liberation is attained.

Sandals, symbolizing surrender to the Divine.

Sūtra 27　　तस्य सप्तधा प्रान्तभूमिः प्रज्ञा ॥ २७ ॥

tasya saptadhā prānta–bhūmiḥ prajñā

The *yogi's* awareness develops in seven stages of ultimate insight.

तस्य	*tasya*	his (the *yogi's*)
सप्तधा	*saptadhā*	is sevenfold
प्रान्त	*prānta*	final, ultimate
भूमिः	*bhūmiḥ*	level, stage
प्रज्ञा	*prajñā*	discrimination, insight

In the previous *sūtra*, it was explained that the *yogi* whose discrimination is purified by the practice of Kriyā Yoga and *samādhi* achieves unwavering discriminative wisdom (*aviplavā viveka khyāti*). This unwavering discriminative wisdom is the vehicle for removing primal ignorance (*avidyā*). Now, in this *sūtra*, discriminative wisdom itself is explained in seven levels. This wisdom develops from unstable, partial realizations up to the perfected, unwavering knowledge that removes ignorance and brings about final liberation. Each stage is developed as discriminative wisdom is stabilized, until each of the seven insights are perfected and established beyond doubt.

The first four ultimate insights are called liberation from action (*kārya vimukta prajñā*). Their achievement requires effort, but once they are attained, no further effort is required. The last three insights are known as liberation from the mind (*chitta vimukta prajñā*). These three automatically appear after the first four are attained, and they bring about the complete cessation of the mind.

Liberation from action (*kārya vimukta prajñā*)
1. **Realization of what is to be avoided (*heya śhūnya avasthā*).** In this first stage of discriminative wisdom, the aspirant completely understands the limitations and pains inherent in all forms of desire, attachment, and experience. The *yogi*, having totally understood the true nature of *prakṛiti* and the futility of worldly desires as the means to happiness, is freed from preoccupation with all objects, animate or inanimate, gross or subtle. There is nothing else to be realized about pain, suffering, or the objects of creation.
2. **Awareness of the means for that removal (*heya hetu kṣhīna avasthā*).** In the second stage of realization, the *yogi* recognizes that primal ignorance (*anādi avidyā* or the conjunction of undifferentiated consciousness with the primordial energy of creation) is the cause of bondage. Having thus realized the root cause of suffering, and knowing that removing the cause removes the effect, nothing else remains to be understood concerning the removal of suffering, and no further effort in this regard is required.
3. **Awareness of spiritual evolution (*prāpya prāpta avasthā*).** In the third stage of ultimate insight, the *yogi* realizes the nature of the spiritual goal. Having achieved awareness of the nature of pure consciousness and its relationship to creation, the mind knows that *nirodha samādhi* (the complete

cessation of mental modifications) is the final goal, so no further inquiry is required concerning the nature of the spiritual goal.

4. **Awareness of fulfillment and accomplishment (*chikīrṣha śhūnya avasthā*).** In the fourth stage of realization, the mind has recognized and gained the means to liberation, and discriminative knowledge becomes unwavering (*aviplavā*). It is forever freed from all further efforts to attain liberation.

Liberation from the mind (*chitta vimukta prajñā*)

5. **Awareness of the purpose of experience and liberation (*chittasattva kṛitārthatā*).** The discriminative intellect (*buddhi*) has fulfilled its dual purpose of experience (*bhoga*) and liberation (*apavarga*). There remains nothing more to accomplish and the activities of the intellect (*buddhi*) totally cease.

6. **Awareness of fulfillment of the work of the *guṇas* (*guṇa līnatā*).** In this stage of liberation, the three *guṇas*, which are the constituent qualities of *prakṛiti* that create the *chitta* and all its consequent states of mind, resolve back into their primordial, unmanifest state never to rise again for that individual *puruṣha*. With the dissolution of the *guṇas*, the embodied soul (*jīvātma*) realizes the cessation of all mental states.

7. **Awareness of one's own Self (*ātmasthiti*).** In this stage of liberation, the embodied soul (*jīvātma*) realizes its true nature as the absolute *puruṣha* (pure, undifferentiated consciousness). With this Self-realization, the *jīvātma* is completely and permanently separated from the three *guṇas*, and becomes identical with or merged in the absolute *puruṣha*.

With the attainment of these seven kinds of ultimate insights (*prajñā*), a *yogi* completes final emancipation. The *yogi* at this stage is called proficient (*kuśhala*). When the mind stops functioning for the purpose of experience and liberation and resolves back into its cause, the *yogi* is called liberated (*mukta*) and proficient (*kuśhala*). The *yogi* remains free and wise while living. The state of being liberated while keeping the body is called *jīvanmukta*.

Note

In the previous *sūtra*, it was explained that unwavering discriminative wisdom is the means of removing primal ignorance and thus bondage. Now, in this *sūtra*, the actual removal of ignorance and bondage is explained in seven steps. These seven steps are the process by which unstable glimpses of wisdom become the unwavering discriminative wisdom required for liberation, and then how the embodied *puruṣha* becomes free from its association with the mind and body. Each of these steps is complete in that nothing can be done to further the knowledge or work at that particular level. It should also be understood that defining these seven stages is an act of philosophy, and the enlightened *yogi* moving through them does not have any notion or awareness of stages or distinctions. Instead, the *yogi's* awareness is simply and completely absorbed in discriminative wisdom.

In the first step, the problem is fully realized. Until this level of knowledge is perfected, there remains a doubt about the nature of creation and suffering. We read in Sūtra II:15 that all experiences cause suffering, but just reading it does not bring liberation. We doubt, so we test and try. We continue to seek pleasure, and then we fail to see how the suffering that follows was connected to the pleasure. But if we persist in the practices of Kriyā Yoga, the mind becomes purified and more capable of determining subtle causes. As discriminative wisdom dawns and begins to stabilize, the truth of Sūtra II:15 is known completely. At this point, there is no more doubt about the nature of suffering, and all efforts to determine the nature of suffering cease forever.

The second stage is the direct experience of discriminating the nature of *puruṣha* and its relationship to *prakṛiti*. This is the generic description of discriminative wisdom that is used throughout the *Sūtras*, but in this particular stage, the knowledge specifically refers to the identification of *puruṣha* (consciousness) with *prakṛiti* (qualities of creation, mental content) as primal ignorance and the direct cause of bondage. This is the truth of Sūtra II:24, and until it is realized fully, doubt remains and the mind works in various ways to resolve the doubt. Once this second stage is achieved, all doubts are removed, and all efforts cease. There is nothing further to be known about the cause of suffering.

The third stage is the realization of the means to remove suffering. Until this level of knowledge is perfected, there remains a doubt about how suffering is permanently removed. In this knowledge, it is recognized that *nirodha samādhi*[1] or *asamprajñāta samādhi* (complete cessation of all thoughts, the state beyond all knowledge) is the final state. The mind is so pure at this point that it is on the verge of dissolution. It has already attained the highest level of *samprajñāta samādhi*, but that was not the end. Why?

In the second stage, the complete independence of pure consciousness from its content is recognized. Yet, this recognition is a form of content also. Therefore, the absolute state must be free from content. Thus, the *yogi* sees that *nirodha samādhi* is the highest possible state, just as a mountain climber sees the peak and knows there is no higher peak beyond it. Therefore, all doubts about, and efforts to know, the highest state are removed forever.

The fourth stage is beginning the slippery slope on the far side of the hill. The nature of suffering, its cause, and the means for its removal have been known completely in the previous three stages. There is nothing left for the mind to do or achieve, so it begins the slide into oblivion. No more effort of any kind is required. These four stages are known as liberation from action.

The fifth state begins what is called liberation from the mind. In the fourth state, the mind begins to slide effortlessly into dissolution. In the fifth state, the

---

1   The term *nirodha samādhi* is mentioned by Vyāsa in his commentary. *Nirodha* means blocking or cessation, so *nirodha samādhi* is the *samādhi* of cessation or *asamprajñāta samādhi*. In practice, the blocking element of *nirodha*, which is an effort, culminates in *dharma megha samādhi*. There is no effort of any kind in *asamprajñāta samādhi*.

slide is finished, or say all activities of the *guṇas* cease for that *jīva*. The *guṇas* are only active for the purpose of experience and liberation. Those purposes have been completely and permanently fulfilled. There is no cause for further mental activity of any kind.

The sixth state is the resolution of the *guṇas* back into their source. This means that the *chitta* (mind) resolves back into *pradhāna* (the great unmanifest). Said differently, the *guṇas*, which had been active since the beginning of creation, cease all activity, and resolve back into a state of balanced and unmixed rest. This is like the gates of the jail being opened and the prisoner (*jīva*) being set free.

The seventh and final state is when the *jīva* becomes merged with the absolute *puruṣa*. It is the ending of *saṁsāra* (the cycle of suffering through birth and death). The individualized spirit and the universal, undifferentiated spirit are united (*yoga*), never to be separated again, just as a pail of water emptied into the ocean can never be reclaimed.

A question arises about *jīvanmukta* (liberated within the body). The commentators disagree about whether the body can remain alive after this seventh step. Many say that the seventh step is absolute and final, and does not allow for the possibility of the body continuing to function. The *guṇas* have completely fulfilled their purpose and have resolved back into primordial nature (*pradhāna*). These last stages, therefore, require the body to have finished all its *karma*.

Others say that the body has its own momentum (*prārabdha karma*), and that it continues to function until that momentum is finished even if the individualized *jīva* has merged in *puruṣa*. The body may still have a universal purpose, say to serve or support other, unenlightened *jīvas*, for which it continues to function. In this case, *prakṛiti* functions in the form of that body by the presence and pervasiveness of the absolute *puruṣa*; no vestige of individuality is needed.

It is said that in the sixth stage, the *guṇas* resolve back into their cause (*pradhāna* or the great unmanifest). If the *guṇas* merge into their unmanifest state, then there is no way the body or mind could continue to function because the body, mind, and the rest of creation are all exclusively comprised of the three *guṇas*. This would support the first argument, that these final stages of liberation can only occur with the dissolution of the body.

But, the resolution of the *guṇas* can also be understood from the perspective of the *puruṣa*. The *puruṣa* is the sense of self. In the average person, this sense of self is fully identified with, or say polluted by, the mind, body, and senses. As the *yogi* progresses through the various levels of *samprajñāta samādhi* and achieves discriminative wisdom, this sense of self is gradually purified of its association with the mind, body, and senses until it is established in its own true nature (see Sūtra I:3).

In this progression, the "I" begins as "I am this mind-body complex with all these friends, relatives, and possessions." Gradually, it is recognized that "I am who I am even as people and possessions come and go." Then, this sense of who I am gets simpler and simpler. It goes from being a complex personality to simply a living person to just a collection of energies. Finally, it sees that "I am separate from the collection of energies".

The identification of the liberated self (*jīva*) with the absolute Self (*puruṣa*) is qualitatively different from the kinds of identification that are known in daily life. We cannot know what it is like until we get there, but we can understand it by analogy. In life, we see that our perspectives change as we mature. For example, we may not remember how it felt to be afraid of ghosts or how some other anxiety we may have had felt. We may feel so separated from those feelings that we wonder how it was that they even arose in the first place. Another example could be feeling devastated at the breakup of a romantic partnership, and then a year later wondering what we ever saw in the partner in the first place.

The point is that something that felt very real at one point becomes unreal later. They say that for the liberated *yogi*, the world has no reality. A partial feeling of unreality can be experienced by us in an airplane. On the ground, the trees, buildings, cars, and people all seem real and large, but as the plane takes off, they look smaller and smaller until they no longer exist for us. Yet, to all those left behind, they are exactly as they always had been.

In the same way, the identification with the body that now feels so unquestionably real can be removed. For the *puruṣa* that completely merges into the Absolute, the realities of the body, and the whole creation for that matter, dissolve. The dissolution of the reality of the creation for the liberated *puruṣa* could be called the merging of the *guṇas* back into their unmanifest cause because they have no reach, and thus no reality, to the *puruṣa*.

And, just as the trees and buildings that looked smaller and smaller until they no longer existed for the airplane passenger remain the same for those left behind, the body of the liberated *puruṣa* may continue to function the same for all others. This would support the second argument, that the functioning of the body has to do only with its *prārabdha karma* and not with the bound or liberated state of the indwelling *puruṣa*.

Whether the idea of *jīvanmukta* is understood as final liberation or just partial liberation is immaterial to the question of suffering. There is no doubt that once discriminative wisdom has become unwavering, the cause of suffering, which is the identification of the *puruṣa* with the mind, body, and senses, is removed. When the cause is removed, the effect ceases to be. Therefore, suffering cannot occur to the *puruṣa* after unwavering discriminative wisdom.

In the next *sūtra*, it is explained that the sustained practice of the various limbs of *yoga* purifies the mind and brings about unwavering discriminative wisdom.

Mahā Ārati lamp and equipages for worship.

Sūtra 28   योगाङ्गानुष्ठानादशुद्धिक्षये ज्ञानदीप्तिराविवेकख्यातेः ॥ २८ ॥

yogāṅgānuṣhṭhānād–aśhuddhi–kṣhaye jñāna–dīptir–ā–viveka–khyāteḥ

The sustained practice of the limbs of *yoga* destroys impurity [of the mind], at which point the light of knowledge reaches up to discriminative wisdom.

योग	*yoga*	of *yoga*, union
अङ्ग	*aṅga*	of the accessories, limbs
अनुष्ठानाद्	*anuṣhṭhānād*	by the sustained practice
अशुद्धि	*aśhuddhi*	impurity
क्षये	*kṣhaye*	on the destruction
ज्ञान	*jñāna*	of knowledge
दीप्तिः	*dīptiḥ*	the light
आ	*ā*	reaching up to, leads to
विवेक	*viveka*	of discernment
ख्यातेः	*khyāteḥ*	the wisdom

In the preceding *sutra*, it was said that discriminative wisdom is developed through seven stages. In this *sutra*, Patañjali indicates the means by which an aspirant attains discriminative knowledge (*viveka khyāti*).

By the sustained practice of the limbs of *yoga*, the five afflictions (*kleshas*), which are ignorance (*avidyā*), egoism (*asmitā*), attraction (*rāga*), aversion (*dvesha*), and fear of death (*abhiniveśha*) are removed (see Sūtra II:3). The *kleshas* are the impurities of the mind that are the root causes of bondage of the embodied soul (*puruṣha*). The removal of the *kleshas* means the mind becomes purified or free from the passion of *rajas guṇa* and the torpidity of *tamas guṇa*. In that pure state of mind (*sattva buddhi*), true knowledge manifests by itself.

The more that sustained practice increases, the more the impurities of the mind, which are the obstacles to knowledge, decrease. By this process, the mind of the *yogi* is gradually illuminated with knowledge until discriminative wisdom (*viveka khyāti*) is attained. That is, the *yogi* realizes that the undifferentiated consciousness (*puruṣha*) is his or her essential nature, distinct from the mind, body, and senses, which are all made by combinations of the three *guṇas* of *prakṛiti*.

The sage Vyāsa, in his classical commentary on the *Sūtras*, lists nine types of causes that are found in the scriptures. Normally, we think of three causes— material, instrumental, and purpose. For example, in the creation of a clay pot, the material cause is clay, the instrumental cause is the potter, and the purpose may be to create art or an object to earn money. Here, nine different types of causes are explained.

A cause is seen operating in more ways than one, and Vyāsa encourages the aspirant to apply this knowledge of the nine causes to as many objects as possible. However, only two of the causes are relevant to this *sutra*, causes six and seven, which are attainment and separation. In deference to Vyāsa, a full treatment of the nine causes with various examples is given below.

1. **Cause of birth (*utpatti kāraṇa*).** Cause of birth is a material cause. In the *Nyāya Vaiśheṣhika Darśhana*, this material is called *samavāṣhika kāraṇa*. The mind is the material cause of knowledge. *Utpatti* (birth) doesn't mean that something new is created that did not exist before, but rather that the knowledge that had been unmanifest appears in its manifest state through the mind. As a seed is the cause of a tree, similarly the mind is the cause or origin of knowledge. The seed of all knowledge exists in *mahat* (cosmic mind). The *karmāśhaya* (the reservoir of impressions of past actions) exists in the *chitta*, giving rise to birth, life span, and experience (see Sūtras II:12–13).

2. **Sustaining cause (*sthiti kāraṇa*).** Just as eating food sustains the body, serving the purposes of *puruṣha* sustains the mind. In Sūtras II:18 & 21, it is explained that *bhoga* (experience) and *apavarga* (liberation) are the two purposes of *puruṣha*, and that the mind exists only for the sake of fulfilling these purposes. Therefore, experience and liberation are the sustaining causes of the mind. When experience and liberation are achieved, the mind has served its purpose and it dissolves into its cause, *mūla prakṛiti* (the unmanifest state of *prakṛiti*).

3. **Cause of manifestation (*abhivyakti kāraṇa*).** Light and knowledge of form are the two causes of visible objects. Light is the cause of visibility, and knowledge of form is the cause of the appearance of the object in the mind. Both light and knowledge are invisible by themselves, but they create a field of visibility and knowledgeability, respectively. Light and knowledge together bring visibility of the object; without both, there could be no experience of visible objects. Therefore, they are taken together as the cause of visibility in objects.

4. **Cause of modification (*vikāra kāraṇa*).** Fire is the cause of changing an object. Rice changes its form in the cooking process. Fire is the cause of that modification. Similarly, when the mind ponders an object, it is modified by taking the form of that object. Therefore, the object of thinking is considered the cause of the modification of the mind.

5. **Cause of knowledge (*pratyaya kāraṇa*).** In this case, the reference is to the cause of inferential knowledge. For example, when smoke is seen, the knowledge that there must be a fire is inferred, and the smoke is the cause of that knowledge.

6. **Cause of attainment (*prāpti kāraṇa*).** Vāchaspati Miśhra says, "It is natural for causes to manifest their effects." This manifestation of the previously existing latent effect is called *prāpti*. All effects exist within their cause in a latent form. When the effect manifests, it is neither exactly the same as nor entirely different from the cause.

   Just as virtue brings the attainment of happiness, the practice of the accessories (eight limbs) of *yoga* brings the attainment of discriminative knowledge (*viveka khyāti*). Sometimes the progression of cause and effect is blocked. In the case of water, the natural downhill flow may be blocked by a dam. This blocking is called *aprāpti* or non-achievement. When the dam is removed by some means, then the water will naturally flow again.

In the mind, the natural inward flow toward knowledge of its true nature (*puruṣha*) is blocked by vice (*adharma*) and inertia (*tamas*). By the practice of the accessories of *yoga*, which include virtuous action, all blocking energies are removed. With the removal of these impediments, the natural operation of *buddhi sattva* becomes established and smooth. The purified mind thus reaches its natural state in which discriminative knowledge (*viveka khyāti*) brings Self-realization (see Sūtras II:24 – 27).

7. **Cause of separation (*viyoga kāraṇa*).** Something can be achieved by separating from its opposing cause, such as virtues are achieved by separating from vice. In this case, the cause of separation is the root cause of the achievement. The practice of the limbs of Aṣhṭāṅga Yoga brings separation from the impurities in the mind (*aśhuddhikṣhaya*), which is the cause of achieving discriminative knowledge (*viveka khyāti*). Just as an axe is the cause of the separation of wood, discriminative knowledge is the cause of the separation of *puruṣha* and *prakṛiti*, which is the attainment of Self-realization.

8. **Cause of differentiation (*anyatva kāraṇa*).** As the goldsmith is the cause of changing gold into a gold bracelet, so the mind changes the essential principles of creation (*tattvas*) into objects of desire. Gold has its own inherent worth, but it is unattractive in block form. The goldsmith creates a form that is variously judged by different people, though the gold itself is no different. Similarly, the objects of creation have their inherent nature, but the mind judges those objects according to its desires. For example, the ideas concerning a beautiful woman may vary from person to person. Her husband is made happy by seeing her, while another woman may get jealous, a lustful man becomes passionate, and the wise remain indifferent. In all these cases, the woman is the same and the mind is the cause of differentiation.

9. **Cause of support (*dhṛiti kāraṇa*).** The body supports the senses and the senses support the body in its capabilities and welfare. Without the *prāṇa* (life energy), the body would be dead. Similarly, the elements—earth, water, fire, air, and ether—support the body, and the body supports the elements. All animals, birds, herbs, vegetables, and humans are the supporting cause of each other.

Of these nine causes, only two causes—the cause of attainment (*prāpti kāraṇa*) and the cause of separation (*viyoga kāraṇa*)—are relevant to this *sūtra* as direct causes of discriminative knowledge. The practice of the accessories (limbs) of *yoga* cause the destruction of impurities in the mind and body, which is the separation from the obstacle. When all the impurities are destroyed, the mind and body automatically bring discriminative wisdom and the attainment of enlightenment.

Note

In the previous *sutra*, the seven stages of discriminative wisdom were given. In Sūtra II:26, it was stated that unwavering discriminative wisdom is the vehicle for removing ignorance and attaining liberation (the separation of *puruṣha* and *prakṛiti*). Unwavering discriminative wisdom (*aviplavā viveka khyāti*) can only occur when all the impurities of the mind are removed. Impurities, by definition, are those contents that distract the mind and block the perfection of all forms of knowledge.

Now, in this *sutra*, the relationship between the practices of *yoga* and the attainment of knowledge and liberation is established. The practices of *yoga* purify the mind, ultimately removing all the obstacles to unwavering discriminative wisdom. This one, simple concept is the purport of the *sūtra*.

The extensive information presented in the classical commentaries on this *sutra* is primarily intended to be a rebuttal against skeptics who don't see the relationship between practice and philosophy. The nine forms of causation are presented for two reasons. The first is to show that there are many ways one object can be the cause of another. Two of these principles of causation are applicable in the relationship of the practices of *yoga* to discriminative wisdom.

The two types of causation that are relevant to this are separation and attainment. The practices of *yoga* are the cause of separating the obstacles from the mind. The mind and ego function in the world in a known, predictable way![1] The practices of *yoga* counteract that functioning because they limit the expression of self-interest and weaken the afflictions. For this reason, the limbs of *yoga* are guaranteed to work if they are practiced consistently, sincerely, and properly.

The practices of *yoga* are the cause of attainment because they bring about discriminative knowledge in the intellect. The intellect is comprised of the three *guṇas*. Normally, the wisdom of *sattva* is limited by the influences of *rajas* and *tamas*. When these influences have been weakened and made dormant by the practices of *yoga*, the light of knowledge flows perfectly in the intellect. The perfection of knowledge is known as discriminative wisdom.

The second reason the nine types of causation are presented is that they help us discriminate the realities of creation. The more clearly we can see the workings of cause and effect in creation, the more eager we will be to understand the cause and effect relationship between the mind and the world, and between the mind and consciousness. The more enthusiastic we are in this, the more we practice and the more the impurities of the mind are removed.

The most significant philosophical tenet of this *sūtra* is that discriminative wisdom arises by itself when the impurities are removed. This means that no special ability is required to attain enlightenment. Instead, all we have to do—

---

1 The terms known and predictable mean they will function according to self-interest and the laws of the afflictions. In contrast, the individual behaviors of any one person are based on such a complex combination of *saṁskāras* that they are very difficult to predict.

all each of us requires—is to purify our minds of the five afflictions, or say the influence of passion (*rajas guṇa*) and sloth (*tamas guṇa*).

Discriminative knowledge is the truth that underlies all experience. It is blocked by the afflictions, just as a dimmer switch blocks the flow of electricity to a light bulb. When the dimmer is removed from the switch, electricity flows unrestricted and the light shines its brightest. In the same way, when the afflictions are removed, the highest knowledge shines unrestrained.

The afflictions are the five energies in the mind that keep us fully invested in the world. We identify with the mind-body complex and then spend extraordinary amounts of energy defending it by pursuing pleasure and avoiding pain. The primary questions that motivate a mind dominated by the afflictions are not *What is truth?* or *What is peace?* but rather *How can I survive?* or *How can I get more?* These primary, motivating questions determine the nature of a person's mind and activities in the world.

The *sutra* says that when the disturbing aspects of the mind that drive all worldly activities are removed, knowledge arises all by itself. How can this be? The active state of the mind in which experiences are known blocks true knowledge (*viveka khyāti*). When this activity is removed, true knowledge dawns and peace is attained.

This means that the experiences of the world are like the images created in the dark by a spinning light. The light appears to make various unbroken shapes so long as it moves quickly enough. But as soon as the light is stilled, the images go away and the light is seen for what it is. In the same way, when the mind is stilled, the experiences of creation disappear, and the light of consciousness is seen for what it is.

All the practices of the eight limbs of *yoga* are for stilling the mind. In the next *sutra*, these eight limbs are introduced.

Hanumān Garh, Nainital, Uttarākhand

Sūtra 29　यमनियमासनप्राणायामप्रत्याहारधारणाध्यानसमाधयोऽष्टावङ्गानि ॥२९॥

yama–niyamāsana–prāṇāyāma–pratyāhāra–dhāraṇā–dhyāna–
samādhayo–'ṣṭāvaṅgāni

Restraints, observances, posture, regulation of breath, withdrawal, concentration, meditation, and absorption are the eight limbs of yoga.

यम	*yama*	restraints
नियम	*niyama*	observances
आसन	*āsana*	posture
प्राणायाम	*prāṇāyāma*	regulation of breath, breath control
प्रत्याहार	*pratyāhāra*	abstraction, withdrawal of senses, introversion
धारणा	*dhāraṇā*	concentration
ध्यान	*dhyāna*	meditation, contemplation
समाधि	*samādhi*	trance, absorption or superconscious state
अष्टौ	*aṣhtau*	eight
अङ्गानि	*aṅgāni*	accessories, limbs

In the previous *sūtra*, it was stated that purifying the mind through the practices of *yoga* prepares the mind for unwavering discriminative wisdom. Now, in this *sūtra*, these practices are described as a complete system called Aṣhtāṅga Yoga (Eight-limbed Yoga). The eight limbs are interdependent and cumulative methods for achieving discriminative knowledge (*viveka khyāti*).

Through these practices, an aspirant controls the outgoing nature of the mind and reverses the flow of the mind to an inward direction by which all pains and miseries, which are based on the five afflictions (*kleśhas*), are weakened and eventually vanquished. Egocentric actions that pull the mind outward, causing rebirth (*janma*), span of life (*āyu*) and enjoyment (*bhoga*) are rooted in the *kleśhas* (see Sūtra II:13) and are similarly weakened and vanquished by the practices of Aṣhtāṅga Yoga.

The last three limbs—concentration (*dhāraṇā*), meditation (*dhyāna*), and absorption (*samādhi*)—are direct means of achieving discriminative knowledge (*viveka khyāti*). They are called internal limbs (*antaraṅga*) because they relate only to the activities of the mind independent of the body and all external phenomena. The first five limbs—self-restraints (*yama*), fixed observances (*niyama*), postures (*āsana*), regulation of breath (*prāṇāyāma*), and withdrawing the mind from the senses (*pratyāhāra*)—are called external limbs (*bāhiraṅga*) because they address the functions of the body and its relationship to the outer world.

The external limbs provide the foundation of a spiritual practice (*sādhana*). The internal limbs are strengthened by the practice of the external limbs. The eight limbs of *yoga* are interdependent and share the same goal, which is discriminative wisdom and liberation of the *puruṣha* (see Sūtras II:17–28).

The eight limbs of Aṣhtāṅga Yoga address all aspects of spiritual life, starting with social relationships and personal and mental disciplines, and culminating with the perfection of knowledge (*viveka khyāti*) and the realization of the distinction between undifferentiated consciousness (*puruṣha*) and the unmanifest reality (*pradhāna*) underlying all aspects of manifest creation (*prakṛiti*). The eight limbs or accessories of *yoga* are:

1. **Self-restraints (*yama*)**. The five precepts of self-restraint concern the relationship of the individual to the society. People normally interact with each other based on their worldly desires and attachments. If the mind is impure, or say fully absorbed in its own self-interest, then all those relationships will create more ego, attachment, and desire, further binding the soul in ignorance. The result will be the perpetuation of rebirth, span of life, and experience.

   The five practices of self-restraint weaken all egocentric actions, attachments, and desires (see Sūtras II:30–39). When they are perfected, life in society and relationships with other individuals becomes *sāttvika* (pure) and divine. The practice of self-restraint is a method of purifying social conduct.

2. **Fixed observances (*niyama*)**. The five observances are practiced to purify one's own body, mind, and senses (see Sūtras II:40–45). The purification of the body, mind, and senses enables one to establish pure relationships with the outer world. Practice of the five *niyamas* is a method of purifying interpersonal conduct by personal discipline.

3. **Postures (*āsana*)**. *Āsana* is a physical activity that removes inertia in the body and instability in the mind (see Sūtras II:46–48). *Āsana* promotes balance and health, and makes the aspirant capable of sitting for meditation.

4. **Regulation of breath (*prāṇāyāma*)**. *Prāṇāyāma* is a controlled way of breathing in which the various aspects of breath—inhale, exhale, and retention—are regulated (see Sūtras II:49–53). The practice of *prāṇāyāma* purifies the *prāṇa* (life energy in the body) and weakens the restless tendencies of the mind. The practice of *prāṇāyāma* makes the aspirant fit for deep meditation.

5. **Withdrawal (*pratyāhāra*)**. The practice of *pratyāhāra* is pulling the mind away from the objects of the senses and focusing it inward (see Sūtras II:54–55). When the thoughts are separated from the senses and their objects, the mind is freed from inertia and restlessness, and becomes pure and ready for meditation.

6. **Concentration (*dhāraṇā*)**. The practice of concentration is the repetition of one thought in the mind (see Sūtra III:1). By persistent practice, the mind is freed from its dull and preoccupied state (*mūḍha*) and from its restless state (*kṣhipta*). The mind becomes pure and capable of maintaining concentration on one object.

7. **Meditation (*dhyāna*)**. When the disturbances caused by inertia (*tamas guṇa*) and restlessness (*rajas guṇa*) are removed, the mind is established in its pure state (*sattva buddhi*), at which point it becomes continuously directed toward a spiritual object (see Sūtra III:2). Through this unbroken flow of concentration, the mind becomes fit for *samādhi*.

8. **Absorption (*samādhi*)**. By the complete elimination of the obstacles of inertia and restlessness, the mind becomes completely pure (see Sūtras III:3 and I:17 – 18). Gradually, it is engrossed in subtler and subtler objects until the awakening of discriminative knowledge (*viveka khyāti*) and Self-knowledge, the perfection of which is liberation.

Note

In the previous *sutra*, it was explained that the eight limbs of *yoga* are for destroying the impurities of the mind, which brings about *samādhi*, discriminative wisdom, and final liberation. Now, in this *sutra*, Patañjali introduces the eight limbs known collectively as Aṣhṭāṅga Yoga. The remaining *sutras* of *Sādhana Pāda* are devoted exclusively to the eight limbs.

The commentary says that the eight limbs are interdependent and share the same goal, which is *yoga* or the union of the embodied soul with its source, the absolute, infinite, undifferentiated consciousness. The limbs are interdependent because they prepare different aspects of the mind-body complex for meditation and *samādhi*.

The *Yoga Sūtras* of Patañjali are an ancient text describing the classical approach to *yoga* and its practices. As is described in detail in the following twenty-six *sutras*, these eight limbs should be understood as means to the final goal. Everything contained in the four books has this as its purpose. There are, of course, secondary benefits to the practices of *yoga* that come along the way to final liberation, but it is important to understand that these benefits are not the purpose of the practices, and many of them become obstacles after a while.

People come to *yoga* for different reasons, and everyone has to start where they are. Many people find great improvements in their lives after just a few months of regular practice. The significance of this should not be underestimated, and at the same time, we have to accept that Patañjali did not have these in mind while composing the *Yoga Sūtras*. From his perspective, even attachment to discriminative wisdom is an obstacle to final liberation (see Sūtra III:50).

The first two limbs of Aṣhṭāṅga Yoga are restraints (*yama*) and observances (*niyama*). Patañjali dedicates 16 *sutras* to these ten essential components of *yoga* practice.[1] It is essential that aspiring *yogis* strive to embody these basic tenets of living. Without them, the other practices of *yoga* are impotent. Practicing *āsana*, *prāṇāyāma*, and meditation without the *yamas* and *niyamas* is like spending an hour in the morning scraping away the walls of the prison and then spending the rest of the day filling in the holes and fortifying the walls. Indeed, meditation can never be fruitful without the support of nonviolence, truthfulness, nonstealing, control of vital energies, and non-hoarding on one hand, and purity, contentment, discipline, inquiry, and surrender on the other.

---

1   In contrast, he dedicates only 3 *sutras* to *āsana*, 5 to *prāṇāyāma*, 2 to *pratyāhāra*, 1 each to *dhāraṇā* and *dhyāna*, and an extraordinary 50 to *samādhi* and *samyama* (the combination of *dhāraṇā*, *dhyāna*, and *samādhi*).

The reason these ten attitudes and practices are so important is because they limit the expression of the selfish ego. The ego naturally flows toward self-interest just as water naturally flows down a mountain. And in the same way, *yogis* practice the *yamas* and *niyamas* in order to reach *samādhi* just as people hike up the mountain in order to reach its peak (see Sūtras II:30–45).

The practice of *āsana* purifies the body and mind by making it less *tāmasika* (heavy and dull) and *rājasika* (restless and unstable). The goal of *āsana* is the ability to sit motionless for extended periods of time in meditation. The three main obstacles to sitting in meditation are pain (discomfort in the knees, hips, and back, usually from lack of flexibility), hyperactivity (passion in the mind activates the body), and sleep (dullness in the mind blocks meditation like fog blocks a vista), all of which are lessened by the practice of *āsana*.

The practice of *prāṇāyāma* purifies the mind and body via the life force. *Prāṇa* is the means by which the mind and body function. When it is blocked or unnaturally limited, the natural flow of the mind and body are disrupted. *Prāṇāyāma* regulates the breath, forcing the *prāṇa* to flow in a predictable way and purifying the *nāḍis* (channels through which *prāṇa* flows). This greatly reduces the energy required to perform natural functions, and the breath becomes smoother and gentler, which is required for meditation.

The practice of *pratyāhāra* is vital for meditation. Normally, the mind is constantly engaged with the senses and their objects. Every moment there is a new sight, sound, or other sense object to experience. There is no end to sense experiences, and they function like the accelerator in a car. *Pratyāhāra* is withdrawing the mind from the senses so that it may concentrate on one internal object. It is like taking your foot off the accelerator; without it, the mind can never stop.

The practices of *dhāraṇā* and *dhyāna* are both refinements of concentration. At first, it is very difficult to keep the mind on one object. These two practices are the intentional repetition of the same thought; the difference is that the concentration in *dhāraṇā* is broken like water poured from a height, while the concentration in *dhyāna* is smooth like oil poured from one container to another. These practices are like pressing on the brake.

The practice of *samādhi* is both deeper and qualitatively different from *dhāraṇā* and *dhyāna*. In the two, there is an awareness of being a person concentrating on an object. In *samādhi*, that awareness is dissolved; there is no awareness of yourself existing separately from the object of concentration. *Samādhi* has many stages, the differences among them being the level of subtlety appearing in the mind. The process by which *samādhi* is perfected is described throughout *Samādhi Pāda*. This is like the car slowing and finally stopping.

All eight limbs of Aṣhṭāṅga Yoga support the attainment and perfection of *samādhi*. For beginning practitioners, the idea of attaining the higher *samādhis* may seem like an impossible fantasy. The point here is that the sincere and consistent practice of the limbs of *yoga* reduces and eventually destroys the impurities of the mind. Then, *samādhi* will be a reality, and not just an idea.

In the next *sūtra*, the five *yamas* (restraints) are described.

Sūtra 30　अहिंसासत्यास्तेयब्रह्मचर्यापरिग्रहा यमाः ॥ ३० ॥

ahimsā–satyāsteya–brahmacharyāparigrahā yamāḥ

The restraints are non-violence, truthfulness, non-stealing, continence, and non-possessiveness.

अहिंसा	*ahimsā*	abstinence from injury, non-violence
सत्य	*satya*	veracity, truthfulness
अस्तेय	*asteya*	abstinence from theft, non-stealing
ब्रह्मचर्य	*brahmacharya*	continence, control (lit. walking in God)
अपरिग्रहाः	*aparigrahāḥ*	abstinence from avariciousness, non-possessiveness
यमाः	*yamāḥ*	restraints

In the previous *sūtra*, the eight limbs of Aṣhṭāṅga Yoga were introduced. Now, in this *sūtra*, the five methods of self-restraint (*yama*) are given. The five *yamas* are a method of purifying social conduct. They purify the mind by weakening the negative and selfish tendencies in thoughts, words, and actions.

1. **Non-violence (*ahimsā*).** *Ahimsā* (non-violence) means not harming any living being physically, not using harsh words to hurt their feelings, and not even thinking badly about them. Violence occurs when someone serves his or her own selfish motives, and includes helping others create pain or violence in any way and supporting the idea of harming others. Reactions based on fear or anger are also considered violence. Even planning to create pain in others and all forms of intimidation and coercion, especially religious intimidation designed to upset someone's spiritual beliefs and ideals, are considered violent. Refraining from all these is *ahimsā* (non-violence).

   The main practice for *ahimsā* is to watch the violence that arises in one's own thoughts, emotions, words, and actions. By keeping the aim of non-violence fixed in the mind at all times, the mind will gradually stop dwelling in violent thoughts all together. *Ahimsā* is the root of the restraints (*yama*) and observances (*niyama*). All the rules of *yama* and *niyama* are for strengthening this root. An aspirant who becomes established in non-violence achieves equanimity of mind.

2. **Truthfulness (*satya*).** Words and thoughts in accord with fact is *satya*. In truthfulness, what is said and thought must conform with the knowledge gained by direct perception (*pratyakṣha*), by inference (*anumāna*), or by testimony (*āgama*). Non-truths such as exaggeration, duplicity, and pretense concerning any object or any action must be removed completely. Without truthfulness, many problems are created in our social lives that obstruct tranquility of mind.

   A question arises about the relative values of truth and non-violence. If telling the absolute truth contributes to violence, should it still be told? The answer is that non-violence is the highest expression of truth, so any action, thought, or word used in support of non-violence is considered truth.

3. **Non-stealing (*asteya*)**. Not taking anything that doesn't belong to you or that isn't given to you is *asteya*. Non-stealing also includes all kinds of indirect and subtle forms of misappropriation, including taking credit for something you didn't do or keeping a lost object without turning it in to the authorities.

   One cannot practice non-stealing without observing non-violence and truthfulness. Again, the practice is to examine one's actions and motives, thoughts and words to see how stealing occurs in gross and subtle ways. Stealing in any form reinforces the undesirable tendencies of the mind that obstruct our spiritual development.

4. **Sexual continence (*brahmacharya*)**. The complete removal of erotic emotions and actions in the mind is the perfection of sexual continence. The method of *brahmacharya* is to control all the sense organs in order to preserve the vital energy in the body. The practice has different rules for monks, nuns, and householders, but the principle of limiting sexual activity to preserve vital energy is the same.

   There are eight kinds of sexual thoughts and actions mentioned in the *Dakṣha Saṁhīta*: thinking about it, talking about it, joking about it, looking with sexual desire, talking privately about it, deciding to do it, attempting to do it, and actually executing it. All eight make the mind restless and waste vital energy. An aspirant who doesn't practice sexual continence cannot control the mind and senses.

5. **Non-possessiveness (*aparigraha*)**. *Aparigraha* means not hoarding wealth and property. An aspirant should not collect any more than what is needed to fulfill his or her essential needs in the world. Hoarding of unnecessary objects creates greed in the mind for more, as well as attachment to the objects already possessed. Desire, attachment, and greed create bondage in the mind. *Aparigraha* gives mental freedom to the *yogi*.

Note

These five practices are called *yama*, which means to restrain, restrict, or control. Yama is also the god of death. The five *yamas* are the practices of restraint that bring about the death of self-interest. Sūtras II:35 – 39 described the perfection of these practices.

The ego's nature is to want what it wants when it wants it. Any limitation imposed on the ego's natural expression will create tension in the mind. If this tension is too severe, the mind will rebel and the limitation will be broken. But, if the tension is moderate and the aim is fixed, the ego will accept the limitation placed on it. Then, the limitation can be gradually increased. Through this process of limitation and adjustment, the ego's power to disturb the mind can be weakened and even eliminated.

There is some confusion among students of Aṣhṭāṅga Yoga about the best way to practice the restraints. The practices of *samādhi* described in *Samādhi Pāda* are for advanced students only. The practices of Kriyā Yoga described in the early part of *Sādhana Pāda* are for intermediate and advanced students only. But the practices of Aṣhṭāṅga Yoga are for all students, although not all the practices are appropriate for all students. While the *yamas* and *niyamas* are universal, they must be practiced according to each person's nature and the condition of his or her mind.

All five *yamas* have gross, subtle, and causal levels. Aspirants begin on the gross level, and progressively move to the subtle levels. Once the *yamas* have been perfected on the subtle level, the *yogi* can address the cause, which is the ego itself. This is a very advanced state.

The practice of non-violence (*ahiṁsā*) is the broadest and most profound practice in *yoga*. On an everyday level, practicing *ahiṁsā* means to watch the mind and limit the expression of violence. Actions, words, and conscious thoughts are the gross level. All gross expressions of violence, including or even especially self-directed violence, should be limited as much as possible. When the gross expression of violence is under control, the aspirant can seek the immediate causes, which come in the form of ego, desire, and attachment. We see how we create violence by defending our self-interest.

Taken to the extreme, every thought based on individuality is violent, so the only true non-violent experience is unwavering discriminative wisdom. In other words, there is no limit to the efficacy of *ahiṁsā*; the perfection of *ahiṁsā* is final liberation.

The practice of truthfulness (*satya*) is more than just not lying. It is also not exaggerating, misrepresenting, manipulating, pretending, or falsifying. These are all the gross level manifestations, and they should be limited as much as possible. Then, once the gross forms of *satya* are stabilized, the subtle levels can be addressed, which include many forms of self-delusion, including feelings of importance and entitlement. These can be very difficult even to see, much less to remove. Still, with a fixed aim and persistent practice, success is possible.

The practice of non-stealing (*asteya*) means more than just not being a thief. The gross forms include not taking anything that wasn't earned, purchased, or given as a gift. This includes food, money, and objects. Less obvious levels are not accepting things like unearned praise or credit, not taking objects discarded or lost, and not accepting payment for incomplete or poorly done work.

The practice of sexual continence (*brahmacharya*) is often misunderstood. The sex drive in human adults is very powerful. Monks and nuns who practice advanced *yogic* methods outside of society have strict rules of celibacy. Married couples and others living in society have different rules of continence. For beginning and intermediate practitioners who live in society but still have the aim of attaining peace and control over the mind, the sex drive should be limited gently and gradually, just like every other desire. Placing too strict a limit on any desire too quickly will result in a violent backlash.

Why is the sex drive such a significant force? The answer has many levels. On the physical level, sexual pleasure is the most intense of all external sensations.

The mind is very easily attracted and addicted to it. On the emotional level, humans are social creatures. The intimacy associated with sex fulfills a significant part of that social longing.

There is also another reason why the sex drive is so significant. All sense experiences contribute to the desire for sex. How? Whenever the life force (*prāṇa*) gets excited, which it does at every sense experience, it extracts vital energy from every part of the body. This vital energy descends into the seminal region, where it seeks release. This is the natural human experience.

This means that the only way to break this flow is to curb the zeal for all sense experiences. The less an aspirant seeks to gratify the cravings of all ten senses, the weaker the sex drive will be. Unfortunately, some aspirants have read about *brahmacharya* and attempt to practice celibacy without withdrawing the mind from the senses. They find themselves in an extremely difficult predicament.

The practice of sexual continence is very important for serious aspirants of *yoga* because the sex drive activates the mind so strongly. But like all other practices, sexual continence must be done in a *sāttvika* way for it to be most effective. It should be practiced with gentle persistence and dispassion. Otherwise, it is like trying to stop a faucet with a balloon. If you don't turn off the tap, sooner or later the balloon will pop.

The fifth *yama* is non-accumulation (*aparigraha*) of unnecessary possessions. Everyone needs at least a few possessions to live. The most austere ascetics may have only a cloth to wear, a blanket, and a begging bowl, but they still need these things. A king may require a palace in order to perform his royal duties. Both can practice *aparigraha* by keeping only those items necessary for their position in life. A family needs more possessions than a recluse. The point is not how many items a person has, but that they have as few as possible.

The difference may seem subtle but it has a large impact on the mind. We cannot possess objects without their possessing us. When an object is needed as part of one's duty in life, then the mind can be around it without owning it. But every object that is not so needed is retained only out of attachment. Time, energy, and money are required to maintain it, protect it, and possibly even replace it when it wears out. Furthermore, the mind is never content with what it has. The more it has, the more it wants. Until the mind feels that it possesses nothing of the world, it will not be able to become stable in *samādhi*. Again, the key to practicing *aparigraha* is to slowly reduce unnecessary possessions, getting used to each new level of simplicity before reducing further.

In the next *sūtra*, the importance of the five *yamas* as a spiritual practice is described.

Sūtra 31　जातिदेशकालसमयानवच्छिन्नाः सार्वभौमा महाव्रतम् ॥ ३१ ॥

jāti–deśa–kāla–samayānavachchhinnāḥ sārvabhaumā mahāvratam

They (the five restraints) become a great vow [when they are practiced] universally, not limited by space, time, life state, and circumstances.

जाति	*jāti*	class, life state
देश	*deśa*	place, space
काल	*kāla*	time
समय	*samaya*	occasion, circumstance
अनवच्छिन्नाः	*anavachchhinnāḥ*	not limited by, unrestricted by
सार्वभौमाः	*sārvabhaumāḥ*	universal
महाव्रतम्	*mahāvratam*	great vows

In the previous *sūtra*, the five restraints (*yamas*) were introduced as non-violence (*ahiṁsā*), truthfulness (*satya*), honesty (*asteya*), sexual continence (*brahmacharya*), and non-possessiveness (*aparigraha*). Now, in this *sūtra*, the manner in which they should be practiced in order to achieve perfection in *samādhi* is described.

In the course of everyday life, an aspirant faces many difficulties in observing the five restraints. In certain situations, at certain times, the practices conflict with some aspect of life. Several examples of this kind of difficulty are as follows:

A spiritual aspirant is trapped in a snow storm in the remote woods. Should he kill a rabbit to eat for his survival?

A truthful man sitting outside sees a deer running, followed by a hunter. The deer hides behind his cottage. The hunter arrives and asks, "Did you see a deer around?" Should the man tell the hunter where the deer is hiding?

What about sexual continence? Is moderation acceptable?

What about a householder who has a large family? If he has no possessions, how can he take care of his family?

Many varieties of these questions arise, and an aspirant may become confused by the conflict between worldly necessity and spiritual ideals.

For life in the world, discrimination is necessary and an aspirant must choose the highest good. This *sūtra*, however, makes it clear that if one takes the five restraints as a great vow, they must be practiced universally and unconditionally without consideration of class, space, time, or circumstances. For example, for the renunciate who takes this great vow, it would not be acceptable to kill certain classes of animals and not others, to kill animals in certain places like the tundra but not others, to kill an animal only as a part of a ritualistic sacrifice and not at other times, or to kill in certain situations like war but not in others. All five restraints will be practiced in the same unconditional way by one who takes the great vow. If the restraints are not observed universally, then it is not considered a great vow.

For the householder aspirant who must perform worldly duties, observing the great vow is not possible. For the renunciate who is totally dedicated to achieving Self-realization, the restraint of non-violence and the other restraints are always practiced without fail in all conditions of life, everywhere, always, and in all circumstances. By upholding the great vows, the aspirant attains universality.

Note

The five practices of restraint (*yamas*) were introduced in the previous *sūtra*. These practices are very important for all aspirants at all levels, but they cannot be practiced the same by all people. In this *sūtra*, the highest level of practice is indicated.

Life in the world is complicated because we have duties to ourselves and to others. Often these duties conflict with each other, and there is no way to perform both perfectly. Even the most saintly of householders must find compromises at times. Therefore, the absolute nature of this *sūtra* is not appropriate for householders.

In order for the practice of *yama* to become the great vow, all five restraints must be practiced at all times, places, and conditions. No compromise is possible. There is no room left for individual self-expression (ego), so the great vow is a very hard austerity. For those who can maintain it, it is like an express elevator to the top.

An objection arises. One cannot even live in society without compromise, so this great vow is an unattainable ideal. Even Arjuna from the *Bhagavad Gītā* had to fight in the war because of his duty as a warrior.

The objection is correct for everyone except the most austere renunciates. For those *yogis* who have renounced all participation in worldly activities, who have separated themselves from society, and who are highly determined to achieve Self-realization, the unconditional nature of the great vow is a primary means of liberation.

The *sūtra* does not say that the only way to attain liberation is through the great vow. It is not trying to contradict all the other paths of *yoga*, such as Karma Yoga and Bhakti Yoga, that also lead to the same goal. Instead, it is showing the awesome extent to which the *yamas* can be practiced.

Nor does this *sūtra* take away from the value of practicing the restraints at more moderate levels. In verse VI:17 of the *Bhagavad Gītā*, moderation is given as a requirement for achievement in *yoga*. The verse says that *yoga* is most effective for those who are "moderate in eating, recreation, exertion, and sleeping." In other words, eating, sleeping, or exercising too much or too little is harmful to the practice of *yoga*.

The key phrase is "too much," because what is too much for one person may not be enough for another. For example, an artist living in a warm climate may only need two small meals a day, while a logger working in a cold environment may require three large meals to stay healthy. In both cases, their diet could be considered moderate. The same is true for exercise and sleep. All bodies require some exercise and some sleep. Depending on the type and condition of the body, what is moderate for one could be either excessive or insufficient for another.

All aspirants benefit from being non-violent, truthful, honest, continent, and generous. These are all aspects of virtue (*dharma*), and until liberation is established, *dharma* requires effort. Our mind is purified every single time we practice the *yamas*. We do the best we can, over time our best improves. When we climb a mountain, we progress by taking one step after another. If we give up and stop walking, we will never reach the goal. But, if we start again after every rest, if we get up again after every fall, in time we are guaranteed to reach the top.

In practicing the *yamas*, the top is when they are practiced universally and become the great vows. This means that the great vows are achieved, and not taken as promises that may or may not be upheld.

The five observances (*niyama*) are introduced in the next *sūtra*.

Sankaṭ Mochan Hanumān Mandir, Mount Madonna Center, California

Sūtra 32   शौचसन्तोषतपःस्वाध्यायेश्वरप्रणिधानानि नियमाः ॥ ३२ ॥

shaucha–santosha–tapah–svādhyāyeshvara–pranidhānāni niyamāh

The observances are purity, contentment, austerity, self-study, and surrender to God.

शौच	*shaucha*	purity, cleanliness
सन्तोष	*santosha*	contentment
तपः	*tapah*	austerity
स्वाध्याय	*svādhyāya*	self-study
ईश्वरप्रणिधानानि	*Īshvara–pranidhānāni*	self-surrender, worship of God
नियमाः	*niyamāh*	observances

In Sūtra II:30, the five restraints (*yamas*) were explained. Now, in this *sūtra*, the five observances (*niyamas*) are explained. The purpose of practicing the restraints and observances is to cultivate morality, character, and *yogic* discipline. The practice of restraints and observances is considered an austerity (*tapah*) of the mind, body, and senses. As such, they are the foundation of spiritual life. This *yogic* discipline purifies the mind and develops one-pointed concentration.

1. **Cleanliness or purity (*shaucha*).** Cleanliness means to purify the body as well as the mind. The gross body is cleaned externally and internally. External cleanliness means to wash the body, including the hair, nails, eyes, and nose. All the rules of hygiene and healthy living are to be observed. The internal body is cleaned by the six purificatory methods of Hatha Yoga called *shat karma*.[1] Also, eating the right food in the right amount at the right time combined with moderate exercise purifies the digestive system.

   The mind and body are interconnected, so keeping the body clean develops purity of thought in the mind. The mind is further purified by developing positive qualities such as love, compassion, and honesty. The mind is also purified by constant repetition of a *mantra*, a name of God, or prayers. A pure mind is freed from egoism, attachment, and desires, and thus fit for one-pointed concentration.

2. **Contentment (*santosha*).** Contentment means wanting nothing you don't already have, and being satisfied with what you do have. Yogic discipline cannot be perfected without contentment (*santosha*) because without it, the restlessness of the mind will never stop.

   One method of cultivating contentment is to accept whatever comes as a gift from God. When the mind learns to accept the pairs of opposites as the law of nature, the ego will stop fighting for more and expressing discontent-

---

1 The six methods of *shat karma* clean the inside of the body, which the *yogis* value as much as cleaning the outside of the body. The methods are called *dhauti, vasti, neti, nauli, trātak,* and *kapāla bhāti.*

ment. By cultivating acceptance, the mind remains calm and equal in all situations. Equanimity of mind is necessary for one-pointed concentration.

3. **Austerity (*tapaḥ*).** The practical application of restraints and observances is austerity. The term *tapaḥ* literally means to heat up. It is analogous to a goldsmith who heats a lump of gold to remove the impurities.

   Controlling worldly desires by the force of will through particular methods is austerity. Some examples are fasting, maintaining a vow of silence, living on a fruit or milk diet, and practicing other vows like honesty, non-stealing, and non-violence. The practice of *prāṇāyāma* is also considered an austerity.

   Austerity is classified in three broad categories: of body, speech, and mind.

   a. **Austerity of the body** involves the force of will. Examples are the willful forbearance of the extremities of heat, cold, hunger, and thirst.
   b. **Austerity of speech** includes complete vocal abstention, speech that expresses only positive attitudes, and the chanting of God's name and the scriptures.
   c. **Austerity of the mind** is the subtlest and most demanding form of austerity. It requires complete renunciation of all negative thoughts, moods, and emotions.

Austerity performed for spiritual advancement is distinguished from self-inflicted torture. Some *yogis* are seen lying on a bed of nails; some keep one arm up for years, atrophying the arm and making it dysfunctional; some starve the body by eating too little. All such austerities are nothing but self-torture and are considered demonic.

The purpose of practicing austerity is to get control over the desires that cause restlessness in the mind. The ego of individuality is weakened through the practice of austerities in all our actions and thoughts. Austerities are developed gradually without harming the body or the mind. The discipline of austerity strengthens the will, and then will power strengthens austerity.

4. **Self-study (*svādhyāya*).** Self-study is the study of scriptures that talk about the path of liberation. By studying the scriptures and reflecting deeply on their meaning, *yogis* understand how their own egos, attachments, and desires create the world they perceive, and thus how suffering and misery are also self-created. Without applying the teachings of the scriptures to our own lives, the study of scriptures will not bring liberation of the embodied soul. In order to achieve liberation, the study of the scriptures with reflection on their meaning, and practical application of their teachings to daily life are necessary.

5. **Surrender to God (*Īshvara praṇidhāna*).** Surrender to God means keeping the divine presence in the heart by surrendering the ego to God (Īshvara). In Sūtra I:23, Patañjali says, "By surrender to God, the state of liberation becomes imminent." In Sūtra I:29, it was said, "From that surrender to God comes Self-realization and the obstacles disappear." Both *sūtras* mean that the practice of *Īshvara praṇidhāna* is a profound method of purifying the mind. Why?

In all our actions, words, thoughts, and emotions there is "I" consciousness. This "I" consciousness colors everything by its nature of individuality, and thus creates its own limitation. By the practice of *Īshvara-praṇidhāna*, this "I" consciousness subsides in all our action, words, thoughts, and feelings.

In the practice of surrender to God, two main methods are used. First is the mental assertion, "Not my will, but Thy will be done." The second method is the practical application of selfless service. When the mind is well established in surrender to God, the mind becomes steady and peaceful.

Chanting the *mantra* Om, which is the manifest form of Īshvara as sound, is also a method of surrender to God (see Sūtra I:28). Surrender to God is a path of devotional *yoga* (Bhakti Yoga). In the path of devotion, the "I-ness" is offered to God in all actions and thoughts. In this way, the mind merges in devotion to God and *samādhi* is attained.

Note

These five observances (*niyamas*), combined with the five restraints (*yamas*), are the core and foundation of spiritual life. Ideally, they are to be practiced consistently and reasonably according to the nature and capacity of the aspirant. They all support each other, and the perfection of any one of them is the perfection of all of them.

Purity means inner and outer cleanliness of the body and mind. The ego expresses itself most strongly through negativity because negativity is what separates us from each other. The complete removal of negativity is the end of individuality, which is the death of the ego. Therefore, the practice of purity is an effective means of weakening the ego through reducing negativities.

Outer purity means washing the body, wearing clean clothes, and maintaining clean living and working spaces. It also means living a virtuous life and associating with good people. Inner purity means cultivating good thoughts and speech, and acting with a pure and good motive. It also means having a right diet and lifestyle.

Contentment is considered a practice of *yoga*, as opposed to a state of mind that arises when life is pleasant. *Santoṣha* means cultivating and practicing that peaceful state of mind no matter what the external circumstances of life are. This is difficult to do because the ego wants to pursue pleasure and avoid pain. Instead, the aspirant practicing contentment accepts what comes of its own accord and doesn't seek anything else.

This doesn't mean not to act. Our worldly duties have come to us unsought, so we must perform them to the best of our ability. This means that *santoṣha* requires us to accept ourselves and our duties, and not try to be something we are not.

Austerity as a practice of *yoga* is very broad. It means discipline, and all the methods of *yoga* are disciplines of one form or another. Disciplines are the means for controlling the ego, so placing limits on the expression of desires breaks the ego's domination over the mind. In the *Bhagavad Gītā*, austerities are categorized according to the predominant *guṇa*. The three *guṇas* are *sattva* (purity), *rajas* (passion), and *tamas* (ignorance).

Austerities that are *sattva* predominant calm the mind, increase dispassion, and prepare the aspirant for meditation. It is said that *sattva* is bitter at first and sweet in the end, which means that *sāttvika* austerities are not pleasing to the ego when they are performed, but the effect, which is the reduction of self-interest and suffering, is beneficial and sweet. They also make the body and mind more resilient and tolerant of the extremes of life such as heat, cold, hunger, and thirst. When the aspirant is unmoved by the pairs of opposites, *samādhi* arises.

In contrast, *rājasika* austerities are sweet at first and bitter in the end. Even though they may be strenuous or difficult, *rājasika* austerities are gratifying to the ego, which is often proud of its feats and accomplishments. It may think, "I have become a great *yogi* for I can meditate in cold water for hours," or "My mind has become so pure; no one else I know can hold his breath as long as I can." Because these austerities strengthen the ego, they perpetuate suffering, which is indeed a bitter result.

Tāmasika austerities are bitter in the beginning and bitter in the end, which means they are forms of self-torture that perpetuate negativity of mind. Aspirants may believe they are performing proper austerities, but an excess of *tamas* confuses the mind. If peace does not increase, the austerity was not pure.

Self-study means investigating the mind and world with the intention of separating truth from illusion. All scriptures that teach liberation of the embodied soul from bondage can be used as aids in this investigation. The two classical questions in this regard are, "Who am I," and "How did this world around me arise?" But this practice of *svādhyāya* is not a study in philosophy.

Svādhyāya is the direct investigation into the nature of experience and liberation. It may use philosophy as an aid, and indeed, the philosophies of liberation were created specifically to be tools for self-study, but the practice itself is much more than just philosophy. The aspirants must exert great effort in searching their minds, thoughts, words, and motives to understand exactly who they are and why they do what they do. The knowledge they acquire in this process is specific to them and their paths, and no one can ever take it away from them.

The practice of surrender to God as an observance (*niyama*) is an everyday technique of limiting the ego. It is the process of aligning our actions, words, and thoughts with the natural order. We try not to dwell on what we want for ourselves, but rather on what is needed for the whole.

It is also the practice of seeing the divine force in ourselves and in the outer world. Skeptics think that God is dead (or never existed) because they don't see God anywhere. But spiritual aspirants look for God in the form of life, love, and selflessness that appear all over the world. By concentrating on that divine energy, faith, hope, and trust increase, while fear, anxiety, and the ego's selfish nature automatically diminish.

Sūtra 33   वितर्कबाधने प्रतिपक्षभावनम् ॥ ३३ ॥

vitarka–bādhane pratipakṣa–bhāvanam

When the mind is disturbed by negative thoughts, one should dwell on their opposites.

वितर्क	*vitarka*	negative thoughts, evil thoughts
बाधने	*bādhane*	on opposition by, on oppression by
प्रतिपक्ष	*pratipakṣa*	to the contrary, opposite thoughts
भावनम्	*bhāvanam*	dwelling on, habituation

In the previous three *sutras*, the practices of restraints (*yamas*) and observances (*niyamas*) were explained. In theory, they are simple, but many obstacles arise in practicing them, even for experienced *yogis*. Therefore, Patañjali gives an effective method to remove those obstacles: dwell on their opposites.

Obstacles arise because of the aspirant's negative habits and tendencies that were formed by the latencies (*saṃskāras*) of past actions. These undesirable habits and tendencies can overpower the mind in spite of the aspirant's resolve. Or say, negative thoughts and behaviors do not disappear just because an aspirant improves his or her motives and begins a daily *sādhana* (spiritual practice).

In such situations, Patañjali suggests countering these undesirable thoughts that obstruct our self-development by dwelling on their opposites. By encouraging and dwelling on positive thoughts, negative tendencies that the aspirant developed previously are opposed and weakened. For example, when the mind is possessed by hatred and the person expresses hate in action, those hateful thoughts should be replaced by thoughts of love, and the hateful action should be replaced by expressing love in action.

One may also feel hate coming from others, in which case, one should replace that feeling with the feeling of love coming from others. In this way, all undesirable tendencies, which are in the mind in the form of thoughts or feelings and which may be expressed in action, should be replaced by their opposites.

As hatred is replaced by dwelling on love, anger is replaced by dwelling on compassion; jealousy is replaced by friendship; and deceit is replaced by honesty. Because the experience of the world is colored by the mind's projections, this method gives an aspirant the ability to change that projection from negative to positive. Dwelling on the opposite is a method for overcoming the obstacles that arise in the practice of yogic discipline.

A renunciate asked his master, "How can one overcome the feeling of enmity?" The master answered, "When one can beg food from the house of an enemy, then the feeling of enmity exists no more."

Note

In the previous three *sutras*, the *yamas* and *niyamas* were explained in theory. Now, in Sūtras II:33–34, practical advice is given to help overcome the obstacles that may arise. The restraints and observances are simple. Don't be violent. Don't lie, steal, or hoard. Control your desires. Be clean, content, and disciplined. Reflect, and surrender your ego to God. But practicing them is very difficult because many things get in the way.

Most of the time, what gets in the way are past tendencies. The whole reason we practice *yoga* is to purify our minds, bodies, and behaviors. This means that when we start, we are impure. These impurities don't go away just because we decide to start practicing *yoga*.

We find that while we agree with the theory of non-violence, we also don't want to get bitten by mosquitos or have mice in the house. We love the idea of remaining content no matter what happens, but sometimes people do things that make us so mad. No, the practice of the restraints and observances is very difficult in reality.

So what are we to do? Patañjali tells us that we can dwell on the opposite quality. If we feel angry, we should dwell on compassion. We can think about how much the other person must be suffering if they have come to be as cruel, insensitive, or miserable as they are.

If we feel proud of our possessions and desirous of obtaining more, we can dwell on freedom and non-attachment. We can think about how free it is, or must be, to not have to worry about objects. Nothing to defend, maintain, or replace. No jealousy or competition from others. Just peace of mind. Then we can give away everything we don't need and start feeling that peace.

If we feel sexually excited at the wrong time, we can dwell on dispassion. We can think about the body as inert like a piece of wood, or as filled with waste fluids like sweat, urine, and phlegm.

The same techniques can be applied to all negative tendencies of the mind. Their efficacy is pure brilliance. The method is simply to remove the cause of the negativity. All of our urges, both positive and negative, arise because of the content of our minds. When we find the practice of *yama* and *niyama* difficult, it is because our minds are filled with negative thoughts. If we replace the negative thoughts with positive thoughts, the practice of *yama* and *niyama* becomes easy and natural. In other words, dwelling on the opposite quality removes the struggle and practice becomes delightful.

An objection arises. Patañjali says, "Just dwell on the opposite," but it is not so easy. The mind is out of control. What can we do if we can't just switch it?

The answer is to try. How do toddlers become potty trained? At some point, they learn to feel their bladders and wait until they get to the bathroom. If they feel their bladders but do nothing to hold it, they never become trained. In the same way, we have to learn to recognize our negative thoughts and turn them to positive thoughts. It is not a magical formula; it is just practice.

In the next *sūtra*, Patañjali describes the different kinds of evil actions and how they can be removed.

Sūtra 34 वितर्का हिंसादयः कृतकारितानुमोदिता लोभ क्रोध मोह पूर्वका
मृदुमध्याधिमात्रा दुःखाज्ञानानन्तफला इति प्रतिपक्षभावनम् ॥३४॥

vitarkā himsādayah krita–kāritānumoditā lobha krodha moha pūrvakā
mridu–madhyādhimātrā duhkhājñānānanta–phalā iti pratipaksha–
bhāvanam

**Negative thoughts cause violent or harmful actions. They are either per-
formed directly, initiated through others, or tacitly approved. They may
be caused by greed, anger, or delusion, and are in mild, medium, or
intense degrees. Knowing that their result is endless pain and ignorance is dwelling on the opposite.**

वितर्का	*vitarkā*	negative thoughts, evil thoughts
हिंसादयः	*himsādayah*	causing injury to others, violent or harmful actions
कृत	*krita*	done
कारित	*kārita*	caused to be done by others
अनुमोदितः	*anumoditah*	permitted to be done or approved
लोभ	*lobha*	greed
क्रोध	*krodha*	anger
मोह	*moha*	ignorance, delusion, attachment
पूर्वका	*pūrvakā*	preceded by, caused by
मृदु	*mridu*	slight, mild
मध्य	*madhya*	middling, medium
अधिमात्रः	*adhimātrah*	intense
दुःख	*duhkha*	pain
अज्ञान	*ajñāna*	ignorance
अनन्त	*ananta*	infinite, endless
फल	*phala*	result, fruit
इति	*iti*	thus, so
प्रतिपक्ष	*pratipaksa*	to the contrary, opposite thoughts
भावनम्	*bhāvanam*	thinking, dwelling in the mind

In this *sūtra*, Patañjali describes what evil actions are, the way they are performed, how they are caused, in what degrees they occur, their fruit, and how
they can be removed.

Evil or negative thoughts (*vitarkā*) are those that cause harm to oneself or to
others. Harmful or violent actions are performed in three ways: direct involvement (*krita*), by employing someone or using some outer agency to harm another (*kārita*), or by permitting, tacitly approving, or conniving to harm another
(*anumoditah*). In all three ways, the person is responsible for the injury.

Generally, we don't feel responsible for the harm done to someone by others,
even if it occurs in our presence. We simply remain indifferent. Actually, it is a
way of approving the act of violence. For example, a person doesn't shoot a deer
or send someone to shoot a deer, but by watching someone shoot a deer without taking any contrary action, they assume some interest in it. Their act of

watching with interest is a form of participation. It is against the rules of the restraints (*yama*) and observances (*niyama*).

The three main causes of performing evil action are greed (*lobha*), anger (*krodha*), and attachment (*moha*). All three causes are contrary to the rules of restraint and observance.

The following example shows how the rules of non-hoarding (*aparigraha*) and contentment (*santoṣha*) are broken. A dissatisfied person whose extensive needs are not fulfilled commits evil actions out of greed (*lobha*) to acquire greater possessions. Whenever any obstruction rises, the mind reacts with anger (*krodha*) to remove the obstruction. Because the mind is attached (*moha*) to the objects, it commits additional evil actions to guard and protect them. These evil actions range in degree from mild (*mṛidu*) to medium (*madhya*) to intense (*adhimātra*).

The fruit of evil actions is endless pain and ignorance in which there are untrue cognitions. Both pain and ignorance are the inevitable results of evils (*vitarkā*) and are the cause of bondage of the soul.

The cure for removing this endless pain and misery is dwelling on their opposite. By the persistent practice of the restraints (*yama*) and observances (*niyama*), the evils (*vitarkā*) are removed.

In the next eleven *sūtras*, the perfection of the *yamas* and *niyamas* is described.

Note

In the previous *sūtra*, the method of overcoming negativities by dwelling on the opposite was given. Now, in this *sūtra*, that method is supported by the practice of seeing the harm caused by various activities.

The essence of this verse is that seeing the harm in negative thoughts is the way to dwell on their opposites. Often we are lulled into bad habits because we don't see the harm they cause. We say things like, "Just this once," or "No one will notice." By doing this, we weaken our will and bring harm to ourselves and others. When we are able to clearly perceive the harm our actions cause, it is much easier to turn away from them.

This *sūtra* says that there are three forms of violence motivated by three different causes, and with three levels of intensity.[1] The point is that there are many degrees of harmful activities; skipping your morning bath is not as harmful as killing your ex-lover.

But for the *yogi* intent on perfecting *samādhi*, understanding subtle forms of violence and harmful activities is very important. The most poignant example in the commentary is the harm caused by vicarious participation in violent actions. If we are witness to a violent action but do nothing to prevent or minimize it, the *sūtra* says that we are responsible for a harmful action. We may not

---

1 The classical commentaries subdivide each level of intensity into three more categories of mild, medium, and intense, making nine. Therefore, the total categories of harmful activities would be 81.

be as responsible as the person directly performing the action, but the mind will still be affected in a negative way.

An objection arises. Sūtra I:33 stated that the *yogi* should cultivate an attitude of indifference for the non-virtuous. Now, it is saying that if we don't stop a violent act, we are responsible for the violence. Which is the correct attitude, indifference or intervention?

The answer is that they are talking about different things. Sūtra I:33 was talking about attitudes toward people, and this *sūtra* is talking about participation in action. Furthermore, the examples given in the commentary are not talking about indifferent people. They are talking about people who watch with interest or listen with interest. Why do they watch? They watch because they are excited by it in some way. And excitement always relates to the ego, so watching strengthens the ego. In this case, the excitement relates to a harmful act, so it perpetuates suffering on several levels.

For aspirants of *yoga*, committing harmful actions is undesirable because it strengthens the ego, distracts the mind, and weakens the will. The more clearly we understand how our actions may be causing harm to ourselves and to others, the easier it is for us relinquish them and to deepen our practice of *yama* and *niyama*.

In the next *sūtra*, the external result of non-violence is described.

Statue of Mahatma Gandhi at Nainital Lake, Uttarākhand.

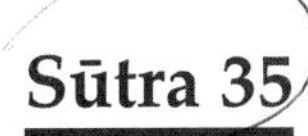

Sūtra 35　　अहिंसाप्रतिष्ठायां तत्सन्निधौ वैरत्यागः ॥ ३५ ॥

ahiṁsāpratiṣṭhāyāṁ tatsannidhau vairatyāgaḥ[1]

All hostilities are given up in the presence of one who is firmly established in non-violence.

अहिंसा	*ahiṁsā*	non-violence
प्रतिष्ठायाम्	*pratiṣṭhāyām*	on being firmly established
तत्	*tat*	in one's (the *yogi's*)
सन्निधौ	*sannidhau*	vicinity, presence
वैरत्यागः	*vairatyāgaḥ*	giving up of hostility

From this *sutra* to the end of *Sādhana Pāda*, Patañjali explains the eight limbs of yoga individually. These next eleven *sutras*[2] give the result or perfection of each restraint (*yama*) and observance (*niyama*).

What is the specific result for a *yogi* who attains perfection in non-violence (*ahiṁsā*)? This *sutra* says that anyone who comes in the vicinity of that *yogi* becomes free from all fears and hostile thoughts. For example, a tiger and a deer could sit together in that perfected *yogi's* presence, unafraid of each other and unafraid of the *yogi*. The reason is that the mind of the *yogi* has become so pure (*sāttvika*) and full of love and compassion that the energy of non-violence projects out through the *yogi's* aura. All living beings who come into the presence of the *yogi*, such as a humans, animals, or birds, are so affected by the energy of non-violence that they give up their hostile nature even if they normally have enmity to each other.

Perfection in non-violence can only be realized by a *yogi* who has perfected all the restraints and observances through the regular practice of all eight limbs of *yoga*. Perfection in non-violence means that all violent thoughts are completely eliminated from the *yogi's* mind.

Note

In the previous five *sutras*, the restraints and observances were introduced as the foundation of spiritual practice. They directly oppose the negative tendencies in the mind. Now, in this *sutra*, Patañjali begins a new section showing the extreme results of these ten practices.

Perfection in the *yamas* and *niyamas* brings about extraordinary consequences as a direct result of the complete purification of the mind. There is no logical basis for deducing these effects, but they can be realized directly when perfection is attained.

This *sutra* explains the incredible result of absolute non-violence. Violence, ultimately, is any thought based on the ego. For life in the world, ego-based

---

1　Some commentators have added *sarva praṇināṁ bhavati* to this *sutra*, which means "non-violence appears in the minds of all living beings around [that *yogi*]."

2　There are ten *yamas* and *niyamas*, but Patañjali gives two *sutras* to purity (*śhaucha*).

thoughts are necessary. But for a renunciate *yogi*, the world is considered unreal, and the ego-based reality is rejected. When the *yogi's* renunciation is complete, there is nothing left for him or her to accomplish because both mind and ego are completely absorbed in the absolute, infinite consciousness (*puruṣha*).

For such a *yogi*, there is no possibility of violence or even harmful thoughts because he or she doesn't distinguish between the welfare of one body over another. There is no thought of identification with anything of the world, including the body, so there is nothing left to defend. Only love and equanimity are present in their mind.

What is the effect of this complete absence of self-interest? No one is threatened. Every living being has an intuitive sense of danger, which is an important tool for survival. The law of the jungle is kill or be killed. Even though we don't feel our lives threatened all the time in today's sophisticated societies, the nature of life has not changed. Life is based on competition because of the ever-present functioning of the ego. The ego defines itself by what it is and what it has, which is known by comparing to what it isn't and what it doesn't have.

The ego also wants to be victorious in everything it does. In the jungle, mere survival is victory, but once survival itself is not a concern, the ego refines its comparisons and enters into competitions, such as having a better car or house, or going to a more prestigious college. This cannot be avoided so long as the ego functions in the mind. We all know it intuitively, which is why we defend ourselves constantly from and against others.

This *sūtra* is now talking about an enlightened *yogi* for whom this sense of competition is utterly missing. There is no force or energy within that *yogi* that tries to take anything from anyone. Instead, they are there only to give. The effect of this complete turnaround is dramatic.

The intuitive sense of danger that arises around other people simply doesn't get activated. Just as a crow rests on a cow's back and people rest under a tree without fear of attack by the cow or by the tree, so these *yogis* inspire complete trust in the people around them. They, in turn, are overcome by the sense of tranquility, and temporarily abandon their competitive and violent natures. This peaceful effect goes away when they leave the presence of the *yogi* because their impure minds return to their normal activities, but the memory of that peace leaves a new sense of potential for them, and they may be inspired to become better people as well.

In the next *sūtra*, the effect of perfect truthfulness is described.

Sutra 36   सत्यप्रतिष्ठायां क्रियाफलाश्रयत्वम् ॥ ३६ ॥

satya–pratiṣṭhāyaṁ kriyā–phalāśhrayatvam

On being firmly established in truthfulness, [the *yogi's* words] bear fruit as actions.

सत्य	*satya*	truthfulness, veracity
प्रतिष्ठायाम्	*pratiṣṭhāyām*	on being firmly established
क्रिया	*kriyā*	of action
फल	*phala*	fruit, result
आश्रयत्वम्	*āśhrayatvam*	the dependence of, basis

The practice of truthfulness in speech, thought, and action purifies the *yogi's* mind. When the *yogi's* mind is completely purified, it is called being firmly established in truthfulness. In that state, the mind is no longer controlled by the ego, which means that it is a universal mind or divine mind.

In the divine mind, knowledge of the past and future are always present. The *yogi's* words, thoughts, and actions are not guided by egocentric desires, but rather are guided by the divine mind. Whatever that *yogi* thinks, says, or does comes true. The *yogi's* actions will bring results based on truth. A *yogi* who has achieved such a high state of truthfulness will not speak, think, or act in any way that is not in conformity with the divine plan. Hence, all his or her words will come true.

Note

Continuing with the fruits of perfecting the *yamas* and *niyamas*, this *sutra* explains that perfection in truthfulness (*satya*) results in everything the *yogi* says coming true. How is this possible?

First of all, this *sutra* does not mean that the *yogi* can change the outcome of sporting events or the stock market just by declaring someone a winner. It means that whatever words are spoken by the perfected *yogi* will correspond to the result. Because their mind is so completely established in truthfulness, they will only speak what they know will come true. If there is any doubt, they will not speak about it as if there were no doubt.

Secondly, the purified mind is devoid of self-interest. Self-interest is the limiting factor in the mind, so without it, the mind is not limited by individuality. Its capacity of perception is extremely subtle, so it has the great ability to comprehend any situation in its entirety. Therefore, it can perceive the consequences of certain actions ahead of time.

Thirdly, such complete purification of the mind can only occur through the intense focus of will by the *yogi*. Without such a strong will, the *yogi* could not have achieved perfection, but would have settled at some lower level of achievement. This intensity of will is another reason that all the *yogi's* words bear fruit as action.

Again, this means that the *yogi* would not manipulate the world for personal benefit because he or she is no longer identified with any particular mind-body complex. In fact, the concept of "personal benefit" doesn't even arise. The will of such *yogis* has dissolved into the divine will, so they can only want what is in accordance with the world order.

This power of having words bear fruit in action is gradually achieved. As the mind is purified through the practice of truthfulness (and all the other practices of *yoga*), the *yogi's* will is strengthened along with the ability to comprehend past and future causes.

In the next *sūtra*, the perfection of non-stealing (*asteya*) is described.

Sūtra 37　अस्तेयप्रतिष्ठायां सर्वरत्नोपस्थानम् ॥ ३७ ॥

asteya–pratiṣhṭhāyāṁ sarva–ratnopasthānam

On being firmly established in non-stealing, all kinds of wealth present themselves.

अस्तेय	*asteya*	non-stealing
प्रतिष्ठायाम्	*pratiṣhṭhāyām*	on being firmly established
सर्व	*sarva*	all
रत्न	*ratna*	jewels, gems, wealth
उपस्थानम्	*upasthānam*	approaching with, present themselves

The desire for more and more leads to all forms of stealing. Taking anything that doesn't belong to us is considered stealing.

Through the practice of non-stealing, the desire to have more begins to subside and a person finds contentment with what they already possess. When a *yogi* develops a pure state of mind, he or she becomes desireless and unattached, and dwells in peace. Spiritually minded people get attracted to such a *yogi* like moths are attracted to a candle flame.

The phrase, "All kinds of wealth present themselves," means that people who get attracted to such a *yogi* offer all kinds of jewels and wealth to show their respect and to express their love and devotion. Everything is available to that *yogi*, but the *yogi* remains unattached to everything.

The *sutra* also suggests that a *yogi* who is established in non-stealing develops the power of clairvoyance and can see wealth buried in the ground.

Note

Stealing in all its forms is a function of the individual ego. It sees its own interests without seeing or valuing other people and their interests. Because of a strong desire for wealth, recognition, and power, a person begins to steal.

Stealing does not just mean breaking into someone's house or car and taking something without permission. For *yogis*, it also means not taking ideas that aren't theirs, nor even credit for what they didn't do. Actually, the term *asteya* means non-covetousness. So long as the mind craves or covets wealth of any form, it is not completely pure.

Complete purity is achieved through *yoga*. All the practices of *yoga* are designed to weaken and remove the influence of the selfish ego. Because the ego has so many faces, the *Sutras* describe so many practices to combat it.

This *sutra* speaks to an ironic truth. When a *yogi* becomes firmly established in non-stealing, wealth presents itself. This means that all kinds of wealth and power become available to one who covets nothing.

How and why does this happen? The answer is that the *yogi* has become completely trustworthy. They are the perfect guardians of wealth and power because they don't want anything for themselves. Others recognize this and donate their money in full confidence that the *yogi* will remain indifferent and unaffected by it, and they will use it for the good of the world. The irony is that wealth comes freely to one who doesn't want it but is so hard to achieve for those who covet it.

Of course, this freely given wealth and power can become a trap for the *yogi* who is not firmly established in *asteya*. Wealth and power are very attractive to the ego, which can reawaken if any dormant desires are allowed to sprout. There are many stories of *yogis* whose passion for the world was rekindled by unsought wealth and power.

In the next *sūtra*, the benefit of sexual continence is described.

Sūtra 38   ब्रह्मचर्यप्रतिष्ठायां वीर्यलाभः ॥ ३८ ॥

brahmacharya–pratiṣhṭhāyāṁ vīryalābhaḥ

On being firmly established in sexual continence, vigor is obtained.

ब्रह्मचर्य	*brahmacharya*	sexual continence
प्रतिष्ठायाम्	*pratiṣhṭhāyām*	on being firmly established
वीर्य	*vīrya*	vigor
लाभः	*lābhaḥ*	gained, obtained

In Sūtra II:30, sexual continence (*brahmacharya*) was explained. In this *sutra*, the result of sexual continence is given. Gaining vigor (*vīrya*) is that result. Vigor is not merely physical power, but it also includes mental power and power of the senses.

Vīrya also means semen. The semen in its purified state becomes subtle energy called *ojas*. *Ojas* is the energy of vigor, virility, and brilliance. For a *yogi* who is established in sexual continence, the *ojas* energy starts moving toward the cerebrum. Such a *yogi* is called *ūrdhva retaḥ*. *Ūrdhva* means upward and *retaḥ* means sexual energy. A *yogi* who is *ūrdhva retaḥ* achieves invincible powers (*siddhis*).

Note

Sexual continence does not simply mean to be celibate. It means to retain the vital energy of the body by not indulging in sensual pleasures. Sensual pleasures include any contact of the senses with their objects for the purpose of enjoyment. Actually, trying to be celibate for extended periods of time without restraining the senses is impossible.

The body and mind get energy from food, from the air, and from the sun. People use energy in many ways, but generally most is spent in selfish activities, especially seeking pleasure and avoiding pain. For a *yogi* seeking liberation, not only does this waste precious energy, it disturbs the mind.

The practice of *brahmacharya* really means using the life energy for spiritual purposes. Instead of dissipating energy in all forms of enjoyment, the energy is channeled for one purpose (purification of the mind), and it becomes highly focused and powerful. It is like a garden hose with an adjustable nozzle. The water can be spread widely and softly over a short distance, or it can be focused narrowly and travel very far. Also, calm water is soft to the touch, but a block of ice is as hard as a brick and high pressure water is powerful enough to penetrate metal. In the same way, the life energy can be soft and dissipated, or it can be highly focused, powerful, and penetrating.

This *sutra* says that when a *yogi* is firmly established in *brahmacharya*, the subtle energy is highly focused (vigorous) and capable of extraordinary powers. Such power is extremely seductive to the ego, so it can be dangerous if not used for spiritual purposes.

In the next *sutra*, the benefits of *aparigraha* (non-possessiveness) are described.

Symbols of Lord Śhiva.

Sūtra 39   अपरिग्रहस्थैर्ये जन्मकथन्ता संबोधः ॥ ३९ ॥

aparigrahasthairye janmakathantā sambodhaḥ

On becoming steady in non-possessiveness, knowledge arises of how and why birth comes.

अपरिग्रह	*aparigraha*	non-possessiveness, non-hoarding
स्थैर्ये	*sthairye*	in the confirmation, on becoming steady
जन्म कथन्ता	*janma kathantā*	how and wherefore of birth
संबोधः	*sambodhaḥ*	the knowledge

In this *sūtra*, the perfection of *aparigraha* (non-possessiveness) is explained. The greatest attachment or feeling of possession is the identification of the "I" with the mind-body complex. From this basic sense of identity, which is egoism, the notion develops that "I am the performer and enjoyer of actions and objects." This possessiveness expands through a deepening attachment to objects and experiences. In this way, possessiveness naturally arises from beingness. This sense of self-identity, the ego of individuality, is hard to renounce.

By not hoarding unnecessary objects, the mind starts to develop non-attachment to all objects. Non-attachment weakens the desire for acquiring and possessing objects. The mind gradually develops non-attachment even for one's body. Then, in the absence of desire and attachment, the ego stops identifying itself as a performer and enjoyer, and instead dwells in a state of dispassion. In that state, the intellect (*buddhi*) becomes very pure and achieves knowledge of past births. "Who I was in past birth, where I was, and what I will be in future births" can be known.

Why don't we always remember past births, since the latencies (*samskāras*) of past births already exist in the mind? The identification of the ego with the body is the cause of forgetting our past identities. There are two faces to the ego: the one that owns the gross body and the one that owns the subtle body. The subtle body contains all the *samskāras* (latent impressions of past experiences) and *vāsanās* (desires, tendencies, urges to act), and it is the cause of the gross body.

The ego that had identified the previous body as "I am" no longer exists after the death of that body. When the individual soul (*jīvātma*)[1] reincarnates, a new ego develops and says, "I am this mind-body complex." The mind-body complex of the past life is completely forgotten. So in each birth this ego relates only to the new body, and does not remember the past births.

A *yogi* who is well established in non-possessiveness has purified his or her mind of the attachment to the current gross body ego, and thus becomes capable of knowing about each incarnation of the individual soul (*jīvātmā*).

---

1 In this case, the term *jīvātma*, which is not from Sāmkhya, is being used instead of "subtle body." The *jīvātma* is the embodied *puruṣa* that reincarnates until liberation is attained.

Note

The practice of *aparigraha*, which is the final restraint (*yama*), is to not hoard any object that is non-essential to maintaining life in the world. The key word in this practice is non-essential. The *sūtra* does not say that we should burn all our possessions. It means that we should limit our possessions to those that are necessary for our life in the world.

When the ego is permitted free reign, it wants to possess everything. Nothing is ever enough, and it constantly seeks to acquire more even when some external limit is placed on it. This tendency of the ego keeps the mind very active and entirely absorbed in the outer reality. Therefore, it is a tremendous obstacle to *sādhana* (spiritual practice).

All aspirants need to place limits on the ego. In fact, all the practices of *yoga* can be understood as different ways to limit the ego. With *aparigraha*, the limit is on possessions. In society, we are identified and judged by our possessions. Where we live, what we wear, and what we drive are all significant factors in our social worlds. The question of what is needed to live in society is a gray area. At first, we may believe that everything we own is necessary, but if we look carefully, we can see many things that aren't needed. If we have the courage to give them away, then we are practicing *aparigraha*.

This very act of giving away what is unneeded purifies the mind. As the mind becomes more pure, it sees that other possessions are not needed, so it gives them away also. Through this process, everything but the essentials are given up. What is the result? The result is the decrease of attachment in general and the increase of dispassion. This dispassion changes the way we relate to everything: our possessions, our families, even our bodies. The feeling that they belong to "me" disappears.

The main problem with possessions is that they don't come for free; they come with attachment. To say that it is impossible to own something without attachment is redundant because the very notion of ownership is a form of attachment. By definition, the more we own, the greater our attachment.

An objection arises. What about the great king Janaka? He was an enlightened sage who happened to be a king with great wealth, huge palaces, and thousands of servants. He is an example of a person who owned a tremendous amount without attachment.

The objection is correct from an external perspective, but not from an internal one, where it counts. Yes, King Janaka's wealth was great by any standard, but he did not feel like it belonged to him. Instead, he felt that it was his duty as king to manage the property in a way that benefitted the society as a whole. The difference may seem like semantics, but the effect on the mind is profound.

The mind that "owns" possessions must protect and maintain them. Anxiety is created because there are so many external forces that get in the way, such as thieves, competitors, careless people, and extreme weather. The ego has identified itself as the owner of these possessions, so any threats to the objects are also threats to the ego itself. This anxiety is a powerfully driving force in the mind whose external orientation thwarts any attempt at meditation.

The pure mind that doesn't identify with any objects of the world, including those objects required for life in the world, develops dispassion even for the body. The ego that had been identifying the "I" with the body atrophies and finally disappears. Simultaneously, the feeling of "I" expands beyond the body until it becomes universal. The universal mind is capable of recognizing the *saṁskāras* (latent tendencies) of the body and knowing their sources, which were the previous incarnations of the subtle body or *jīvātma* (individual soul).

The commentary explains that there are two faces to the ego: one that identifies with the gross body and one that identifies with the subtle body. When the ego's identification faces the gross body, the mind's understanding is limited to that body. When that identification is weakened and finally eliminated, the ego only identifies with the subtle body. It thus becomes capable of remembering its previous incarnations because the subtle body is what transmigrates from one gross body to another.

In the next two *sūtras*, the results of perfecting physical and mental purity are described.

Śhri Hanumānji

Sūtra 40 शौचात्स्वाङ्गजुगुप्सापरैरसंसर्गः ॥ ४० ॥

śhauchāt–svāṅga–jugupsā–parair–asaṁsargaḥ

From [the perfection of] cleanliness, [there arises] indifference to one's own body and cessation of contact with others.

शौचात्	*śhauchāt*	from cleanliness or purity
स्वाङ्ग	*svāṅga*	to one's own body
जुगुप्सा	*jugupsā*	indifference
परैः	*paraiḥ*	with others
असंसर्गः	*asaṁsargaḥ*	non contact

Purity is of two kinds: external purity, which is purity of the body and its outer surroundings, and internal purity, which is purity of the mind in thoughts, feelings, and actions. Mind and body are interrelated. External purity develops internal purity and vice-versa.

In reality, the physical body is an impure object. It is only a bundle of flesh, bones, secretions, and waste products. None of these components is attractive by itself, but we don't see the body as such. We see it as beautiful and get attached to it. By developing a habit of cleanliness, a person sees the body with all its components and waste products. Dispassion for one's body develops and this creates non-attachment for one's own body and the bodies of others.

This non-attachment is not created by hateful ideas about the body, but rather it is created by the true knowledge of the gross body. Non-attachment to one's own body stops the desire for physical contact with others. It is a state of purified mind which is conducive to achieving *samādhi*.

Note

In this *sūtra*, the result of external purity is described, and the relationship between *śhaucha* (purity) and *brahmacharya* (sexual continence) is established. The gross body is impure, but when the mind is impure, the body appears to be an attractive source of pleasure. Through the process of trying to purify the gross body, its flaws and limitations are seen clearly, and dispassion arises for both one's own body and the bodies of others.

When aspirants see how impure the body is, they start to practice *śhaucha* (purification of the body). They bathe regularly and wear clean clothes. They eat a healthy diet of freshly cooked food in the right amounts at the right times. They exercise moderately. Furthermore, these practices purify the mind in addition to the body when the motive is *sāttvika* (pure). Then, as the mind gets purified, it sees even more impurities in the body. There may be an excess of phlegm or bile, or the digestion may be weak. All of these create problems in meditation. So, the aspirant may practice *ṣhaṭ karma*, which are methods to fix these problems.

The practices of *ṣhaṭ karma* create dispassion for the gross body. The more an aspirant tries to get rid of the impurities in the body, the more they realize that the nature of the gross body is impure; there is no possibility of having a totally pure gross body. But since the gross body is needed for life in the world, the *yogi* does not destroy it, but instead treats it only as a tool for *sādhana* and service.

Attraction to the gross body as a source of pleasure actually comes from a dullness of mind. That dullness seeks excitement, which it finds in the contact of the senses with objects. But, when the mind is extremely pure, the contacts of the senses with their objects creates a disturbance in the mind, not excitement.

As with all the restraints (*yamas*) and observances (*niyamas*), the practices of purification (*śhaucha*) should be gradual. The beginning practices are disciplines of cleanliness such as bathing, brushing your teeth, flossing, wearing clean and untorn clothes, keeping your living and working areas neat and clean, improving your diet and lifestyle, which includes limiting and eliminating intoxicants and stimulants. In time, these have a real effect, and as long as the effort doesn't stop, the rest takes care of itself.

In the next *sūtra*, internal purity is explained.

Sutra 41 सत्त्वशुद्धि सौमनस्यैकाग्र्येन्द्रियजयात्मदर्शनयोग्यत्वानि च ॥४१॥

sattva–shuddhi saumanasyaikāgryendriya–jayātma–darshana–
yogyatvāni cha

From purification of the mind, [there arises] cheerfulness, one-point-edness, control of the senses, and fitness for the vision of the Self.

सत्त्व	*sattva*	mind
शुद्धि	*shuddhi*	purity
सौमनस्य	*saumanasya*	cheerfulness
एकाग्र्य	*ekāgrya*	one-pointedness
इन्द्रिय	*indriya*	senses
जय	*jaya*	control
आत्म	*ātma*	the Self
दर्शन	*darśhana*	vision, the knowledge
योग्यत्वानि	*yogyatvāni*	fitness for
च	*cha*	and

In the preceding *sutra*, Patañjali explained how physical cleanliness leads to dispassion for one's own body as well as toward physical contact in general. In this *sutra*, Patañjali gives the result of mental purity (*sattva shuddhi*).

The mind as an evolute of *prakriti* is constituted by the three *guṇas*. *Sattva guṇa* is the quality of purity, goodness, and knowledge. *Rajas* is the quality of activity and passion. *Tamas* is the quality of inertia and ignorance. When *rajas* and *tamas* are predominant in the mind, the impurities of ego, attachment, and desire give rise to anger, fear, greed, lust, violence, and all other forms of negative thoughts.

When these negative thoughts and feelings are eliminated, it is called *sattva shuddhi* (the pure state of mind). In this state, *sattva guṇa* predominates in the mind; *rajas* and *tamas guṇas* are reduced so much that they cannot oppose the quality of *sattva*, even though they remain as a support. In this pure state of mind, one achieves cheerfulness or joy, which is an attribute of *sattva guṇa*. Concentration flows naturally in one-pointedness and the senses remain under control. *Rajas guṇa* (passion) and *tamas guṇa* (inertia) are so weak that they cannot disturb the mind and senses. As a result, the mind is established in purity and becomes fit to realize the Self.

Note

There are two kinds of purity—external and internal—which are separate but related. External purity and its fruit are described in the previous *sutra*. Attachment to one's own body and attraction to others' bodies are two of the greatest pulls of worldliness. When external purity is achieved, these two pulls are so greatly weakened that they cease to influence the mind. Now, in this *sutra*, the fruits of internal purity are described as cheerfulness, one-pointedness, control of the senses, and fitness for the vision of the Self.

In order to understand this *sūtra*, we have to understand what is meant by mental purity. According to the *Sūtras*, mental purity means free from the pull of the world. One way to understand it is in terms of the *guṇas*. A pure mind is *sāttvika*, while the impurities are the predominance of *rajas* and/or *tamas*. These latter two create what we call the normal condition of being human. In it, there is a strong sense of individuality and the mind is completely identified with the variety of experiences that occur. There may be times of great happiness or great sadness, but they do not last for long. Mostly, the experience is of fluctuation and instability.

The purpose of *yoga* is to bring about liberation of the embodied soul. The purpose of life, on the other hand, is first to have a broad spectrum of experiences (*bhoga*) and then to become free from the effects of those experiences (*apavarga*). *Yoga*, therefore, is a vehicle for moving from immersion in experience to freedom from experience.

The philosophies of *yoga* do not say that experiencing the world is bad or wrong. And yet, the philosophies and practices of *yoga* are for those people who are eager to finish their experiences of the world. The average person has no problem generating new experiences; indeed, they are unrelenting. But often the specific experiences generated are not exactly desired. Many people are confused about life, about how the world works, and about how they can find happiness in the world. Even though the practices of *yoga* can be used toward this worldly end, the original purpose of the philosophy is to free the aspirant from all individualized experiences, not just the obviously bad ones.

It is for these reasons that the term "impure" refers to the aspirant's inclination toward experience. Purity, therefore, is the absence of all worldliness. It is highly desirable by itself because it brings cheerfulness, one-pointedness, control of the senses, and fitness for the vision of the Self. But even more importantly, it is absolutely required for liberation. So long as the mind is attracted to the world in any form, the *vṛittis* (thoughts) will continue to revolve, thus perpetuating bondage of the soul. Why?

There is only one possible way that the mind can be attracted to the world. It is called egoism, and it means that the notion of "I" is linked to the mind-body complex. This linkage is based only on ignorance, and ignorance is bondage.

The *sūtra* states that cheerfulness is the first attribute of purity. At first, it may seem odd that they should be linked, but upon further examination it is obvious. Purity is the absense of worldliness, which means that the aspirant no longer looks to experiences of the world to generate lasting happiness. The body, of course, continues to function as normal, but the world is no longer considered a remedy for the problem of suffering in life.

Purity and one-pointedness are also inextricably linked. In this case, the term "one-pointedness" refers to the mind's ability to concentrate on one object during meditation. In order for perfect concentration to occur, all extraneous thoughts must be removed from the mind. When the mind is attracted to the world, the world stays with the mind at all times. By definition, when any aspect of the external world is in the mind, there cannot be one-pointed concentration. The idea of the world requires at least three things: "I," the body, and at least one object to be experienced.

True one-pointed concentration only occurs in *samādhi*. Before *samādhi*, the sense of separate existence is always present in the mind. Even *dhyāna*, which technically is the uninterrupted repetition of one thought in the mind, is not true one-pointed concentration because that repeated thought still contains the "I" as meditator separate from the object of concentration. It is only in *samādhi* that the separateness of the "I" and the object dissolves, leaving only the one object in the mind.

Control of the senses is a very significant benefit of purity. The senses are the vehicles for experience. Their nature is to go out and contact their objects. The ears contact sound; the skin seeks texture and temperature; the eyes, color and form; the tongue, flavor; and the nose, odor.

But the senses don't work alone. They always carry the mind with them. The mind consciously directs the senses when there is a specific desire, but in the absense of such a directed will, the senses flit hither and thither. We see examples of this all the time. In the middle of a conversation, some object attracts the eye, and the mind loses its train of thought. A particular smell triggers a memory, and an intricate daydream begins. The temperature changes, and everyone starts talking about the weather. In these cases, the contact of the senses with their objects initiates action in the mind.

So long as there is an underlying hope for happiness in the experiences of the world, there can be no control of the senses. This hope (or impurity) is like an unrestrained license for the senses. It is like a general order for the troops to keep on the lookout for any meaningful activity.

In contrast, the purified mind has no hope that any contact of the senses with their objects will bring lasting happiness. Instead, it recognizes that these contacts always bring alternating notions of pleasurable and painful sensations. They arise, get noticed, and then disappear, no matter whether they are sought or rejected. The problem is not in the senses, but in the mind. Therefore, the purified mind treats the senses as instruments and nothing more. Their benefits and dangers are known and acknowledged. Instead of being mercenaries on the lookout for pleasure and meaning, the senses are considered rebels or seditionists whose activities disrupt and destabilize the mind. They are watched and guarded by the purified mind, which has no desire for their bounty.

Finally, the *sūtra* says that only the pure mind is fit for the vision of the Self. The Self cannot be perceived by the senses nor even understood by the mind. Instead, the phrase "vision of the Self" refers to the realization that comes when all mental activity ceases.

The Self is pure, undifferentiated consciousness. It is the basis for all forms of worldly experiences even though it never changes. All the content of these experiences is generated by the three *guṇas*. We say that pure consciousness is the basis for this content because without it, the *guṇas* simply do not function. And yet, so long as the *guṇas* are active in the mind, the Self is hidden. This is known as the impure mind. But when the mind is made so pure that the activities of *rajas* and the confusion of *tamas* are rendered insignificant, all mental content is stilled and the underlying consciousness can be perceived as the Self of all.

Purification of the mind is the perfection of *śhaucha*, but it is a result of all the practices of *yoga*. The more the mind and body are purified through *sādhana*, the less interesting the world of experience becomes. The less interesting the world of experience becomes, the more the mind is purified. These two feed each other until supreme dispassion is attained. Supreme dispassion is the direct cause of the vision of the Self.

In the next *sūtra*, the perfection of contentment is described.

Sūtra 42　　संतोषादनुत्तमः सुखलाभः ॥ ४२ ॥

saṅtoṣhādanuttamaḥ sukhalābhaḥ

Unsurpassed happiness is gained by contentment.

सन्तोषाद	*santoṣhāda*	by contentment
अनुत्तमः	*anuttamaḥ*	unsurpassed, extreme
सुख	*sukha*	happiness
लाभः	*lābhaḥ*	acquisition, gained

In the previous two *sutras*, the perfection of external and internal purity was given. Now, in this *sutra*, the perfection of contentment is described as unsurpassed happiness. In normal states of mind, the predominance of *rajas guṇa* (quality of activity and passion) keeps the mind preoccupied with thoughts of external objects and plans to procure them. Whatever happiness the mind feels when it obtains the desired object is short-lived, quickly replaced with discontentment because new desires arise in the mind.

True contentment is achieved only when the mind is free from the qualities of *tamas guṇa* and *rajas guṇa*. In that contentment, the mind wants nothing and remains satisfied with what it already has. There is complete elimination of new desires that cause unhappiness.

By achieving perfect contentment, one achieves a state of extreme happiness (bliss). This happiness far exceeds the happiness that arises from acquiring objects of desire. In fact, Vyāsa says that even the pleasures of heaven do not compare to the unsurpassed happiness of true contentment: "Whatever pleasure there is in the world of desires and whatever larger happiness there is in the world of heaven, they are not one-sixteenth the joy that comes from the absence of desires."

Note

Continuing with the description of the perfection of the *yamas* and *niyamas*, this *sutra* describes the happiness that comes from true contentment. There are several kinds of happiness that can be experienced in the world. The most common form is that which results from pleasure of the senses. When we contact or possess a desired object, we experience pleasure, which is a form of happiness.

Another type of happiness comes from success. When we work hard to achieve something, a different type of happiness arises that lasts longer than the pleasures of the senses. The ego is gratified, and feels proud of its accomplishments. A third type of happiness comes from serving others. A deep satisfaction arises in the mind when our hard work benefits others. This satisfaction lasts much longer than either of the other two.

Most people spend their greatest efforts pursuing the first kind of happiness. The people who achieve the most worldly success spend their greatest efforts pursuing the second kind. Saints and sincere devotees spend their greatest efforts serving others and thus experiencing profound happiness. But this *sutra* is talking about something all together different.

In these three types of happiness, some form of desire is being fulfilled. In the first, physical desire is gratified. In the second, achievement and self-importance are attained. In the third, feelings of love and connection are deepened. This *sutra*, however, is talking about the unsurpassed happiness that comes from the absence of desire.

Why is it unsurpassed? Because nothing can diminish it. In the three types of worldly happiness, there is always the threat of its going away. With sense gratification, it is guaranteed to go away quickly. With worldly success, there is always some competitor who tries to take it away. With service, there is a desire for results (that the efforts will be beneficial and not harmful), and there is almost always a hidden desire for recognition. In any case, these forms of happiness are dependent on the right conditions for their fulfillment.

True contentment means accepting everything that comes unsought, and not seeking anything that doesn't come unsought. Life happens according to God's will or the laws of nature, depending on your philosophy. Without desires of attraction and repulsion, a profound happiness arises. And since there is never anything to attain or achieve, there are no conditions that can affect it. It is unsurpassed and unshakable. The sage Vyāsa even says that it is far greater than the highest happiness of heaven.

In the next *sutra*, the perfection of austerity is described.

Sūtra 43   कायेन्द्रियसिद्धिरशुद्धिक्षयात् तपसः ॥ ४३ ॥

kāyendriya–siddhir–aśhuddhi–kṣhayāt tapasaḥ

Upon destruction of impurities through austerity, there comes perfection in the body and sense organs.

काय	*kāya*	body
इन्द्रिय	*indriya*	senses
सिद्धि:	*siddhiḥ*	perfection, occult powers
अशुद्धि	*aśhuddhi*	impurities
क्षयात्	*kṣhayāt*	due to destruction
तपस:	*tapasaḥ*	austerities

In the previous *sutra*, the perfection of contentment was described. Now, the perfection of austerity is explained. Austerities purify the mind, body, and senses, just as heating purifies metal. The word *tapasaḥ* comes from the root *tāpa*, which means to heat. Just as metal is heated to separate the dross and purify the metal, enduring the pain (heat) of austerities (*tapasaḥ*) purifies the body and sense organs. In *tapasya* (the practice of austerities), some limitation is accepted. Hunger and thirst are endured in fasting, heat and cold are endured throughout the year, and the pain caused by limiting desires is endured in *yogic* discipline.

The purpose of practicing austerities is to purify the mind, body, and sense organs, all of which function by the flow of *prāṇa* (life force). Making the life force (*prāṇa*) healthy and strong also purifies the body and sense organs. The regular practice of *prāṇāyāma* (breath control) is also considered an austerity because the life force is strengthened.

A *yogi* who is completely purified by the regular practice of austerities (*tapasaḥ*) develops a healthy body and perfect functioning of the sense organs. This *sūtra* can also mean that a *yogi* develops *siddhis* (occult powers) by performing austerities. When impurities are destroyed through the practice of austerities, minor occult powers like clairvoyance and clairaudience are developed.

Note

In this *sūtra*, the perfection of the practice of austerities is described. *Yogic* austerities are practices that generate a purifying heat in the mind and body. But exactly what is being purified, and how? There are four levels to the answer of this question: the problem, the cause of the problem, the solution, and the results of implementing the solution.

The *sūtra* specifically says that austerities bring about perfection of the body and senses. For the *yogi* aspiring to achieve liberation from all suffering, perfection of the body and senses means that they simply become agents of the discriminating intellect and not distractions for it. In the normal condition of life, the senses and their objects keep the mind actively engaged in the pursuit of pleasure and the avoidance of pain. This is a considerable problem for aspiring *yogis* because it is the primary obstacle to one-pointed concentration and meditation. Unless this restlessness of the mind can be curbed, progress in *yoga* will always be limited.

What is the cause of this restlessness? Using the language of Sāṁkhya, the intellect is the vehicle through which the indwelling spirit experiences the world, and the mind, body, and senses are the vehicles through which the intellect generates those experiences. All experiences of the world are generated by the intellect recognizing and responding to the contact of the senses with their objects. Without this, no experiences are possible.

The intellect is the source of the manifest "I am," which means that the indwelling Self can only be known by the intellect. Normally, though, the intellect functions outwardly through the mind, body, and senses in such a way that the indwelling spirit is united with the intellect as if they were one. So long as this outer orientation is active, the separation of the intellect and the Self, which is the goal of *yoga*, is impossible.

This means that the practices of *yoga* must be designed to curb the outer flow of the mind and strengthen the inner resolve of the intellect. This is where austerity (*tapasya*) comes in. Most people are highly attached to their bodies. They are elated by pleasurable sensations, troubled by discomfort, and dismayed by pain. They find it difficult to concentrate on one task because the mind, body, and senses are constantly pulling them from one object or idea to another. Thus, they have very little control over their reactions to external stimuli, which creates high levels of anxiety. In these ways, the intellect—and by association, the Self—is ruled not only by the mind, body, and senses, but also by the external circumstances of life.

For the *yogi* with discrimination, however, the reverse is true. He or she becomes the ruler of the mind, body, and senses, engaging them when needed, and setting them to rest when not needed. Even if an opportunity for pleasure arises unexpectedly, *yogis* are not distracted because they understand the cyclical nature of experience. Instead, concentration and awareness are the characteristics of their intellects, which means that the predominant experience for such *yogis* is peace and stability.

To understand how austerities purify the mind, we have to understand how the ego and intellect work together. The intellect is the dual functioning of discrimination and will. The ego is the principle of ownership that directs the will. When the ego has complete control over the will, every thought, word, and action is oriented toward generating pleasure and avoiding pain for itself.

How does the intellect become free from the ego's subjugation? The answer is through austerity. Austerities are disciplined actions that counteract the ego's natural tendency toward comfort, security, and pleasure. Each act of austerity strengthens the will and weakens the ego's control. The outward flow of the mind is contained, the ability to concentrate improves dramatically, and the experience of peace dawns.

In practice, though, not all austerities are considered equal. The Bhagavad Gītā categorizes the exercising of the will, called *dhṛti* (firmness), according to the predominant *guṇa*. *Sāttvika* firmness is when the mind, *prāṇa*, and senses are restrained from their outgoing nature so that the mind may be concentrated in *samādhi*. *Rājasika* firmness is when the mind, *prāṇa*, and senses are directed outward toward the three positive aims of life: *dharma* (virtue), *artha* (honest wealth), and *kāma* (appropriate pleasures). *Tāmasika* firmness is when the mind, *prāṇa*, and senses are used for selfish, misguided, and destructive ends. The *yogic* practice of austerities is the means to move from *tāmasika* and *rājasika* uses of the intellect to *sāttvika* uses.

Relating this back to the earlier discussion, *tāmasika* firmness is when the intellect is used exclusively with ego-driven or self-interested motives. *Rājasika* firmness is when the motives are mixed; the ego still expects to achieve pleasure and satisfaction through its outgoing efforts, but now it is hoping that these efforts benefit others as well. This could be called a "win-win" approach. The *sāttvika* firmness, on the other hand, rejects the outgoing desires of the ego entirely in order to remain established in one-pointed concentration.

An objection arises. If the *rājasika* approach is "win-win," what is the motivation to become *sāttvika* and completely absorbed in meditation? The answer is that the ego is still expecting to get a result. This expectation is based on desire and attachment. And, so long as desire and attachment remain in the mind, some form of suffering will also remain.

The *rājasika* person does not fully accept this understanding and has hope that their experience of pleasure will exceed their experience of pain. The *sāttvika* person, on the other hand, fully accepts it. Their hope for achieving happiness through the activities of the world has been extinguished. This is called dispassion for the world. One who cultivates dispassion turns away from the activities of the senses and employs their greatest efforts in meditation.

The purification of the mind, body, and senses through austerity is often compared to the purification of gold through heating. Gold is purified by melting it, which separates the dross from the metal. Then, charcoal powder is applied to the mixture. The charcoal powder burns away the dross without leaving any residue. The end result is simply purified gold.

The practices of austerity "heat" the body and mind by disappointing the ego's desire for comfort and gratification. All the attachments and desires present in the mind are revealed for what they are: sources of misery. This is like separating the dross from the metal. This process takes place all the way to discriminative wisdom. Then, supreme dispassion (*paravairāgya*) arises, which is the charcoal powder that burns away all the final impurities (*vyutthāna saṁskāras*) while burning away itself. The result is *asamprajñāta samādhi*, which is the self isolated in the self or liberation.

The commentary mentions that perfection of the body and senses can also be understood as developing *siddhis* (supernormal abilities). As the mind becomes purified and one-pointed concentration is perfected, extraordinary powers become available to the *yogi*. They are achieved by tremendous exercises of will (see *Vibhūti Pāda*), which are made possible by intense austerities. Ironically, to achieve them requires great control over the ego, but their use is a great temptation to the ego and can expand and strengthen its influence over the intellect. Therefore, the scriptures describe these powers as obstacles to liberation.

In the next *sūtra*, the perfection of self-study is explained.

Sūtra 44   स्वाध्यायादिष्टदेवतासंप्रयोगः ॥ ४४ ॥

svādhyāyādiṣhṭadevatā–samprayogaḥ

By self-study comes communion with the desired deity.

स्वाध्यायाद	*svādhyāyāda*	from self-study
इष्टदेवता	*iṣhṭadevatā*	desired deity
संप्रयोगः	*samprayogaḥ*	union, communion

In the previous *sutra*, the result of perfecting the practice of austerity was described. Now, in this *sutra*, the perfection of self-study is explained. Self-study (*svādhyāya*) means investigating the nature of the Self, generally through three methods: study of the scriptures, deep reflection into the mind and its causes, and absorption into a deity by repeating its *mantra*. In this *sutra*, the term *svādhyāya* is specifically used for repetition of a *mantra* with the mind completely absorbed in the meaning and form of the deity.

The term *iṣhṭadevatā* means a form of God chosen by the devotee as a vehicle for worshiping the Absolute. By continuous recitation of the *mantra* with the mind fixed on its meaning and the form of the deity, a divine presence arises in the heart of the devotee. This divine presence removes the mind from worldly desires and attachments, and the *yogi's* mind becomes pure, full of faith, devotion, and dispassion. When this state of self-study (*svādhyāya*) is well established, the *yogi* comes into communion with the desired deity.

Note

The practice of self-study has several forms, all oriented toward investigating the nature of the Self. This *sutra* is speaking about the specific devotional practice in which the mind is absorbed in the repetition of a *mantra* of the chosen deity. This practice works by switching the mind from its normal preoccupation with worldly reality and bodily existence to an internalized, concentrated state. It is only in highly concentrated states that the mind can contemplate the subtle nature of the Self.

The *sutra* says that self-study brings about communion with the desired deity. From a devotional standpoint, the *yogi* merges with the form of God that had been worshipped through the *mantra*. Communion means that the selfless qualities of the deity are adopted by the devotee. The mind is habitual by nature, and whatever it dwells on grows in the mind. When a devotee perfects self-study, the mind dwells completely on the form and qualities of God and thereby takes on those qualities.

A question arises. The Self (absolute *puruṣha*) is pure, undifferentiated consciousness. It is beyond all names, forms, and qualities, and thus it is beyond the possibility of comprehension by the mind. The mind is limited by time and space and cannot conceive of anything outside of them. So how, then, can we concentrate on God when God cannot be conceived by the mind?

The answer is that a form of God is created for the purpose of contemplation and devotion. The form itself is not God, but it is endowed with positive qualities that purify the mind. The more pure the mind gets, the quieter it gets, and the more the formless radiance of the Infinite shines. Eventually, all the impurities of the mind are washed away, and nothing separates the mind from God.

In devotional practices, the image and form of God must be attractive to appeal to the heart of the devotee. So many forms of God have been created because there are so many different types of people in the world. Ultimately, it doesn't matter which form of God one worships so long as the mind is purified by dwelling on the positive qualities of that form. It is the constant dwelling on the love and selfless nature of the God that brings about the desired result and not the particular form of God.

The other two primary means of *svādhyāya* are reflection or inquiry and the study of scriptures. Inquiry is an intellectual approach in which the mind is used to discriminate the various activities and functions of the mind and body. Each activity is recognized in its real form, and then its cause is sought. All physical objects have elemental causes. The elemental causes have subtle causes, and the subtle causes have a universal cause. When the mind is absorbed in the universal cause, it is capable of seeing the Self.

The study of scriptures means using accepted teachings of liberation and the removal of suffering to guide the aspirant's life and spiritual practices. It can take either a devotional or an intellectual approach, depending on the aspirant and/or the scripture studied. The *Bhagavad Gītā*, for example, is studied by both devotees and intellectuals, while the *Sāmkhya Kārikā* is primarily a *jñāni* (intellectual) text. Regardless of the text, studying scripture and applying its teaching brings the mind away from the outer world and toward the inner Self.

The obstacles to *samādhi* and peace are selfishness, attachment, and desire. The practice of self-study works to minimize these three no matter which method or which form of God is used. The Self, or energy of consciousness, permeates everything in creation, so anything in creation can be used to rediscover the truth about the Self.

Those who perfect self-study achieve communion with the chosen deity, which means that they embody all the positive, universal, and selfless characteristics of the divine.

In the next *sūtra*, the result of surrender to God is described.

Sūtra 45　समाधिसिद्धिरीश्वरप्रणिधानात् ॥ ४५ ॥

samādhi–siddhir–īshvarapraṇidhānāt

From surrender to God, superconsciousness is attained.

समाधि	*samādhi*	trance, superconsciousness
सिद्धिः	*siddhih*	success, the attainment
ईश्वरप्रणिधानात्	*Īshvarapraṇidhānāt*	from self surrender

This *sutra* concludes Patañjali's explanation of the results of perfecting the *yamas* (restraints) and *niyamas* (observances) by stating that the perfection of surrendering to God brings about *samādhi* (superconsciousness). The practice of surrender to God is described in several places through the *Yoga Sūtras*. It is a method of achieving *samādhi* in Sūtra I:23, an aspect of Kriyā Yoga in Sūtra II:1, and one of the five *niyamas* in Sūtras II:32 & 45.

In this practice of surrender to God (*Īshvara praṇidhāna*) as one of the *niyamas*, a devotee's ego of being a performer, enjoyer, or sufferer is gradually reduced. Consequently, the mind of the devotee naturally flows toward God (*Īshvara*) without any obstructing thought waves. This process purifies the mind, which strengthens dispassion for the world. The more dispassion is strengthened, the more the mind surrenders to God. Total surrender to God brings success in trance (*samādhi*).

Even though Patañjali clearly establishes devotional surrender to God as an independent method of achieving *samādhi* in Sūtra I:23, "Or by devotional surrender to God [*samādhi* can be obtained quickly]" (*Īshvara praṇidhānādva*), without practicing the other seven limbs of Aṣhṭāṅga Yoga, the devotee cannot cultivate dispassion. Therefore, the practice of surrender to God (*Īshvara praṇidhāna*) in conjunction with the practices of Aṣhṭāṅga Yoga accelerates success in achieving *samādhi*.

Note

In this *sutra*, the perfection of *Īshvara praṇidhāna* is described as success in *samādhi*. Immediately, a couple of questions arise. Given that the practice of surrender to God is described variously throughout the text, which form is referenced here? Which type of *samādhi* is achieved? And, is this success independent of the other *yamas*, *niyamas*, and limbs of *yoga*?

To answer these questions, we have to break things down and ask simpler questions. In the practice of *Īshvara praṇidhāna*, who surrenders what, and to whom? What is *samādhi*, and how is it achieved? In answering these questions, the larger questions of the *sutra* will become obvious.

All the practices of *yoga* speak to the mental content of the aspirant. No matter what may happen in the outer world, every experience of life is known only through its mental content. In the *Sutras*, this mental content is known as the *chitta vṛittis*. *Yoga* itself was described in Sūtra I:2 as the control of *chitta vṛittis*.

If *yoga* is the control of mental content, then it must mean that the mental content is not under control most of the time. In fact, mental content has tremendous momentum of its own, and it is self-perpetuating. It is driven by selfishness, desires, and attachment, which are collectively known as the ego.[1] The forms the ego takes are as varied as there are people, but the general functioning is the same in everyone.

The ego's job is to generate beneficial experiences for itself. This means pursuing pleasure in all its forms and avoiding pain in all its forms. Ironically, it does not matter how successful these efforts are; both the experiences of pleasure and pain increase the strength of the ego. The practices of *yoga*, on the other hand, are unique in that they specifically weaken the ego. They all function in different ways, but the end result is the same.

This *sūtra* is specifically talking about the practice of surrender to God, in which God's will is consciously used instead of our own will. Will means intention; to act in a way that brings about a desired end. Without conscious intervention, all of our acts of will are selfish because the will (*buddhi*) is controlled by the ego. Surrender to God means to act intentionally for the benefit of God, whether or not the action brings benefit to us.

An objection arises. God's will is mysterious and infinite. There is no way that we mortals could ever comprehend it. Therefore, any attempts at fulfilling "God's will" must instead be disguised acts of self-interest.

The objection is partially true, but there is one essential factor that makes all the difference: intention. It is correct that we cannot know God's will, but the very intention to serve it purifies the mind. God is universal, so any time we act in a way that benefits the whole and not just ourselves, we weaken the selfish ego. The weaker the ego gets, the more capable the mind becomes of seeing the needs of the whole and the more capable it is of surrendering to God.

In this sense, it doesn't matter what form of God we choose or what ideas we have about God. So long as self-interest is constantly replaced by universal interest, there will be progress in *yoga*. Furthermore, there is a tremendous benefit to this process: the mind calms down. All thought waves are motivated by self-interest. Every thought is directly or indirectly seeking pleasure or avoiding pain. When the selfish ego has been substantially weakened, the mind stops dwelling on past events and worrying about future events. Instead, space is created, and in that space the mind becomes capable of one-pointed concentration. The perfection of one-pointed concentration is *samādhi*.

---

1 The ego is the *ahaṁkāra*, which is simply the individualizing principle in the mind. The *ahaṁkāra* itself does nothing but own experiences and separate one thing from another. Technically, the term *egoless* would be impossible for any living being. Colloquially, however, we use the term *ego* to refer to the selfish tendencies of an embodied being, and as such, the term *egoless* would mean an enlightened person whose mind has been purified of all selfish tendencies.

For a beginning practitioner, surrender to God simply means taking other people into consideration and wondering about the question of God. As we progress, we take ownership of fewer and fewer aspects of experience. We attribute the activities of creation to a higher power, and see that we are simply agents of that power. Gradually, our notions of self-identification go from seeing ourselves as a complex personality in a body to a collection of God-given energies and tendencies. Finally, when discriminative wisdom dawns, we recognize the "I" as pure consciousness alone.

This pure consciousness alone is God, and the perfection of surrender is when all other forms of identifications are relinquished for this ultimate and final identification. All individual notions are surrendered for the one, universal notion.

What then is *samādhi*? *Samādhi* is a special kind of one-pointed meditation in which the notion of "I" is merged in the object of concentration. Normally, all forms of mental activity are divided in such a way that the subject (the "I") is identified as separate from the object.

There are many types of *samādhi*, each classified according to the nature of the object of concentration, so which one is this *sūtra* referring to? The answer is all of them. When the practice of surrender is proficient, the lower *samādhis* are attained. As the practice gets perfected, the higher *samādhis* are attained. Finally, when all vestiges of individuality are wiped out through complete surrender to God, *asamprajñāta samādhi* is attained, which is final liberation.

While it is true that surrender to God can work alone in theory, in practice it is very difficult. The forces of the ego are extremely subtle, ubiquitous, and pervasive. It is virtually impossible to successfully disempower them without the various levels of practice throughout all eight limbs of Aṣṭāṅga Yoga. For those with a devotional bent, surrender to God can be the beacon by which all the other practices are guided.

The next three *sūtras* describe *āsana* (postures), the third limb of Yoga.

Coconut offering at yajña ceremony

Sūtra 46   स्थिरसुखमासनम् ॥ ४६ ॥

sthira–sukham–āsanam

The posture should be steady and comfortable.

स्थिर	*sthira*	steady
सुखम्	*sukham*	easy, comfortable
आसनम्	*āsanam*	posture

In Sūtras 30 to 45, the perfection of the restraints (*yama*) and observances (*niyama*) were explained. Now, in this *sutra*, the third limb of Aṣhṭāṅga Yoga, *āsana* (the posture) is explained.

The term *āsana* is often used to describe the wide variety of postures developed primarily through the Haṭha Yoga system. But in this *sutra*, it is used in its literal meaning, which is "seat." Sitting postures are primarily used in concentration (*dharanā*), meditation (*dhyāna*) and trance (*samādhi*), which are collectively called the internal limbs (*antaraṅga*) of Aṣhṭāṅga Yoga.

The word *sthira* means absence of all motions, so the *sutra* is indicating that while seated, the body should be free of all movements. The body should be positioned with the head, neck, and spine in alignment, but not rigid. As such, one should be able to sit comfortably (*sukham*) for a long time.

The eleven postures used for sitting meditation as listed by Vyāsa in his classical commentary are: *padmāsana* (lotus posture), *vīrāsana* (warrior posture), *bhadrāsana* (nobleman's posture), *svastikāsana* (easy lotus posture), *daṇḍāsana* (stick pose), *sopāśhrayāsana* (squat posture, in which a cloth is wrapped around the back and legs and then tied), *paryaṅkāsana* (corpse pose), *krauñchaniṣhadana* (a bird's resting pose), *hastiniṣhadana* (sitting posture of an elephant), *uṣhṭraniṣhadana* (sitting posture of a camel), and *samasaṁsthāna* (the squatting pose in which the heels and toes of both feet press each other).

In Haṭha Yoga system, 84 different postures (*āsana*) are listed. These different positions of the body are designed to make the body flexible, light, strong, and healthy.

Note

This *sutra* begins a discussion on the third limb of Aṣhṭāṅga Yoga. *Āsana* (posture) is positioning the body in a specific way designed to achieve a desired result. In the context of the *Yoga Sūtras*, the practice of *āsana* is designed to support *samādhi*. In order for the mind to be fully absorbed in *samādhi*, the body has to be absolutely still. Any movement of the body disturbs the mind and prevents one-pointed concentration.

Most people find it difficult to sit absolutely still for extended periods of time. Their "seat" is unsteady and uncomfortable. There are many causes for discomfort in the body, and all of them must be overcome before stability and comfort can be established. For most people, practicing the various *āsanas* described in the Haṭha Yoga system is the best way to become steady and comfortable in their body generally, and in their sitting practice specifically. The various postures have tremendous health benefits also, but it should be remembered that for Patañjali, the postures were not an end in themselves but rather a means to another end (*samādhi*).

This guideline that *āsanas* should be steady and comfortable can also be applied to all practices of the postures. The postures are not achievements in themselves, so their practice should be steady and comfortable. Sometimes, students push too hard, straining themselves in the posture. This is contrary to the aim of *āsana* and should be avoided. Students should find their limits at the edge of steadiness and comfort.

Progress in *āsana* is made through repeated practice. Gradually, we find that the body becomes stronger, more open and flexible, and steadier. The real indication of progress, though, can only be seen in meditation. When the body can be held motionless and comfortable for a long time without distracting the mind in any way, one is approaching perfection in *āsana*, which is described in the next *sūtra*.

In the next *sūtra*, the means for mastering posture are described.

Sūtra 47 प्रयत्नशैथिल्यानन्तसमापत्तिभ्याम् ॥ ४७ ॥

prayatna–śhaithilyānanta–samāpattibhyām

[Posture is mastered] by relaxation of effort and absorption in the infinite space.

प्रयत्न	*prayatna*	effort
शैथिल्य	*śhaithilya*	looseness, slackening, relaxation
अनन्त	*ananta*	endless, infinite space
समापत्तिभ्याम्	*samāpattibhyām*	by meditation, by absorption in

Having described the nature of meditative posture in the preceding *sūtra*, this *sūtra* gives the means to perfect the meditative posture. The body and mind get distracted away from the steadiness (*sthira*) and comfort (*sukha*) of a meditative posture (*āsana*) by pain. In the course of extended meditation, pain arises from rigidity in the posture and restlessness that comes from body consciousness.

When the body is forced to sit still in a particular meditative posture, the mind notices physical pressure and starts feeling pain. By loosening effort, the body becomes relaxed in the sitting position. It does not mean letting the body drop down by bending the spine, head, or neck. The spine, head, and neck should remain straight but not stiff. If the body remains rigid in the sitting position, then it will tire quickly and extended sitting becomes impossible.

The second distraction in the meditative posture is the mind. When the mind becomes conscious of the body and the outer world, two things happen. The mind starts identifying with pain in the sitting position, and it becomes restless from thoughts of the outer world. This *sūtra* says that while sitting in a meditative posture, body consciousness may be removed by fixing the mind on infinite space. The phrase *ananta samāpattibhyam* means absorption of the mind in infinite or endless space (*ananta*). *Ananta* is also the name for the mythological serpent who upholds the earth, so it can also mean absorption of the mind in that mythological serpent.

When the mind is switched from body consciousness to endless space, the rigidity of the body relaxes and one can sit for a longer period of time without any physical pain or mental restlessness. By the regular practice of sitting in a meditative posture in this way, a *yogi* achieves perfection in the sitting posture (*āsana siddhi*).

In the beginning of meditation practice, the aspirant should maintain a straight and steady posture and the mind should be aware of any unsteadiness in the posture. One should try to keep the body straight by tolerating pain to some degree. After some practice, the sitting posture becomes natural and effortless.

The results of perfecting the sitting posture (*āsana*) are described in the next *sūtra*.

Note

In the previous *sūtra*, the proper method for sitting postures (*āsana*) is described. Now, in this *sūtra*, the means of perfecting sitting postures is explained. Steadiness and comfort are the proper method, relaxation of effort and concentration on the infinite are the means of perfecting the method. Why?

Extended steadiness is not possible if the body is uncomfortable. The body cannot be comfortable if it is strained, exhausted, or activated. Therefore, the way to make the body comfortable and stable is to relax effort and disengage the mind from the world.

There are a variety of traditional sitting postures. The traditional meditation posture is the full lotus, in which each foot rests on the opposite thigh. This position provides the most stable base if it can be held comfortably for extended periods of time. If it cannot, then variations can be adopted in which one foot rests on the floor, or even both feet are on the floor. Sitting on a pillow or small platform can also make the posture more comfortable.

But no matter which position is adopted, discomfort and distraction will arise if there is not relaxation of effort and concentration on the infinite. Proper alignment of the body is necessary for relaxation of effort. If the body is too stiff to hold a proper alignment, then the aspirant should practice a variety of *yogic* postures that increase flexibility as described by Haṭha Yoga. Even when proper alignment can be established, the aspirant must allow the body to relax. This means that all effort becomes suspended once the posture is firmly established.

But steadiness is not a natural state for the mind and body. The three *guṇas* are constantly changing, encouraging the body to move. Whenever the body is held in one position for too long, some level of discomfort arises. Usually, the mind identifies with the discomfort ("I am uncomfortable"), and feels a strong urge to move and find comfort. This urge distracts the mind and body and makes steadiness impossible. Even if the aspirant decides not to move, significant effort must be employed to control the body's urge to move. This effort is exhausting and thus prohibits extended periods of sitting.

Therefore, the only way to become stable in a sitting posture is to remove the identification of the mind with the body. The method described in the *sūtra* is to concentrate on the infinite. Technically, though, the infinite is not something that can be conceived of by the mind because the infinite is beyond space and time and the mind always functions within space and time. So how can the mind concentrate on the infinite?

The intention to concentrate on the infinite requires that all other concepts in the mind be abandoned, at least temporarily. This includes the identification of the mind with the body. When the mind doesn't identify with the body, any discomfort that may arise in the body is not recognized by the mind. The pain doesn't distract the mind, and the mind doesn't encourage the body to move.

Another major obstacle to sitting for extended periods of time is the mind's worldliness. Worldliness means seeking pleasure and gratification in the objects of the world, including physical pleasures, wealth, and fame or recognition. Achieving these things is not easy, so the mind first has to plan and scheme extensively, and then engage the body in pursuit of its plans and goals. The body goes where the mind tells it to go. If the mind is busy with worldly hopes and plans, the body will feel the urge to become active. Then effort will be required to keep the body still, which is contrary to the perfection of *āsana*.

The solution is to concentrate the mind on the infinite as much as possible. But this is the highest form of meditation and difficult to perfect. For beginning and intermediate aspirants, any form of concentration will help steady the posture. No matter what, the mind can be returned to the object of concentration again and again, even if the mind notices discomfort in the body. Actually, returning to the object of concentration lessens the discomfort.

All of the practices of *yoga* are perfected by repetition. Humans are habitual creatures. The more we do something, the more deeply we do it. This is true for both virtues and vices. By establishing a daily routine of sitting meditation, the mind and body become habituated to it. Naturally and gradually, the resistance and obstacles to relaxation of effort and concentration on the infinite are weakened. The body becomes more comfortable and the mind becomes more focused. Moderate effort should be employed; enough to stretch our limits, but not so much that the mind rebels and all practices are stopped. In time, the posture is perfected.

In the next *sūtra*, the benefit of mastery of posture is described.

Ārati worship

Sūtra 48   ततो द्वन्द्वानभिघातः ॥ ४८ ॥

tato dvandvānabhighātaḥ

From that (mastery of posture), the pairs of opposites no longer disturb.

ततो	*tato*	from that, thereafter, then
द्वन्द्व	*dvandva*	pairs of opposites
अनभिघातः	*anabhighātaḥ*	no assault, cessation of disturbance

In the previous two *sutras*, the proper method of sitting and the means for its perfection were described. Now, in this *sutra*, the result of perfecting the sitting posture is described as being free from the disturbing effects of the pairs of opposites.

The pairs of opposites take both physical and mental forms. Physical sensations such as heat and cold, hunger and thirst are experienced by the body, whereas emotional and mental phenomena such as joy and sorrow, likes and dislikes are experienced by the mind. A master *yogi* doesn't get affected by the pairs of opposites, because the *yogi's* mind rises above the pairs of opposites when the sitting posture (*āsana*) is perfected.

When the sitting posture becomes relaxed and the *yogi's* mind is absorbed in the infinite, bodily pain and mental distractions are no longer identified. This removal of internal and external disturbances causes the mind to flow naturally toward the object of meditation.

What are the mechanics by which the perfection of *āsana* brings about the end of all mental disturbances? Perfection in *āsana* means relaxation of effort and absorption in the infinite. All "efforts" are expressions of ego, so the relaxation of effort weakens the ego. Also, the ego defines itself by its limits ("This is me and that is not me"). In concentration on the infinite, the ego can't find any boundaries and thus becomes dormant. So, when the meditative posture (*āsana*) is perfected, the ego doesn't identify with any of the physical and mental pairs of opposites.

Note
The *sutra* states that when sitting (*āsana*) is perfected, the pairs of opposites no longer disturb the mind of the *yogi*. The pairs of opposites are also known as life in the world. All experiences are known only in relation to their opposites. In the middle of a summer heat wave, a room air-conditioned to 70 degrees feels cold. In the middle of an icy winter, a room heated to 70 degrees feels hot. The room is the same temperature, but our experience of it is very different because of what we are comparing it to. The same is true of all experiences of life. Pain and pleasure are only known relative to each other and depend on our expectations.

The purpose of life is to experience this world of opposites (*bhoga*) and then to become free from it (*apavarga*). *Bhoga* is the active mind seeking pleasure. It is the core obstacle to yoga. When the mind is activated, steadiness in sitting is impossible. But removing the pull of the world is very difficult. Even for one with relatively high levels of dispassion, some aspect of the world distracts the mind. For each person, it may be different. For some, aversion to experiences such as hunger, thirst, cold, and death might activate the mind. For others, attraction to comfort, fame, wealth, and pleasure enters the mind. As soon as either one fills the mind, perfection in sitting is impossible. The effort to sit and meditate must be increased when anything but the infinite fills the mind.

The *sutra* says that perfection in *āsana* means the pairs of opposites lose their power to disturb the *yogi*. Ironically, the *yogi* must turn away from the pairs of opposites in order to perfect the posture. The point is that until perfection in *āsana* is achieved, there is a type of mental effort on the part of the *yogi* to relax the physical effort and concentrate on the infinite. But once perfection is achieved, the world of opposites, including the body and mind, ceases its pull on the *yogi*. Undisturbed concentration on the infinite becomes possible, and the highest levels of *samādhi* are attained.

In the next *sutra*, the third limb of Aṣhṭāṅga Yoga (*prāṇāyāma*) is introduced.

Sūtra 49   तस्मिन्सति श्वासप्रश्वासयोर्गतिविच्छेदः प्राणायामः ॥ ४९ ॥

tasmin–sati śhvāsa–praśhvāsayor–gati–vichchhedaḥ prāṇāyāmaḥ

On this (perfection of posture), the cessation of movement of inspiration and expiration of breath is called regulation of breath (*prāṇāyāma*).

तस्मिन्	*tasmin*	on this (that, the posture)
सति	*sati*	having been, being
श्वास	*śhvāsa*	inhalation, inspiratory
प्रश्वासयोः	*praśhvāsayoḥ*	and exhalation, of the expiratory breath
गति	*gati*	movement
विच्छेदः	*vichchhedaḥ*	break, stoppage
प्राणायामः	*prāṇāyāmaḥ*	regulation of breath

When mastery over the sitting posture is accomplished and all mental and physical disturbances caused by the pairs of opposites have ceased, then *prāṇāyāma* (breath control) is practiced. The term *prāṇāyāma* is made from root words: *prāṇa*, which means vital energy, and *ayāma*, which means regulation.[1] Therefore *prāṇāyāma* is a method of controlling the vital energy.

Outside air, taken in through the nostrils, is called *śhvāsa* (inspiration or inhalation). The air held in the lungs that is expelled through the nostrils is called *praśhvāsa* (expiration or exhalation). This process of inspiration and expiration of breath goes on continuously, keeping all living beings alive and healthy. *Prāṇa* (vital energy) is not the physical process of inhalation and exhalation of breath (*śhvāsa-praśhvāsa*), but rather it is a subtle energy derived from the natural flow of inspiration and expiration. In *prāṇāyāma*, when breathing is regulated, the *prāṇa* is also regulated, which supports concentration (*dhāraṇā*).

In expiration (*praśhvāsa*), when the air from the lungs is exhaled out, the inward flow of air (*śhvāsa*) is suspended. This is a natural *prāṇāyāma* that can be developed by consciously extending exhalation.

In inspiration (*śhvāsa*), when outside air is inhaled into the lungs through the nostrils, the outward flow of air (*praśhvāsa*) is likewise suspended. This is also a natural *prāṇāyāma* that can be enhanced by consciously extending the inhalation.

In the suspension of breath after the inhalation and exhalation, both inhalation and exhalation are suspended. This is also a *prāṇāyāma* that can be developed by concentration on the suspension of breath.

In this way, three varieties of *prāṇāyāmas* are practiced, one after another: inhale (*pūraka*), exhale (*rechaka*), and retention (*kumbhaka*).

---

1   The term *yāma* literally means restraining or ending, so adding the prefix *a* (non) would normally imply expanding or beginning. In the case of *prāṇa*, however, commentators disagree about the etymology of the term *ayāma*. Some say that it refers to the expansion of *prāṇa* through restraining the physical breath in a methodical way. Others say that it means restraining the *prāṇa* by focusing it on one point. From a practical standpoint, there is no disagreement; *prāṇāyāma* is the method of regulating the breath in order to control the mind.

So long as the mind is in a restless state, *prāṇāyāma* will not be conducive to *samādhi*. When the mind is free from all disturbances, *prāṇāyāma* will make concentration deep, which becomes *samādhi* in its higher states. To remove the restlessness of mind while practicing *prāṇāyāma*, one should fix the mind on one spiritual object like the concept of God, infinite luminosity in the heart center, or the feeling of void.

In *prāṇāyāma*, the thoughts in the mind are controlled by fixing the mind on one object or point of concentration. There is an exact correlation between thought distractions and the movement of *prāṇa*. When the mind is in a state of restlessness, the movement of breath will be irregular, which causes irregularity in the flow of *prāṇa*. By the practice of *prāṇāyāma*, the movement of breath is regulated, which automatically regulates the flow of *prāṇa* and also removes mental disturbances.

Note

In the previous three *sūtras*, the perfection of the sitting posture (*āsana*) was described. Now, in this *sūtra*, the practice of *prāṇāyāma* is introduced. Just as the practice of *āsana* described earlier is different from the 84 postures described in Haṭha Yoga, the practice of *prāṇāyāma* described here is different from the variety of breathing practices described in Haṭha Yoga.

Prāṇa is the subtle life force that causes all experiences of the world. *Prāṇa* is *rajas guṇa* (quality of activity), so all movements of mind, breath, and body can only happen when the *prāṇa* is active. The body can live for weeks without food and days without water, but it can only live for a few minutes without air. The *prāṇa*, more subtle than air, is the very life force and the mind and body cannot live for a moment without it.

The *prāṇa* is intimately connected with the breath and with the mind. Regulating one regulates the other two. Actually, *prāṇa* is the link that connects the mind and the breath. In order for perfection in *yoga* to be attained, all three need to be calm, smooth, and subtle.

In everyday life, the mind is highly active and distracted at least to some degree. The breath is irregular, alternating between deep and shallow, fast and slow, smooth and irregular according to our moods, emotions, and experiences. The mind and the breath feed each other in a cycle that naturally ends only at death. The *yogi*, however, recognizes the importance of regulating the breath as a means of controlling the mind, and therefore practices *prāṇāyāma*.

The natural cycle of breathing is inhale, momentary pause, exhale, momentary pause, inhale, etc. Regulating any of these aspects is known as *prāṇāyāma*. Extending the inhale, making it long, smooth, and subtle is one form. Extending the exhale, making it long, smooth, and subtle is another form. Recognizing the pause and allowing it lengthen is the third form of *prāṇāyāma*.

The idea of *prāṇāyāma* is not to have one super-long breath, but rather to control all the breaths. Because of the tremendous momentum generated by years of unregulated breathing, extending the breath must be done gradually. If the inhale is extended too much too quickly, the exhale will not be smooth. If the pauses are held too long, the mind will panic and the breath will become frantic, which, of course, is opposite to *yoga*.

Because of the connection between the mind and the breath, the practice of *prāṇāyāma* requires controlling both. The mind should be concentrated while the breath is regulated. The practice described in this *sutra* suggests that the mind should be concentrated on the infinite. The commentary specifically mentions three versions of this: the infinite God, luminosity in the heart center, and the feeling of an immense void. Another version is to concentrate on the primordial sound of Om.

The mind can also be concentrated on the breath itself, with the aim of extending the breath and making it more subtle. Just as a devotional person concentrates first on a form of God in order to transcend all forms as the mind becomes more subtle, a *yogi* concentrates on the breath in order to transcend the breath as the mind becomes subtle.

Obviously, this *prāṇāyāma* is an advanced practice because it requires high levels of stability and concentration. The *sūtra* says "Upon the perfection of *āsana*," which means after the posture has become unmoving and comfortable and the mind is fixed on the infinite. Then the body and mind have minimal physical requirements, and the breath can be suspended easily for extended periods of time.

To prepare for this practice, beginning and intermediate students can concentrate on a *bīja mantra* (seed or single-syllable sound that invokes energy), such as *om* or *rām*, and link it to the breath. As concentration deepens, the *bīja mantra* can be extended, which automatically extends the breath. Also, all the Haṭha Yoga *prāṇāyāmas* prepare the mind and breath for this *prāṇāyāma*.

In the next *sutra*, the practice of *prāṇāyāma* is further explained.

Installation of Hanumānji Murti (prānapratiṣṭha)

Sutra 50   बाह्याभ्यन्तरस्तम्भवृत्तिर्देशकालसंख्याभिःपरिदृष्टो दीर्घसूक्ष्मः ॥५०॥

bāhyābhyantara–stambha–vrittir-desha–kāla–samkhyābhih–
paridrishto dīrgha–sūkshmah

That (*prāṇāyāma*) is external, internal, and suspended. [When] regulated by space, time, and number, [they become] prolonged and subtle.

बाह्य	*bāhya*	external
आभ्यन्तर	*ābhyantara*	internal
स्तम्भ	*stambha*	suppressed, total restraint
वृत्ति	*vritti*	stage, manifestation
देश	*desha*	place
काल	*kāla*	time
संख्याभिः	*samkhyābhih*	and number
परिदृष्टो	*paridrishto*	regulated, measured
दीर्घ	*dīrgha*	prolonged, long
सूक्ष्मः	*sūkshmah*	subtle

In the previous *sūtra*, the term *prāṇāyāma* (regulation of breath) was introduced as the suspension of inhalation and/or exhalation. Now, in this *sūtra*, that suspension is divided into three types (internal, external, and generally suspended), which are performed according to measurements of space, time, and number.

1. **External operation of breath (*bāhya vritti*)** is practiced by exhaling and then suspending the breath, which naturally wants to inhale. The complete expiration of breath causes the suspension of breath. In this *prāṇāyāma*, as distinct from the Haṭha Yoga *prāṇāyāmas*, the suspension of breath is not forcibly held (locks are not used). It is a natural extension that comes from making the breath subtle. If the following inhale is rapid, forced, or rough, the suspension was held too long.

2. **Internal operation of breath (*antar vritti*)** is practiced by inhaling and then suspending the breath, which naturally wants to exhale. In this case, inspiration of breath is the cause of the suspension of breath. The suspension is not forcibly held, but rather extended naturally as the breath becomes more subtle. If the exhalation is rapid, forced, or rough, the suspension was held too long.

3. **Suspension of breath (*stambha vritti*)** is the practice of suspending both the external and internal operations of breath. This practice is different from the previous two in that it is not caused by either the complete exhalation or the complete inhalation. Instead, when the mind has become highly concentrated on the infinite, the breath becomes very subtle and can be stopped at any time.

These three types of *prāṇāyāmas* are to be practiced observing space, time, and number. This gradually makes the breath prolonged and subtle.

1. **Regulated by space (*deśa paridṛishṭa*)**. The measurement of space in *prāṇā-yāma* is used in two ways. The external space is observed during exhalation (the external operation of breath) by measuring the distance from the nostrils to the furthest point to which the breath extends.[1] That length of breath is observed and gradually shortened. It is called observation of external space.

   Internal space is observed in inhalation (internal operation of breath) by feeling the inner space. The breath goes in and fills the heart region. It is observed by feeling the touch of breath inside the body. Internal space covers from the top of the head to the soles of the feet. In the suspended stage after inhalation, the breath is held in the internal space, which is observed by feeling the sensation of touch all over the body. This observation of internal touch purifies the mind and the *nāḍīs* (subtle nerve channels), and makes the breath subtler.

2. **Regulated by time (*kāla paridṛishṭa*)**. The measurement of time is used in *prāṇāyāma* to control and extend the inhalation, exhalation, and retention of breath. The time can be fixed by seconds on a clock, by counting the duration of time, or by repetition of a *mantra*, like the sacred syllable Om, a name of God, or the Gāyatrī Mantra. In practicing *prāṇāyāma*, observation of space and time are practiced together to make the breath long and subtle.

3. **Regulated by number (*saṁkhyā paridṛishṭa*)**. One round of *prāṇāyāma* includes inhale, hold, exhale, hold, which corresponds to one cycle of breath. Each round of *prāṇāyāma* takes a certain period of time. In addition, *prāṇāyāma* practice is determined by a specific number of rounds.

   A typical healthy person inhales and exhales fifteen times in a minute. It means one inhalation and exhalation takes four seconds. It is called one unit (*mātrā*). Twelve units take 48 seconds, which is called one stroke (*udghāta*). When a person takes one *udghāta* (48 seconds) to complete one round of *prāṇāyāma* (one cycle of inhale-hold-exhale-hold), it is considered mild (*mṛidu*) *prāṇāyāma*. When a person takes two strokes or 96 seconds to complete one round of *prāṇāyāma*, it is considered medium (*madhya*) *prāṇāyāma*. When a person takes three strokes or 144 seconds, it is considered intense (*tīvra*) *prāṇāyā-ma*. The number of rounds practiced daily is regulation by number.[2]

By regular and prolonged practice of *prāṇāyāma*, the breath can be effortlessly suspended for lengthy periods. The breath is then considered to be long and subtle, which is highly supportive of deep concentration and *samādhi*.

---

1 This length of external measurement of breath is often measured in finger widths, for example ten fingers. In traditional texts, it is said to be determined by the movement of a fine piece of cotton wool. The furthest distance that the wool can be moved by the breath is the external space of *prāṇāyāma*. The breath is said to have become subtle when the wool doesn't move even when placed at the opening of the nostrils.

2 In progressing from mild to medium to intense level of *prāṇāyāma*, first the number of rounds or repetitions of a *prāṇāyāma* is increased before attempting to increase the length of the *prāṇāyāma*.

In verse IV:29 of the *Śhrīmad Bhagavad Gītā*, *prāṇāyāma* is explained as:

Apāne juhvati prāṇaṁ prāṇe'pānaṁ tathāpare
Prāṇāpānagatī ruddhvā prāṇāyāmaparāyaṇāḥ

Some offer as sacrifice the act of exhalation into that of inhalation. Others offer the act of inhalation into that of exhalation. There are still others given to the practice of *prāṇāyāma* who offer the suspension of breath.

Note

In this *sūtra*, the discussion of *prāṇāyāma* is continued. The practices of regulation of breath (*prāṇāyāma*) described in the *Sūtras* by Patañjali are not the same as the Haṭha Yoga *prāṇāyāmas*. They are only advanced practices that still the body, breath, and mind in support of *samādhi*.

Patañjali states that there are three types of *prāṇāyāma* practice—internal, external, and suspended—that should be regulated according to space, time, and number. The methods are extremely simple; they are extensions of the natural breathing rhythm. The regulation of this natural rhythm is gentle and gradual, which directly makes the breath smooth and subtle. Haṭha Yoga *prāṇāyāmas*, on the other hand, force the breath past comfortable limits in a controlled way.

Though some commentators disagree, the external operation of breath means to naturally extend the exhalation and the pause after the exhalation. These delay the inevitable inhalation. Internal operation of breath means to naturally extend the inhalation and the pause after the inhalation. These delay the inevitable exhalation. Suspension of breath means to stop the breath at any point in the process of inhalation or exhalation.

These three should be regulated by space, time, and number. Regulation by space in external operation means to be aware of how far out the exhalation extends (past the nostrils) with the intention of ever reducing the distance. The *yogi* must walk a fine line between extending the breath and the pauses enough to calm it, but not so much that it excites the mind and causes the inhalation and following breaths to become more forceful.

Regulation by space in internal operation means to be aware of how the breath fills and touches the body. Starting in the heart region, the breath should be felt filling the entire space of the body from the top of the head to the soles of the feet. This subtle sense of touch purifies the mind and body, and improves concentration because it removes the mind from specific sensations. The space inside the body cannot be pinpointed exactly. It is a subtle sensation that requires the mind to be open and expanded, which means it cannot be directed toward worldly objects. The more the mind is concentrated on the internal space, the less the specific objects and experiences of the world are in the mind. This is purification of the mind.

Regulation by time means to control the duration of inhale, exhale, and suspension. The duration should be extended gradually in such a way that the breath becomes ever more subtle. The duration of inhalation, exhalation, and suspension can be regulated one at a time or all together in a 1:4:2:pause ratio (with the pause being unregulated, or suspended effortlessly as long as is comfortable).

Regulation by number means to control the repetitions of *prāṇāyāma*. In the beginning, a small number of repetitions can be practiced, gradually extending the number as the mind acclimates.

The quotation from the *Bhagavad Gītā* mentioned in the commentary explains *prāṇāyāma* as a sacrifice or offering (*yajña*). *Yajña* is a means of attaining Self-knowledge. When the incoming breath is offered into the outgoing breath, the outgoing breath is offered into the incoming breath, or when both are offered into the retention, the mind is purified of self-interest. Normally, we use the breath as a means to fulfill our desires (through living in a body). We breathe so that we may continue to live and pursue our self-interested desires in the world.

When we offer the breath into itself, we break that tendency, which purifies the mind. The act of breathing, and thus living, is seen as an integrated process of sacrifice in which every creature and each action functions for the sake of the entire creation. The individual ego, which is the primary obstacle to Self-knowledge, is weakened, making all the other practices of *yoga* more effective.

In the next *sūtra*, the highest type of breath control is described.

Sūtra 51   बाह्याभ्यन्तरविषयाक्षेपी चतुर्थः ॥ ५१ ॥

bāhyābhyantara–vishayākshepī chaturthaḥ

The fourth prāṇāyama transcends the external and the internal.

बाह्य	*bāhya*	external
अभ्यन्तर	*abhyantara*	internal
विषय	*vishaya*	object, range, domain
आक्षेपी	*ākshepī*	transcending, going beyond
चतुर्थः	*chaturthaḥ*	the fourth

After achieving proficiency in the three types of *prāṇāyāmas* described in the preceding two *sutras*, the fourth type of breath control (*chaturtha prāṇāyāma*) can be practiced. In the first three practices of *prāṇāyāma*, awareness is focused on the exhalation and inhalation. The external operation (*bāhya vṛitti*) is observed by feeling the breath going out for a specific distance. The internal operation (*antar vṛitti*) is observed by feeling the breath entering deep inside the chest cavity and filling the body. The suspension of breath (*stambha vṛitti*) is observed by extending the length of the pause after inhalation and/or exhalation, or by pausing at any point during inhalation or exhalation.

By regular and prolonged practice of these three practices of *prāṇāyāma* with awareness, the breath gets subtler and subtler. Eventually the breath stops by itself. This suspension of breath is the fourth type of breath control (*chaturtha prāṇāyāma*). It is considered the highest type of breath control because both external and internal operations of breath are transcended.

There is a subtle but important difference between the third (*stambha vṛitti prāṇāyāma*) and the fourth (*chaturtha prāṇāyāma*). In the third, the breath is deliberately suspended, whereas in the fourth, suspension of breath occurs by itself because of the profound absorption of the mind in the infinite.

Note

In the previous two *sutras*, the practice of *prāṇāyāma* was described as the regulation of inhalation, exhalation, and suspension. This regulation should be increased gradually over an extended period of time with awareness of space, time, and number. The breath is extended and/or paused deliberately.

The regular practice of *prāṇāyāma* with awareness brings subtlety to the breath. This subtlety is further increased by the deepening of concentration. As the mind becomes more perfectly stilled, the breath calms even further, until it can stop at any time. This is the perfection of *prāṇāyāma*.

So long as the mind is actively engaged with the world, the body, or even the breath itself, the breath cannot stop on its own. Holding the breath causes great discomfort and agitates the mind. But as the first three forms of *prāṇāyāma* are perfected, suspending the breath becomes easier because the mind is very still. There is none of the stress and anxiety normally present with the mind's involvement with the world. The more the mind is focused on the infinite, the more peaceful it becomes, and the easier this suspension becomes. In this way, the suspension of breath and concentration of the mind support each other. When this support has become stable and profound, the first three forms of *prāṇāyāma* are transcended, and perfection in *prāṇāyāma* is achieved.

It is very important to understand that this fourth type of *prāṇāyāma* cannot be practiced deliberately. This is what distinguishes it from the other three methods. Instead, it occurs naturally as a result of the mind becoming completely absorbed in the infinite. This corresponds to the highest levels of meditation (*samādhi*), and cannot be forced or faked. Actually, in practice, there is no awareness of the breath being stopped because the mind is completely absorbed in the infinite and no knowledge of the body is present in the mind.

This suspension of breath is required for the higher *samādhis* to become stable. In fact, this *prāṇāyāma* removes the final veils covering Self-knowledge, as described in the next *sūtra*.

Sūtra 52   ततः क्षीयते प्रकाशावरणम् ॥ ५२ ॥

tataḥ kṣhīyate prakāśhāvaraṇam

From that (*prāṇāyāma*), the veil over the light disappears.

ततः	*tataḥ*	from that, then
क्षीयते	*kṣhīyate*	dissolves, destroyed, disappears
प्रकाश	*prakāśha*	light
आवरणम्	*āvaraṇam*	covering, veil

In this *sūtra* and the next, the results of *prāṇāyāma* are given in two ways: the veil over the inner light is destroyed, and the mind is made fit for concentration.

By the regular practice of *prāṇāyāma*, the restlessness of the mind caused by *rajas guṇa* and the inertia of the mind caused by *tamas guṇa* are weakened, while the purity of mind caused by *sattva guṇa* increases. The five afflictions (*kleśhas*)—ignorance (*avidyā*), egoism (*asmitā*), attachment (*rāga*), aversion (*dveṣha*), and fear of death (*abhineveśha*)—veil the light of discriminative knowledge (*viveka khyāti*).

These five afflictions sustain and perpetuate the illusion of finite existence. But, they are gradually thinned out and finally destroyed by the four practices of *prāṇāyāma*. The mind thus becomes illuminated by the light of *sattva*, achieves discriminative wisdom, and no longer regards the relative, impermanent existence of the body and the world as real. Spiritual insight awakens and the *yogi* is freed from the bondage of the cycle of birth and death.

Pañchaśhikhāchārya says: "There is no austerity superior to *prāṇāyāma*. It removes impurities and makes the light of knowledge shine." Manu says: "Just as when gold is melted in fire, its impurities are burned away; in the same way, by the practice of *prāṇāyāma*, the impurities of the senses are destroyed."

Note

In the previous three *sūtras*, the practice and perfection of *prāṇāyāma* were described. Now, in this and the following *sūtra*, the results of perfecting *prāṇāyāma* are explained. *Prāṇa* is the life force animating and connecting the mind and body. Every thought, every movement of and within the mind and body occurs only by the force of *prāṇa*. Without *prāṇa*, there can be no experience.

Prāṇāyāma is the practice of regulating the breath in order to purify the *prāṇa*. The breath and mind together create all experiences of the world. When one is affected, the other changes. Therefore, working with the breath means working with the mind.

The breath and the mind function interdependently; the momentum of one influences the other. Breathing is required for life, but we use different kinds of breath for different activities. We use rapid and deep breathing for intense physical activities, slow and deep for pleasure, rapid and shallow for anxiety, and slow and subtle for concentration. They are necessary for a full and vital participation in the world, and they are the vehicles through which the five afflictions (*kleśhas*) function. Even the highest levels of *samprajñāta samādhi* require some form of subtle breathing and the slight movement of *prāṇa*. And, the momentum of the breath at any level is an obstacle to the next level of *yoga*.

The ultimate goal of *yoga* is complete control of the mind so as to remove all suffering and release the self from bondage. A smooth, calm, and subtle breath is supportive of *yoga*, while all other types are obstacles. In fact, the more subtle the breath, the better for meditation and *samādhi*. Without *prāṇāyāma*, it is very difficult to calm the breath enough for deep meditation.

The *sūtra* states that *prāṇāyāma* removes the veil over the light. The light, of course, is pure consciousness (*puruṣa*). The presence of ignorance and the other afflictions in the mind, all sustained by the movement of *prāṇa*, block or veil awareness of the pure consciousness that is separate from the mind. The perfection of *prāṇāyāma* is the suspension of *prāṇa*, which is also the suspension of the activities of the afflictions. In this suspended state, there is no activity in the mind that blocks the awareness of pure consciousness.

An objection arises. The only thing that veils consciousness is ignorance. But ignorance can only be removed by knowledge, not by the physical control of the breath.

The objection is correct that ignorance veils the light and that knowledge removes ignorance. In everyday life, though, the veiling of the light takes the form of the five root afflictions and their myriad fruits of desire and attachment. These afflictions and their fruits manifest in the breath. For example, clinging to life is seen most dramatically in the panic of someone who can't get enough air.

Making the breath slow and subtle through *prāṇāyāma* precludes the various manifestations of the afflictions. In other words, if the breath is calm, the gross levels of the afflictions can't function, and if the afflictions are fully active, the breath can't be made calm. Therefore, regulating the breath weakens the afflictions, which are the specific aspects in the mind that veil the Self. The weaker the afflictions become, the more the mind is capable of subtle discrimination. When the fourth *prāṇāyāma* is perfected and the breath stops of its own accord, the afflictions are so weak that the mind is prepared to discriminate the subtle principles of the mind, including the ultimate realization that the Self is separate from the intellect (*buddhi*). When this ultimate realization (*viveka khyāti*) is firmly established, ignorance is removed completely and permanently, which is the goal of *yoga*.

This is further explained in the next *sūtra*.

Sutra 53   धारणासु च योग्यता मनसः ॥ ५३ ॥

dhāraṇāsu cha yogyatā manasaḥ

And the mind becomes fit for concentration.

धारणासु	*dhāraṇāsu*	for concentration
च	*cha*	and
योग्यता	*yogyatā*	fitness
मनसः	*manasaḥ*	of the mind

The second result of regular and prolonged practice of *prāṇāyāma* is that it makes the mind fit for concentration (*dhāraṇā*), the refinement of which includes all levels of meditation (*dhyāna*), and trance (*samādhi*).

In Sūtra I:34, it was stated that the mind can be made calm by expulsion and retention of breath. Sūtras II:49–51 gave the definition and methods of *prāṇāyāma*. Sūtra 52 gives the first result of the practice of *prāṇāyāma*, which is dissolving the veils that cover the inner light. Now this *sutra* gives the further affirmation that the purity of mind gained through the practice of *prāṇāyāma* makes the mind fit for concentration.

There are five states of mind described in commentaries on the *Yoga Sūtras*: dull and preoccupied (*mūḍha*), restless (*kṣhipta*), distracted (*vikṣhipta*), one-pointed (*ekāgra*), and restrained (*niruddha*). When all distractions of the mind are removed by *prāṇāyāma* practice, the mind gets steady and fit for one-pointed (*ekāgra*) concentration.

Note

The practice of *prāṇāyāma* removes the veils that hide the inner light and makes the mind fit for concentration (*dhāraṇā*). The term *dhāraṇā* is used in a general way to mean undisturbed, one-pointed concentration, and not in the specific sense of the sixth limb of Aṣhṭāṅga Yoga that precedes the deeper levels of meditation and *samādhi*.

The mind is like a candle flame and the breath is like the wind. So long as the breath flows, the mind cannot be steady. So many forces disturb the mind, yet all of them are fueled by the breath and the *prāṇa*. Until the *prāṇa* is made calm and subtle, true one-pointed concentration is impossible.

As was described in the previous *sutras*, the regulation of breath gradually weakens the afflictions and allows the breath to become very still. Yet, the proper practice of *prāṇāyāma* requires the mind to be concentrated. At first, the breath is not calm and the concentration is not one-pointed. But with persistent practice (*abhyāsa*), the two strengthen each other until the breath becomes so subtle that it stops of its own accord, and the mind becomes absorbed in undistracted concentration.

In the next *sutra*, the fifth limb of *yoga* (*pratyāhāra*) is introduced.

Baba Hari Dass in Mudra

Sūtra 54   स्वविषयासम्प्रयोगे चित्तस्य स्वरूपानुकार इवेन्द्रियाणां प्रत्याहारः
॥ ५४ ॥

sva–vishayāsamprayoge chittasya svarūpānukāra ivendriyāṇāṁ
pratyāharaḥ

***Pratyāhāra* is when the senses separate from their objects, following as
it were the nature of the mind [withdrawn from the senses by concentrating on an internal object].**

स्व	*sva*	their own
विषय	*vishaya*	objects
असम्प्रयोगे	*asamprayoge*	on not coming into contact with, disunion, separate
चित्तस्य	*chittasya*	of the mind
स्वरूप	*svarūpa*	the nature, own form
अनुकारः	*anukāraḥ*	the following of, imitation
इव	*iva*	as it were, as if
इन्द्रियाणाम्	*indriyāṇām*	of the senses
प्रत्याहारः	*pratyāhāraḥ*	is abstraction, sense withdrawal

The practice, perfection, and results of *prāṇāyāma* were described in the preceding five *sūtras*: The natural cycle of breathing is extended, made subtle, and suspended, while the mind becomes concentrated first on the space and time of
prāṇāyāma, and then on the infinite. Now, in this *sūtra*, *pratyāhāra* is explained as
the senses following the mind by separating from their objects.

Abstraction (*pratyāhāra*) is the withdrawal of the senses from the sense objects.
In abstraction, the nose is withdrawn from the function of smelling, the tongue
from taste, the eyes from sight, the skin from touch, and the ears from hearing.
Actually, the mind is behind the activities of the sense organs. If the mind does
not join with the sense organs, then the objects of the sense organs are not experienced. For example, a chess player who is deeply concentrated on the match
doesn't hear outer noises.

When the mind is restrained from outer functions, as in meditation, it turns
inward. The senses, which are meant to function outwardly, follow the mind
and stop their outward function. The traditional analogy is that the senses follow the mind like bees follow the queen; they take off from the hive when the
queen bee leaves and rest when she rests.

Here the term *anukāra iva* (as if imitating) is used to describe the movement of
the senses in relation to the mind. The sense organs stop their respective outer
functions when the mind is inwardly concentrated. Technically, the senses are
not capable of concentrating inwardly, so when the mind stops relating to outer objects, the sense organs follow the mind as if imitating it. In the Vishṇu-
purāṇa it is said, "The *yogi* who is devoted to the practice of abstraction (*pratyāhāra*) should restrain the senses which are attached to their objects (sound, etc.),
and make them imitate the mind."

Note

After describing *prāṇāyāma, pratyāhāra* is now explained. In this *sūtra, pratyāhāra* (abstraction, or withdrawal of the mind from the activities of the senses) is a phenomenon and not specifically a practice. The result of perfecting *prāṇāyāma* is stillness of the breath, which requires the mind to be withdrawn from all outer activities. The senses and the organs of action are the vehicles by which the mind goes out, so the mind must disengage from these in order for perfection of *prāṇāyāma* to occur.

According to Sāṁkhya and Yoga philosophies, there are ten senses (*jñanendriyas* and *karmendriyas*). These organs of sense perception and action include five energies of perception (hearing, touching, seeing, tasting, and smelling), and five energies of action (speaking, manipulating, ambulating, digesting, and procreating). These ten energies work with the mind (*manas*), which both directs and records their functions. Proof of this can be found in everyday life. If you are deeply absorbed in a book, you may not hear someone enter the room. There is nothing wrong with the ears; the mind was so concentrated on the content of the book that it disengaged from the sense of hearing. Even though the sounds reached the ear, the functioning of the ear didn't reach the mind, so no sound was perceived.

In order for *yoga* to be achieved, the normal functions of the mind and body must be suspended. In *āsana*, the five energies of action (*karmendriyas*) must be restrained. All outer action ceases as the body is made motionless in a seated posture. At first, even though the body is still, the mind and senses continue to be active. With some effort, the mind can turn away from all new sense perceptions by closing the eyes, wearing ear plugs, and ignoring any new smells. But even then, the mind continues to revolve around sense objects. It remembers past sensations and experiences, and it imagines future sensations. Even though no actual sensations are being perceived from the outer world, this restless state cannot be considered *pratyāhāra*.

The *sūtra* says that *pratyāhāra* is when the senses withdraw from their objects, in a form of imitating the mind, which has already withdrawn from the senses. This means that *pratyāhāra*, as it is described here, is an automatic process that occurs when the mind is turned inward and concentrated.

We see in this section of the *Sūtras* (starting in Sūtra II:46) that Patañjali is not giving us a diverse set of methods to be practiced independently. *Pratyāhāra* is not something to be done independent of *āsana* and *prāṇāyāma*. The same is true of the later limbs of *dhāraṇā, dhyāna,* and *samādhi*. Instead, each limb forms a progression or deepening of the same practice. *Āsana* is stillness of the body; *prāṇāyāma* is stillness of the breath; *pratyāhāra* is stillness of the senses, while *dhāraṇa, dhyāna,* and *samādhi* mark the stilling of the mind.

Note that there are many methods of *yoga* that are classified as *āsana, prāṇāyāma, pratyāhāra,* and *dhyāna*. Many of these come from the Haṭha Yoga tradition, and not directly from the *Yoga Sūtras* of Patañjali. When these practices are performed regularly with appropriate intensity and with the aim of purifying the mind, they can provide very helpful support for the practices described by Patañjali in this last section of *Sādhana Pāda*. Categorizing the various practices of *yoga* according to the eight limbs is a useful method of guiding the aspirant even if it is not directly supported by the text itself.

The four books of the *Yoga Sūtras* of Patañjali are a philosophical treatise on the science of liberation. They explain both how and why the mind and self get attached and bound to the experiential world, and how and why the mind and self become free from that bondage and experience. In theory, there is one process of moving from the active, distracted mind to the calm, subtle, and eventually dissolved mind. The eight limbs are explained as various stages along that one path.

In practice, though, many methods are applied to combat the various faces of the ego and its attachment to the world. Just as an expert fencer will have many techniques in his or her repertoire, choosing the appropriate one to combat a particular foe at a particular moment, the expert *yogi* practices various methods based on personal strengths and weaknesses as well as the specific problems encountered throughout life.

In the next *sūtra*, the result of *pratyāhāra* is described.

Bābā Hari Dāss making offerings to the Gaṅgā.

Sūtra 55   ततः परमा वश्यतेन्द्रियाणाम् ॥ ५५ ॥

tataḥ paramā vaśhyatendriyāṇām

From that (*pratyāhāra*) comes the highest control of the senses.

ततः	*tataḥ*	from that
परमा	*paramā*	the highest
वश्यता	*vaśhyatā*	control
इन्द्रियाणाम्	*indriyāṇām*	of the senses

In this *sutra*, it is explained that the highest control over the senses is achieved by abstraction (*pratyāhāra*). Vyāsa, in his classical commentary, states four common notions about control of the senses.

1. Some say that non-addiction to objects like sound and touch is control of the senses.
2. Others say that enjoying only those objects not forbidden by the scriptures (*śhāstras*) while rejecting objects forbidden by the scriptures is control of the senses.
3. Still others say that experiencing certain objects by choice, without indulgence and without attachment, is control of the senses.
4. Some say experiencing objects without feeling pleasure and pain (because of the absence of attachment and aversion in the mind) is control of the senses.

In all four of these definitions of sense control, the senses are in contact with their objects and yet there is control over the senses. There is, however, always a possibility of getting trapped in sense indulgence when the senses are in contact with their objects.

The Sage Jaigīṣhavya offers another point of view: "Non-attachment of the senses to their objects (sound, etc.), which arises from the mind's one-pointed focus on Brahman, is control of the senses." When the mind is fixed on the infinite (Brahman), as described in the previous *sutra*, the senses don't chase after their objects because of *pratyāhāra*. When the mind is controlled, the senses are controlled. There is no need to control the senses separately. Therefore, the sense control that arises from one-pointedness of the mind on the infinite is the highest sense control.

Patañjali ends *Sādhana Pāda* with these *sutras* on *pratyāhāra*, the fifth limb of Aṣhṭāṅga Yoga. Each of these five limbs removes mental disturbances and prepares the mind for one-pointed concentration and *samādhi*. The *yamas* and *niyamas* eliminate emotional disturbances, *āsanas* eliminate physical disturbances, *prāṇāyāma* eliminates disturbances caused by the improper flow of the life force (*prāṇa*), and *pratyāhāra* eliminates disturbances caused by uncontrolled sense organs.

The last three limbs, the internal limbs of concentration (*dhāraṇā*), meditation (*dhyāna*), and trance (*samādhi*), are described further in *Vibhūti Pāda*.

Note

With this *sūtra* on control of the senses, Patañjali concludes *Sādhana Pāda*. The senses are vehicles for life in the world. They provide the basis for all phenomenal experiences, generating the pleasures and pains that make us feel alive. They activate the mind, and they are activated by the mind. Without them, nothing in the world is real.

But the senses are the enemies of *samādhi*. Any activity of the senses, whether it is actual, remembered, or imagined, distracts the mind and precludes the one-pointed absorption of *samādhi*. Every sense experience requires "multi-pointedness." There is the subject, which is the owner of the senses (the "I"), the object, which is the material form to be perceived, and the action, which is the perception itself. This is true for direct perception, memory, and imagination[1] because all three aspects of the experience are recreated in the mind (*manas*), no matter where the source of the object may lie.

This means that true "one-pointedness" is not possible in normal interactions with the world. If there is awareness of the world, there has to be "multi-pointedness" because the mind is simultaneously recognizing the subject, object, and act of perceiving. This does not mean that attachment or bondage is necessary. An enlightened sage can interact with the world without identifying with the actions or their results. Indeed, this is one of the goals of *yoga*.

Ultimately, the senses are activated by only one thing: *rajas guṇa*, commonly referred to as passion or worldly desire. Without desire, the senses remain dormant, so controlling desire means controlling the senses. In the case of the enlightened sage, the senses remain active due to the force of *prārabdha karma* (the momentum of past actions) and not from the force of presently active worldly desires.

The commentary lists five definitions of controlling the senses. The first four are considered incomplete or dangerous, while the final definition explains perfect control of the senses. When the mind is completely absorbed in one-pointed concentration on the infinite, no sense cognitions are possible. This is known as the perfection of *pratyāhāra*.

---

1 The five categories of *vṛittis* (thoughts or cognitions) described in Sūtra I:6 are valid cognition (*pramāṇa*), wrong cognition (*viparyaya*), imaginary cognition (*vikalpa*), dreamless sleep (*nidrā*), and memory (*smṛiti*). Direct perception includes both valid and wrong cognitions (correctly or incorrectly corresponding to some physical reality). Imaginary cognitions are notions regarding non-physical reality, such as time, God, or horns on a rabbit, and can be either valid or wrong. Dreamless sleep is a single type of *vṛitti* that precludes any of the other categories. Memory is the repetition of a previous cognition of any category. The list is inclusive in that every notion in the mind is included in one or more of these categories.

The four active categories require "multi-pointedness," with the possible exception of *samādhi* depending on the exact boundaries of the definitions used. Some include the *vṛittis* of *samādhi* in *pramāṇa*, some in *vikalpa* (as they don't necessarily correspond to a physical reality), and some say these five categories are for everyday experiences, and are not meant to include *samādhi*.

A question arises. If the mind is completely absorbed in Brahman, how can the mind-body complex act in the world? The commentary makes it sound like perfect control of the senses is not possible except during *samādhi*.

These first four imperfect methods are excellent techniques for developing control of the senses. The mind cannot be withdrawn from all sense experience at once. It should be done gradually to avoid a reaction and/or rebellion from the mind. At first, the aspirant should moderate his or her experiences to prevent the mind from getting addicted to any one thing.

Then, aspirants can limit their actions to only those prescribed by the scriptures. These include working to support the family, spiritual practices, quality time with friends and family, playing in a non-harmful way, and resting in appropriate amounts. The mind is purified because a limit is placed on the expression of the ego. The ego will resist, for it wants what it wants when it wants it. The more all actions are performed as a duty, the weaker the self-interested ego becomes.

Some say that this limit is necessary only so long as we identify with the ego and thus feel that we are choosing our own activities. Once enlightenment occurs, there is no further identification with the individual ego so no limit is needed. In theory, this is correct, but in practice, it is very tricky because the ego is a master of deception. The veiling power of *rajas* and *tamas* can easily make someone believe they are beyond all identifications when in fact they are still being driven by desire.

Still others say that sense activities needn't be limited so long as the twin urges of attachment and aversion have been conquered. Without attraction and repulsion, experiences are just like bland soup and don't cause a reaction. Again, in theory this is correct, but the danger of being deceived is huge. All actions are motivated by desire. Without desire (attraction or repulsion), no actions would be initiated. Most people who are active in the world but somehow think they are free from attraction and repulsion are likely to be mistaken. This is why the scriptures propose limitations on the types of activity *yogis* perform; it limits the power of the ego to deceive the mind.

When the identification of the self is only with the Self (the absolute *puruṣha* or Brahman), there can be no identification of the self with the mind and senses. In this case, the mind and senses function automatically, without anyone there to reap the consequences. From the outside, the action may look identical. It may appear to be motivated by selfish desire, but in this case, no one says, "This is for me." The self, the "I," only recognizes the infinite consciousness without modification and without qualification, so no matter what the senses may be doing, it doesn't affect the self. In other words, from the perspective of the self, nothing is happening because only the infinite consciousness is known, no matter what the mind-body complex is doing. This is *kaivalya*, the complete liberation from all bondage and all experiences of the mind-body complex.

In this second book of the Yoga Sūtras, *Sādhana Pāda*, the philosophy of yoga has been combined with the practices of yoga (*sādhana*). The philosophy cannot be fully understood without the practice, and the practice is guided and supported by the philosophy. Becoming firmly established in peace is perhaps the greatest challenge in life. There are many obstacles, so great persistence and tenacity are required to succeed.

Sādhana Pāda ended with *pratyāhāra* and control of the senses. No matter what specific practices are performed on a regular basis, if the senses are not controlled or restrained throughout the day, the *yogi's* success in *sādhana* will be severely limited. The senses are controlled by the mind, so the way to control the senses is to control the mind. Keeping the mind positive while the body is engaged in activities that benefit the world order instead of just our own self-interest is a sure road to victory.

May all who seek the Self attain their goal.

Hari om tat sat.

Glossary

jabhāva अभाव – absence, removal, resolved

abhiniveśha अभिनिवेश – clinging to life, or fear of death (fifth of five *kleśhas*, afflictions)

abhyāsa अभ्यास – persistent practice

adhikāra अधिकार – authority, primary, privilege

adhyātma अध्यात्म – spiritual; in regard to the *ātman*

āgama आगम – testimonial knowledge, revealed authority; one of three forms of *pramāṇa*

agni अग्नि – fire, fire element

aham अहम् – "I am"

ahaṁkāra अहंकार – "I amness," ego, identifying principle

ahiṁsā अहिंसा – nonviolence (one of the five *yamas*)

aiśhvarya ऐश्वर्य – sovereignty and spiritual freedom

ājñā chakra आज्ञा चक्र – the energy center located 4 fingers in from the forehead; the sixth *chakra* in the shape of a two petal lotus; the seat of concentration

ākāśha आकाश – space, infinite void, ether element

akliṣhṭa अक्लिष्ट – not painful, non-painful actions or thoughts; non-binding thought

ālambana आलम्बन – support, objects supporting concentration

aliṅga अलिङ्ग – without mark, unmanifest *prakṛiti*; *mūla prakṛiti*

amarṣha अमर्ष – vengeance; results from intolerance

anāhata chakra अनाहतचक्र – the heart *chakra*, the energy center located in the heart region

ānanda आनन्द – ecstasy, rapture, bliss

ānandamaya kośha आनन्दमय कोश – bliss sheath (most subtle of five sheaths or bodies)

ānandanugata samādhi आनन्दनुगत समाधि – see *sānanda samādhi*

ānāpānna sati आनापान्न सति – mindfulness of inhalation and exhalation

an-avachchhedāt अनवच्छेदात् – not being limited, delimitation

an-avasthitatvāni अनवस्थितत्वानि – instability (one of nine obstacles to yoga)

andhatāmisra अन्धतामिस्र – blind nocturnal

aṅgamejayatva अङ्गमेजयत्व – nervousness, unsteadiness, shaking of limbs (one of five symptoms that accompany the distractions to *sādhana*)

anitya अनित्य – non-eternal, impermanent

antaḥ अन्तः – ending in, extending up to

antaḥkaraṇa अन्तः करण – human psyche; internal instruments (*manas, buddhi, ahaṁkāra, chitta*)

antarāya अन्तराय – obstacles, impediments

anu अनु – within

aṇu अणु – the smallest unit that cannot be broken further; atom

anubhūta अनुभूत – experienced

anugama अनुगम – accompanied

anumāna अनुमान – rational processes, inference; one of the forms of *pramāṇa*

anupātī अनुपाती – following upon, depending upon

ānuśhravika आनुश्रविक – heard of, scriptures, revealed, imperceptible

anyaḥ अन्यः – the other

āp आप – water, water element

aparāmṛishṭa अपरामृष्ट – untouched, unsmeared

aparavairāgya अपरवैराग्य – dispassion for worldly objects (lower dispassion), divided into four degrees: *yatamāna, vyatireka, ekendriya,* and *vaśhīkāra*

aparigraha अपरिग्रह – non-possessiveness, non-greed, non-hoarding (one of the five *yamas*)

apavarga आवर्ग – liberation from experience; one of the two purposes of life (see *bhoga*)

api अपि – even, also

āpta आप्त – accomplished person, authority

apuṇya अपुण्य – vice, non-virtue

artha अर्थ – object, form, meaning, object signified

arthamātra अर्थमात्र – only the object

asamprajñāta samādhi असम्प्रज्ञात समाधि – super-consciousness beyond (perfect) knowledge; the Self dwelling in the Self; acognitive *samādhi*

asampramoshaḥ असम्प्रमोषः – not being lost, not being stolen

āsana आसन – seat, posture; the third of eight limbs of Aṣhṭāṅga Yoga

āsanna आसन्न – near, very close

āsevita आसेवित – pursued, practiced, continued

āshaya आशय – accumulation, impression of desires wherein desires sleep; storehouse; dormant *vāsanās* are stored as *saṁskāras* until they mature into action (*karma*)

Aṣhṭāṅga Yoga अष्टांग योग – the Yoga of Eight Limbs, *yama* (restraints), *niyama* (observances), *āsana* (postures), *prāṇāyāma* (breath control), *pratyāhāra* (withdrawing the mind from the senses), *dhāraṇā* (concentration), *dhyāna* (meditation), and *samādhi* (super-consciousness)

aśhuchi अशुचि – impure

asmitā अस्मिता – egoism (second of five *kleśhas*, afflictions), "I-sense," universal sense of being, "I-amness," sense of individuality

asmitānugata samādhi अस्मितानुगत समाधि – see *sāsmitā samādhi*

asteya अस्तेय – non-stealing (one of the five *yamas*)

āsuri आसुरि – demon

asūyā असूया – anger; the feeling of harmful thoughts for those who are happy and successful

asya अस्य – of this

atadrūpa अतद्रूप – not its own form

atha अथ – now, at an auspicious moment of transition

atīndriya अतीन्द्रिय – super-sensuous perception

ātma आत्म – the self, consciousness

avasthānam अवस्थानम् – stability

avidyā अविद्या – the false identification of *puruṣha* with *buddhi*, ignorance, nescience (first of five *kleśhas*, afflictions)

avirati अविरति – lack of enthusiasm; non-abstension or worldliness (one of nine obstacles to yoga)

aviśheṣha अविशेष – non-specific outcome, i.e. that which is productive of further outcomes, specifically the *viśheṣhas*

avyakta अव्यक्त – unmanifest state of creation; the great unmanifest; *pradhāna*

ayu अयु – span of life

bandha बन्ध – bondage; bond, dam, lock; a practice of *ṣhaṭ karma* (six methods of purification), of which there are three: *uddiyāna bandha* (navel lock), *jālandhara bandha* (throat lock), and *mūla bandha* (anal lock)

bhava भव – *saṁskāras* of nescience which are the cause of rebirth

bhāva भाव – state, becoming, being, emotion

bhāvana, bhāvanā भावन, भावना – absorbing, dwelling upon mentally, meditation, by the cultivation; conception

bhava pratyaya भव प्रत्यय – the *samādhi* at rebirth; born with higher consciousness

bhoga भोग – experience, experiencing the outer world, experience of the world through the senses; one of the two purposes of life (see *apavarga*)

bhrānti darśhana भ्रान्ति दर्शन – delusion, confused ideas (one of nine obstacles to yoga)

bhūta भुत – also *mahābhūta* and *pañchabhūta*, gross element, of which there are five: *ākāśha* (space), *vāyu* (air), *agni* (fire), *āp* (water), and *pṛithivī* (earth)

bīja बीज – seed, the principle, object, support

bodha बोध – perception

brahmacharya ब्रह्मचर्य – literally, "walking the path of God"; control of sexual passion, control of vital energy, preservation of vital fluid (one of five *yamas*)

Brahmā ब्रह्मा – creative aspect of God

Brahma ब्रह्म – Absolute God without form (pronounced "Brumm")

buddhi बुद्धि – intellect, individual form

cha च – and, also

chetanā चेतना – consciousness

chiti śhakti चिति शक्ति – conscious principle, light of consciousness; energy of senses

chitta चित्त – mind field; mind, field of consciousness; field of experience

dagdha bīja दग्ध बीज – fried or roasted seed, generally referring to the state of the *kleśhas* after discrimination in which their potency to germinate or grow has been destroyed just as a seed cannot sprout after being roasted in a fire

dākṣhiṇika bandha दाक्षिणिबन्ध – bondage through attachment to ritual

darśhana दर्शन – literally, "sight"; in the light, being in the presence of a sage; the six original schools of thought that form the basis of all Indian philosophies

daurmanasya दौर्मनस्य – depression or frustration

deśha देश – space

dhāraṇā धारणा – concentration

dharma धर्म – righteousness; attributes

dharma megha samādhi धर्म मेघ समाधि – cloud-pouring virtue; the bridge between *samprajñāta samādhi* and *asamprajñāta samādhi*

dhātus धातु – literally, "marks"; the eight constituents of the body such as blood, flesh and bones as classified by Ayurveda

dhyāna ध्यान – meditation

dīrghakāla दीघकाल – a long time

doṣhas दोष – literally, "faults"; the three bodily humors (*vāta*, air; *pitta*, fire; *kapha*, earth) as classified by Ayurveda

draṣṭri द्रष्टृ – the seer

draṣhṭuḥ द्रष्टुः – the seer

dṛiḍhabhūmi दृढभूमि – firmly grounded

dṛiga दृग – seer, pure consciousness, *puruṣha*

dṛiṣhṭa दृष्ट – seen, perceived with the senses; perceptible objects

duḥkha दुःख – pain, suffering

dveṣha द्वेष – repulsion (fourth of five *kleśhas*, afflictions), aversion, hatred following painful experience

eka एक – one

ekāgra एकाग्र – one-pointed (fourth of five states of *chitta*)

ekāgratā एकाग्रता – one-pointedness

eka tattva एक तत्त्व – one principle

ekendriya एकेन्द्रिय – dwelling in one sense (the mind)

etayā एतया – by this

eva एव – like

gandha गन्ध – smell, subtle element of odor

ghora घोर – ferocity, a type of *vyutthāna vṛitti*; *rajas* predominant

grahaṇa ग्रहण – instruments (of experience), the instrumental level, the mind field, instrument of cognition or apprehension, the process and fact of experiencing, subjective experience

grahītṛi ग्रहीतृ – subjective principle, cognizer, apprehender, experiencer

grāhya ग्राह्य – objects (of experience), objects received, object experienced

grāhyeshu ग्राह्येषु – object cognized or apprehended

granthi ग्रंथि – knot, binding, obstruction

guṇa गुण – the attributes of *prakṛiti*: *sattva, rajas, tamas*; quality of creation or nature; quality of matter; energetic quality

guru गुरु – teacher; literally, "bringing light to darkness"

hiraṇyagarbha हिरण्यगर्भ – golden womb

hṛidaya हृदय – heart

ichchhā śhakti इच्छा शक्ति – cosmic will; *rajas guṇa*; one of three cosmic energies

indriya इन्द्रिय – senses, of which there are eleven: *manas* (thinking or recording mind), the five *jñānendriyas* (organs of perception: the ears, skin, eyes, tongue, and nose), and the five *karmendriyas* (organs of action: the vocal chords, hands, legs, genitals, and anus)

īrṣhyā ईर्ष्या – jealousy; results from *rāga*, attraction, as the mind wants all pleasure for itself

Īshvara ईश्वर – Lord of Creation, God, ruler of the creation, a special *puruṣha* not affected by *kleśha, karma, vipāka* nor *āśhaya*; the union of *puruṣha* and *prakṛiti*

Īshvara-praṇidhāna ईश्वर प्रणिधान – surrender to God (one of the five *niyamas*, one of the three methods of Kriyā Yoga, a method to attain *samādhi*)

itaratra इतरत्र – elsewhere, other states

itareṣām इतरेषाम् – of others

iva इव – as though

jāgrat जाग्रत् – waking state; one of four states of mind in Vedanta

japa जप – repetition

jāti जाति – class, species

jīva, जीव – individual being

jīvātma, jīvātman जीवात्म जीवात्मन् – embodied soul; the Self rooted in *buddhi*

jñāna ज्ञान – knowledge, knowledge achieved through yoga; meaning (of a word)

jñāna shakti ज्ञान शक्ति – cosmic knowledge; *sattva guṇa*; one of three cosmic energies

jñānendriya ज्ञानेन्द्रिय – subtle organs associated with sense perception

jyoti ज्योति – inner light, the light of *sattva* (purity)

jyotiṣhmatī ज्योतिष्मती – luminous, radiant, full of light (*sattva*)

kaivalya कैवल्य – liberation (of the soul), isolation of the Self in the Self; freed from the bondage of the cycle of birth and death (*saṁsāra*)

kāla काल – time

kalpa कल्प – imagination

kāluṣhya कालुष्य – impurities of which there are six: *rāga* (attachment), *īrśhyā* (jealousy), *parāpakāra chikīrśhyā* (malevolence), *dveṣha* (hatred), *asūyā* (anger), and *amarśha* (intolerance or revenge)

kārana sharīra कारन शरीर – causal body

karma कर्म – actions that have a binding effect

karmāśhaya कर्माशय – reservoir of impressions of action (*saṁskāra*)

karmendriya कर्मेन्द्रिय – subtle organs associated with action, of which there are five: vocalization, grasping, locomotion, procreation, and elimination

karuṇā करुणा – compassion; suggested attitude toward those who are suffering

kevala केवल – alone, isolated

khyāti ख्याति – discernment (worldly, as opposed to *viveka khyāti*)

kleśha क्लेश – afflictions of which there are five: *avidyā* (ignorance), *asmitā* (egoism), *rāga* (attraction), *dveṣha* (repulsion), and *abhiniveśha* (clinging to life or fear of death)

kliṣhṭa क्लिष्ट – painful, painful action or thought; binding thought

kosha कोष – sheath; level of reality according to Tantra, of which there are five: *annamaya* (food), *prāṇamaya* (vital), *manomaya* (mind), *vijñānamaya* (intellect), and *ānandamaya* (bliss)

kriyā क्रिया – effort, actions

kriyā shakti क्रिया शक्ति – cosmic matter; *tamas guṇa*; one of three cosmic energies

Kriyā Yoga क्रिया योग – the Yoga of Purificatory Action; the three practices of *tapaḥ* (austerity or discipline), *svādhyāya* (Self study or study of scriptures), and *Īshvara praṇidhāna* (surrender to God)

kshetrajña क्षेत्रज्ञ– the knower of the field, pure consciousness, *puruṣha*

kshetram क्षेत्रं – the field, the mind-body complex, *prakṛiti*

kshīṇa-vritti क्षीण वृत्ति – fluctuations of the mind weakened

kshipta क्षिप्त – restless or disturbed (second of five states of *chitta*) *kūṭastha nitya* कूटस्थ नित्य – the eternal, unchanging Self; literally, *kūṭastha* = anvil, *nitya* = eternal ("the anvil is the unchanging block upon which all forms are created")

liṅga लिङ्ग – the indicator of its cause; mark

liṅga mātra लिङ्ग मात्र – mark alone; refers to *mahat*

loka pratyakṣa लक प्रत्यक्ष – ordinary observation of outer objects

madhya मध्य – medium

mahābhūta महाभूत – gross elements, of which there are five (space, air, fire, water, and earth)

mahāmoha महामोह – great stupor

mahat महत् – cosmic mind, cosmic consciousness

mahat tattva महत् तत्त्व – universal form; universal principle

mahattva महत्त्व – magnitude, greatness, most expansive

maitrī मैत्री – amity, love, friendliness; suggested attitude toward those who are happy

manana मनन – contemplating; inference or inferential knowledge; the working of the mind (*manas*)

manasa मनस – recording mind, seat of thinking, mind as receiver of sensation

maṇeḥ, maṇi मणेः, मणि – crystal

mantra मन्त्र – sacred sound, sacred syllable

manvantara मन्वन्तर – lifespan of the creation, epoch

māyā माया – literally, "it is and it is not"; illusion; the creative power of Brahman that makes the absolute, formless God appear as the diverse Creation

mithyā jñānam मिथ्या ज्ञानम् – wrong knowledge

moha मोह – attachment, delusion

mṛidu मृदु – mild

mūḍha मूढ – stupefied (first of five states of *chitta*); dull or preoccupied, stupefication; a type of *vyutthāna vṛitti*; *tamas* predominant

muditā मुदिता – joyful, happy, gladness, delight; suggested attitude toward the virtuous

mukta मुक्त – liberated

mūla prakṛiti मूल प्रकृति – unmanifest state of creation; *avyakta*

muni मुनि – sage, ascetic, teacher

nairantarya नैरन्तर्य – without interruption

nibandhanī निबन्धनी – binder, firmly establishes

nididhyāsana निदिध्यासन – concentration; the practice of meditation; direct experience

nidrā निद्रा – sleep, deep sleep, dreamless sleep (one of five types of *vṛitti*)

nimitta निमित्त – causation

nir-atiśhaya निरतिशय – limitless, unexcelled, unsurpassed

nirbhāsa निभास – illuminative

nirbīja निबीज – seedless

nirbīja samādhi निबीज समाधि – super-consciousness without the support of any seed of creation; complete merging in *purusha*, the Self

nirodha निरोध – control, restraint, suppression; mental control; to retain, to hinder, to arrest, to stop, or to block

nirodha chitta निरोध चित्त – controlled mind

nirodha parinama निरोध परिणाम – the mind fluctuating only with the *samskāras* of restraint; the purifying transformation of the mind in a controlled state

niruddha निरुद्ध – state of being controlled (fifth of five states of *chitta*), the perfection of *nirodha*

nirvichāra निर्विचार – without reflection; suspension of reflection

nirvikalpa निर्विकल्प – without imagination

nirvitarka निर्वितर्क – without reasoning; suspension of reasoning; without gross thought

nitya नित्य – eternal, permanent

nivritti निवृत्ति – without thought; inward direction of the mind

nivritti mārga निवृत्ति मार्ग– mind withdraws into itself; path of involution

niyama नियम – observances, of which there are five: *saucha* (purity), *santosha* (contentment), *tapas* (austerity), *svādhyāya* (self study), *Īshvara-pranidhāna* (surrender to God)

Om ॐ – the primordial sound of creation, the origin of all sound; the name of *Īshvara*

pāda पाद – state (of being), of which there are four: awake, dream, deep sleep, and transcendent

panchabhūta पंचभूत – five gross elements: space, air, fire, water, and earth

panchatayyah पञ्चतय्यः – five fold

para पर – supreme, the highest, transcendent

parama परम – ultimate

paramānu परमाणु – the minutest atom

paramātmā, paramātman परमात्मा , परमात्मन् – supreme Self

parāpakāra chikīrshyā परापकार चिकीर्ष्या – malevolence; the thought and desire to defame and harm others, particularly those that are weaker, in order to build oneself up

paravairāgya परवैराग्य – supreme non-attachment, supreme dispassion

parikarma परिकर्म – purification

parinama परिणाम – change, mutation, alteration, transformation

parishuddhi परिशुद्धि – upon complete purification

paryavasāna पर्यवसान – extending up to, culminating in

prachchhardana प्रच्छर्दन – expulsion, expulsion of breath exhalation, expiration

pradhāna प्रधान – pure unmanifest *prakṛiti*; *mūla prakṛiti*

prajñā प्रज्ञा – awakening of wisdom, realization of the true nature of an object

prakāśha प्रकाश – illumination

prakṛiti प्रकृति – eternal principle of matter, primordial energy of creation

prakṛiti bandha प्रकृति बन्ध – bondage created by identifying with *prakṛiti* or any
    evolute of *prakṛiti*

prakṛitilaya प्रकृतिलय – those merged in *prakṛiti* where the *guṇas* are in equilibrium;
    identification completely with pure *prakṛiti*; rebirth resulting from stopping
    attainment level at *sasmitā samādhi*

pramā प्रमा – accurate perception of a state, condition, fact, or object

pramāda प्रमाद – carelessness, negligence in study, reflection or practice (one of nine
    obstacles to yoga)

pramāṇa प्रमाण – right knowledge or valid proof (one of five types of *vṛitti*)

prāṇa प्राण – breath, vital energy, vital air

pranavaḥ प्रणवः – the word *Om*; *Īśhvara*

prāṇāyāma प्राणायाम – the practice of breath control; expansion of vital energy

pranidhāna प्रणिधान – devotional dedication, self-surrender; literally, "placing
    something down", as in placing the ego in front of God (*Īśhvara-praṇidhāna*)

prasādaḥ प्रसादः – clarity, purity

prasādana प्रसादन – serene, making pleasant

prasaṁkhyāna प्रसंख्यान – the highest discriminative wisdom

prashānta vahita प्रशान्त वहित – the peaceful flow of *sāttvika vṛittis*

prashvāsa प्रश्वास – exhalation, specifically the forced or involuntary exhalation that is
    one of the four symptoms that accompany the nine obstacles to *sādhana*

prasupta प्रसुप्त – dormant, generally referring to emotions or the *kleśhas*

pratibandhī प्रतिबन्धी – opposed to; prevents

pratiṣhedha प्रतिषेध – prevention, negation, removal

pratiṣhṭhā प्रतिष्ठा – established, based

pratyāhāra प्रत्याहार – withdrawing the mind from the senses, the fifth of eight limbs of
    Aṣhṭāṅga Yoga; literally, "against food", or not taking in sense impressions

pratyak प्रत्यक् – inner or inward

pratyakchetanā प्रत्यक्चेतना – inwardly conscious self, *jīvātman*

pratyakṣha प्रत्यक्ष – direct perception, cognition, observation; one of three types of
    pramāṇa

pratyaya प्रत्यय – content of mind, causal principle, cognition principle, object

pravṛitti प्रवृत्ति – with thought; outflowing of the mind, manifestation

pṛithivī प्रथिवी – earth element

pūjā पूजा – devotional and/or ritual offering

puṇya पुण्य – virtue, merit, good actions

puruṣha पुरुष – the Self, eternal principle of consciousness, pure conscious principle; the subjective, pure "I-sense;" individual

pūrva, pūrvaka पूर्व, पूर्वक – preceded by, earliest, former, ancient, first, preceding

rāga राग – attraction, attachment, (third of five *kleśhas*, afflictions)

rajas रजस् – active

rajas guṇa रजस् गुण – quality of activity or passion (one of three *guṇas*)

rajoguṇa रजोगुण – see *rajas guṇa*

rañja रञ्ज – to color, coloring

rasa रस – literally, "juice"; the fluid in the body, such as gastric juices and hormones, as classified by Ayurveda; also the subtle element of taste

ṛṣhi ऋषि – enlightened sage

rūpa रूप – form, nature, appearance; the subtle element of form

sabīja सबीज – with seed

sādhana साधन – spiritual practice

saḥ स: – that practice

sahabhuvaḥ सहभुव: – accompany

sālambya सालम्ब्य – with a support; see *sabīja*

samādhi समाधि – super-consciousness, super-conscious absorption; trance

samāhita chitta समाहित चित्त – harmonized mind, resolution of conflict, even flow of consciousness

sāmānya सामान्य – universal, generic, general classification

samāpatti समापत्ति – engrossment, proficiency, coalescence, mind-field becoming stable in the object

samprajñāta सम्प्रज्ञात – with perfect knowledge or wisdom (*prajñā*)

samprajñāta samādhi सम्प्रज्ञात समाधि – *samādhi* with complete high consciousness; with wisdom (*prajñā*) or perfect knowledge, super-consciousness

saṃsāra संसार – cycle of suffering, wheel of birth and death, worldly existence, flow of the mind toward the world

saṃśhaya संशय – doubt (one of nine obstacles to yoga); opposite of *śhraddhā* (faith)

saṃskāra संस्कार – print of past actions in the mind, latent impression, innate tendency

saṃvega संवेग – desire of emancipation, speed, force

samyama सम्यम – a specific type of concentration in which *dhāraṇā*, *dhyāna*, and *samādhi* alternate in rapid succession, and which gives both profound knowledge of the object and *siddhis*

sānanda samādhi सानन्द समाधि – *samādhi* in which the supportive factor is accompanied by ecstasy or bliss; third level of *samprajñāta samādhi*

saṅjñā संज्ञा – name, definition

saṅkīrṇā संकीर्णा – mixed

santosha संतोष – contentment; accepting what comes unsought and not seeking what does not come unsought (one of the five *niyamas*)

sārūpya सारूप्य – appearance of, similarity in appearance, with the form of

sarva सर्व – all

sarvajña सर्वज्ञ – omniscient, all-knowing

sāsmitā samādhi सास्मिता समाधि – super-conscious trance accompanied by the knowledge of pure "I-sense," *samādhi* in which the supportive factor is merely "I amness;" highest level of *samprajñāta samādhi*

sat सत् – existence, reality, being, pure

sātiśhaya jñāna सातशयज्ञान – knowledge with a limit

satkāra सत्कार – reverence, devotion for truth

satoguṇa सतोगुण – see *sattva guṇa*

sattva सत्त्व – purity, clarity

sattva buddhi सत्त्व बुद्धि – pure intellect

sattva guṇa सत्त्व गुण – quality of consciousness, purity, balance, harmony (one of the three *guṇas*)

satya सत्य – truthfulness, honesty (one of the five *yamas*)

savichāra सविचार – with reflection

savichāra samādhi सविचार समाधि – *samādhi* in which the supportive factor is subtle reflection or thought regarding time, space, and causation

savikalpa सविकल्प – with imagination or ideation

savitarka सवितर्क – with verbal cognition, with gross thoughts of name, form and qualities, with argumentation

savitarka samādhi सवितर्क समाधि – *samādhi* in which the supportive factor is gross thought; first level of *samprajñāta samādhi*; engrossment in gross form

śhabda शब्द – name, word; subtle element of sound

śhānta, śhānti शान्त , शान्ति – peace and calm; a type of *vyutthāna vṛitti; sāttvika* predominant

śharīra शरीर – body

śhāsanam शासनम् – discipline or teaching

śhaucha शौच – purity of action, speech, mind (one of the five *niyamas*)

śheṣhaḥ शेषः – remnant, remainder, leftover

Śhiva शिव – the destructive aspect of God that releases auspicious energy

śhoka शोक – sorrow or grief

śhraddhā श्रद्धा – faith and devotion on that which is true

śhravaṇa श्रवण – listening; study of scriptures; testimonial knowledge

śhruta श्रुत – from listening, hearing, or learning

śhruti श्रुति – revealed scripture; literally, "what is heard"

śhuchi शुचि – pure

śhuddha शुद्ध – pure

śhūnya शुन्य – devoid , without, empty

śhvāsa श्वास – inhalation, specifically the forced or involuntary inhalation that is one of the five symptoms that accompany the nine obstacles to *sādhana*

siddhi सिद्धि – attainment, powers, accomplishments as a result of yogic practice

smṛiti स्मृति – memory, past memory, remembrance (one of five types of *vṛitti*)

sparśha स्पर्श – subtle element of touch

sthiti स्थिति – stability, absorption, established

sthūla स्थूल – gross

sthūla bhuta स्थूल भुत – five gross elements (space, air, fire, water, and earth)

styāna स्त्यान – dullness or mental laziness (one of nine obstacles to yoga)

sukha सुख – pleasure, comfort; those who are happy or comfortable

sūkṣhma सूक्ष्म – subtle

suṣhupti सुषुप्ति – dreamless sleep

sūtra सूत्र – thread, refers to an aphorism

svadharma स्वधर्म – one's own natural duty

svādhyāya स्वाध्याय – Self-study, study of scriptures (one of the five *niyamas*)

svapna स्वप्न – dream state

svarūpa स्वरूप – in its own nature, actual or essential nature or form

svarūpaśhūnya स्वरूपशून्य – devoid of its own form

tadā तदा – then

tadañjanatā तदञ्जनता – taking the form

tamas तमस् – darkness, inertia, stability

tamas guṇa तमस् गुण – quality of inertia, stability, darkness (one of the three *guṇas*)

tāmisra तामिस्र – nocturnal, dark, nature of *tamas guṇa*

tamoguṇa तमोगुण – see *tamas guṇa*

tana तन – of those

tanmātra तन्मात्र – literally, "that measure"; subtle elements, of which there are five: the energies of *śhabda* (sound), *sparśha* (touch), *rūpa* (form), *rasa* (taste), and *gandha* (odor)

tanu तनु – attenuated, weakened

tapas, tapaḥ तपस् , तप: – austerity, discipline (one of the five *niyamas*); literally, "to burn"

tasya तस्य – his; of that

tat तत् – of those, that

tatra तत्र – of those two, there, in that

tatstha तत्स्थ – becoming stable on them

tattva तत्त्व – principles of creation of which there are 25: *puruṣha, pradhāna, mahat* or *buddhi, ahaṁkāra, manas,* five *jñānendriyas,* five *karmendriyas,* five *tanmātras,* and five *mahābhūtas;* objects of senses, mind, "I-sense"

te ते – they

tīvra तीव्र – intense

tu तु – however

turīya तुरीय – transcendent

udāra उदार – fully active, generally referring to emotions or the *kleśhas*

upāya उपाय – means, instruments, methods of concentration

upekṣhā उपेक्षा – indifference, equanimity; suggested attitude toward the non-virtuous

utpannā उत्पन्ना – born or caused

vā वा – or, also

vāchakaḥ वाचकः – signifies, denotes

vaikṛitika bandha वैकृतिक बन्ध – bondage created by attraction to worldly or celestial pleasures

vairāgya वैराग्य – dispassion

vaiśhāradye वैशारद्ये – proficiency

vaitṛiṣhṇya वैतृष्ण्य – freedom from all desires, cessation of all cravings

vāsanā वासना – desire, cause of action, latent impression of past action, motivation

vaśhīkāra वशीकार – control and mastery

vaśhīkāra vairāgya वशीकार वैराग्य – complete renunciation; removal of the mind from all subtle desires; the highest stage of *aparavairāgya* (lower dispassion)

vastu वस्तु – object

vāyu वायु – air element; vital energy, of which there are five: *prāṇa* (located in the heart region), *apāna* (in the anus region), *samāna* (in the navel region), *udāna* (in the throat region), and *vyāna* (pervading the whole body)

Vedānta वेदान्त – a nondual philosophical system in which Brahman (absolute, formless God) is said to be the sole reality, and the universe is simply an illusion based on the creative power of Brahman known as *māyā*

vichāra विचार – reflection, analytical thought process

vichārānugamāt विचारानुगमात् – with reflection, see *savichāra*

vichchhinna विच्छिन्न – interrupted or fluctuating, generally referring to emotions and the *kleśhas*

videha विदेह – bodiless, the state when a yogi's consciousness has left the body; rebirth resulting from attainment stopping at *sānanda samādhi*

vidhāraṇā विधारणा – to restrain, to control, retention (as in breath control and/or retention)

vidyā विद्या – knowledge

vikalpa विकल्प – imagination, fancy, imaginary cognition (one of five types of *vritti*)

vikṣhepa विक्षेप – distraction to concentration

vikṣhipta विक्षिप्त – distracted (third of five states of *chitta*)

vipāka विपाक – maturing, fruition of actions; appears in three forms: *jāti* (class), *āyu* (span of life), and *bhoga* (experience)

viparyaya विपर्यय – false or wrong knowledge or mistaken conception, wrong cognition (one of five types of *vritti*)

virāma विराम – cessation; absence of all *vrittis*

vīrya वीर्य – energy, strength

vishaya विषय – object of experience, sense objects

vishayavatī विषयवती – objective experience

vishesha विशेष – particular, specific, individual; specific characteristics, distinction, specific remainder or outcome

Vishṇu विष्णु – the sustaining energy of God; incarnating avatar (Rām, Krishṇa, etc.)

vishokā विशोका – free from grief or sorrow

vīta वीत – passed, finished, devoid of

vitarka वितर्क – reasoning

vitarkānugamāt वितर्कानुगमात् – accompanied by reasoning, see *savitarka*

vitrishṇa वितृष्ण – one who has lost craving for, indifferent to

viveka khyāti विवेक ख्याति – discriminative wisdom

vritti वृत्ति – modification of the mind field, mental modifications; thought waves, to revolve or fluctuate, activities, fluctuations

vyādhi व्याधि – sickness (one of nine obstacles to yoga)

vyākhyāta व्याख्यात – explained

Vyāsa व्यास – a great sage whose commentary on the *Yoga Sūtras* of Patañjali is among the most significant

vyatireka व्यतिरेक – ascertainment, watching desires as they arise in the mind, as well as their effects

vyutthāna व्युत्थान – literally, "getting up," leaving one state for another, non-meditative state; worldly mindedness

vyutthāna chitta व्युत्थान चित्त – outgoing mind

yama यम – restraints of which there are five: *ahimsā* (nonviolence), *satya* (truthfulness), *asteya* (non-stealing), *brahmacharya* (continence), and *aparigraha* (non-hoarding)

yatamāna यतमान – initial effort to control the mind by removing it from attraction and aversion; first stage of *vairāgya*

yatnaḥ यत्नः – effort (with vigor and enthusiasm)

yoga योग – union, from root *yuj* (to unite, join, connect); yoga is *samādhi* or higher consciousness, super-consciousness *yoga yukta* योग युक्त – joined in yoga

yogi योगि – one whose aim is to attain peace; one who practices yoga

yogi pratyaksha योगि प्रत्यक्ष – direct perception of the reflection of pure consciousness